The Data Ring Main

COMPUTING SCIENCES SERIES
Editor: S.J. Orebi Gann

THE DATA RING MAIN

An Introduction to Local Area Networks

DAVID C. FLINT
Butler, Cox & Partners Ltd.
London

A Wiley Heyden Publication

JOHN WILEY & SONS
Chichester · New York · Brisbane · Toronto · Singapore

Library of Congress Cataloging in Publication Data:

Flint, David C.
  The data ring main.

  (Computing sciences series)
  'A Wiley Heyden publication.'
  Bibliography: p.
  Includes index.
  1. Computer networks. 2. Electronic data processing—
Distributed processing. I. Title. II. Series.
TK5105.5.F57 1983   384   82-23738
ISBN 0 471 26251 X

British Library Cataloguing in Publication Data:

Flint, David C.
  The data ring main.
  1. Computer networks
  I. Title
  001.64'404   TK5105.5

  ISBN 0 471 26251 X

Typeset by Pintail Studios Ltd., Ringwood, Hampshire.
Printed in Great Britain by The Pitman Press, Bath.

To Louise,
for putting up with it all

CONTENTS

FOREWORD

Computing has now progressed so far that it is no longer the exclusive preserve of the research specialist but extends into everyday life, from the microchip which controls a modern washing machine to a company's accounts or word processing operations. The scope and impact of the technology will continue to expand during the 1980s, and this book addresses one of the most influential areas.

The book describes the world of Local Area Networks (usually abbreviated LANs). LANs are the mechanism for connecting elements of a computer configuration together over distances greater than a few feet, but not extending over really large areas. (The boundaries are not precise; nor need they be.) The distance scale is most easily illustrated by examples: LANs would be applicable for interconnection of equipment in a room, in an office, or on a factory site; or inside a car.

The decreasing cost of the computing elements of systems (particularly processor costs, memory costs, and storage costs) does not of itself greatly change the way in which computer developments occur. The ability to connect these items over distances typical of buildings, however, opens up a whole new strategy for computer systems, of genuinely distributing the intelligence in systems to where it is used. Data may be stored in one place and accessed cheaply by many users; building do not have to be extensively rewired every time someone moves office; and new devices may be included in the system easily as and when they are available and needed.

Local Area Networks are the means to this end, and this book gives a clear description of the concepts, the benefits, and the costs, and describes the current state of the art. It will be of interest both to technical readers and to the line manager who wishes to make informed decisions about the tools which are becoming available to him in the running of his business.

The author is an acknowledged expert in the field, being well versed in the world-wide developments which are relevant to the evolution of LANs.

S.J. OREBI GANN

PREFACE

The last three years have seen very rapid developments in the field of Local Area Networks. During the last year hardly a month has passed without one or another supplier claiming a new and revolutionary network product which will solve everyone's problems.

The trade papers, also, continually report claims that 'Broadband will sweep the field', that 'Gateways are the key to networking', or that 'The Super-PABX will be the office controller in the office of the future'. Not all these claims are made by people with a vested interest in the technologies they advocate (though many are).

However self-interested the sales pitches and however dubious the instant explanations, it is clear that something important is happening in computing and communications. And, being new, Local Area Networks are widely misunderstood.

This book is for the people who wish to understand these new technologies and their significance. It explains the changes that are creating the need for new networks, the new technologies, and their implications for information systems. It finishes by explaining how to select a new communications network.

My thanks are due to the various colleagues in Butler, Cox and Partners Limited and clients with whom I have worked on communications assignments. My thanks, also, to Fred Heys, Ken Heard, Dave Marnham, Dan Sze, and Chris Woodward for commenting on parts of the draft, and to Karl Kozarsky for making me cast the LAN versus CBX argument in Chapter 6 in its present, moderate, form.

It is a pleasure to record my debt to Edward Goldblum of Butler Cox and Peter Hull of British Telecom for the care with which each reviewed the whole of the draft, and to Louise Meltzer for help with the drafting and figures. They have undoubtedly saved me from a number of errors though I claim full responsibility for any that remain.

DAVID FLINT

1. THE PROMISE OF A LOCAL AREA NETWORK

Terminals and other digital devices have become much more widely used in commerce and administration as their costs, and those of computers, have fallen. This tendency is likely to accelerate during the 1980s, but the proliferation of digital devices has already begun to concern managers with responsibilities for communications and computing.

This proliferation causes three problems:

1. Devices obtained from different sources and, often, from the same source are unable to exchange information conveniently.
2. Conventional communications systems are too slow for some of the newer devices.
3. Conventional wiring systems are expensive and inflexible.

Computers, word processors, personal micros, and facsimile transceivers are just some of the machines now finding their way into offices and on which workers may wish to prepare and examine documents. Yet it is usually impossible to exchange text between them without losing many of the most valuable features of the machines. Indeed, it is, in many cases, impossible to exchange text at all. The development of public electronic mail systems and local office systems is likely to exacerbate this problem, and others like it (for instance, the exchange of computer graphics).

Existing communications systems may be divided into those that provide only a transparent circuit and those that provide more sophisticated interworking but are tied to one vendor's communications architecture. Neither is a suitable base for the solution of these problems.

A communications system is needed that will allow a wide variety of machines to communicate effectively. Systems that provide a transparent service are unsuitable because they provide only a basic level of service and do not deal with the areas of incompatibility. Proprietary systems such as IBM's Systems Network Architecture (SNA) are also unsuitable because they are based on 1960s concepts of computer communications.

As more powerful machines, first micros and then personal workstations, are installed in offices and other work places, needs will arise for increased bandwidth to match the increased power of the machines. This bandwidth will be needed for file transfer, program loading, and also for the more sophisticated interactions that make an office system more than just a collection of separate machines.

Many conventional systems are based on twisted pairs and cannot, therefore, provide the necessary bandwidth.

When conventional schemes are used, the cost of wiring can add as much as 25 per cent. to the cost of a new system. In addition to the expense there is disruption, because ceilings and walls are opened to allow the installation of cables, and it is often found that existing wiring is damaged during installation and itself needs further work. Conventional wiring schemes are also inflexible, so that moving a terminal usually involves pulling new cables.

These problems are reminiscent of those that were found with UK domestic electrical wiring a few decades ago (Figure 1.1). Cables were of several different kinds and terminated in several kinds of sockets.

This problem was solved, as shown in Figure 1.2, by the ring main and the standardization of plugs and sockets. The ring main is carried to all parts of the building so that it passes close to the proposed location of each new device. It also carries more power than any one cable on the old scheme and this power can be drawn off at any point.

Local area networks offer the same advantages for the connection of digital machines. The construction of a 'data ring main' is, of course, more complex than that of an electrical main. An a.c. power supply may be characterized by frequency, voltage, limiting current, and phase angle. More parameters than this are needed just to specify the transmission of bits, on top of which a variety of character codes and communications protocols must also be specified.

If these problems can be solved, however, the LAN can provide much more than just a cheaper way to wire up existing equipment. Its low error rate can allow simplification of communications protocols. Its high speed can facilitate the

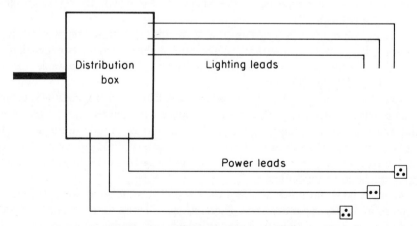

Figure 1.1   Old electrical wiring scheme.

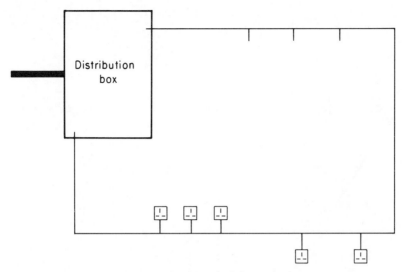

Figure 1.2   Electrical ring main.

sharing and electronic delivery of complex documents. Its low latency can allow programs in separate computers to communicate as if they shared the same computer.

These capabilities create new possibilities for the design of communications networks and computer and office systems. These possibilities can be exploited by both users and vendors to provide more powerful and cost-effective systems.

Unhappily for the potential user, no existing LAN fulfils this promise. There is a wide variety of approaches to the construction of a LAN, due in large measure to the history of the research and development in this field.

HISTORY

Work on what are now called local area networks started in the 1960s as an attempt to find new technologies for telephony. The developers hoped to gain the flexibility inherent in digital transmission whilst also simplifying the problem of wiring a town or building for speech.

These initial developments foundered on the high cost and limited reliability of contemporary electronics. Satisfactory units were much more expensive than conventional switches and wiring schemes. Telephony development has concentrated on digital circuit switches since then.

The idea of a common digital system for all local communications was next picked up in the early 1970s by a number of research laboratories. At Xerox's Palo Alto Research Center (PARC), the University of Cambridge's Computer Laboratory, the Ohio State University, and elsewhere, computer scientists and

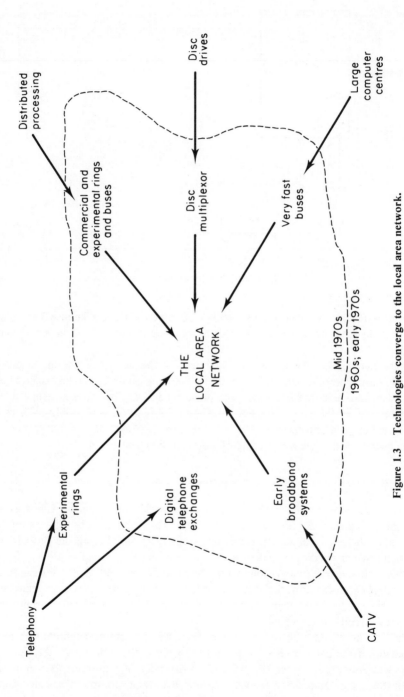

Figure 1.3   Technologies converge to the local area network.

engineers devised novel ways of linking minicomputers. These networks generally used buses or rings with speeds over 2M bit/s. Since they were intended for inter-computer communication, the data were transmitted by computers in packets addressed to other computers and were removed from the network by those destination machines. (Packet switching had been publicized by the ARPANET, to which many of the developers had ready access.)

The 1970s saw three further parallel developments based on cable television (CATV), mainframes, and microcomputers.

During the early 1970s a number of large US organizations began to exploit CATV technology for terminal support and to connect specialized data collection devices to central computers. This development led gradually to the appearance of broadband network products (Smith, 1979).

The need to interconnect a number of dissimilar machines in large computer centres led to the construction of *ad hoc* high-speed networks. This led, in turn, to the development of high-speed buses by specialist vendors.

By 1980 the increasing penetration of microcomputers had created a new market for disc drives. The high cost of the drives made it essential that each should be shared among a number of micros, and multiplexors were developed to support this sharing.

During most of the 1970s the high cost of the interface units restricted the bandwidth that could be provided to a few ten, or a few hundred, thousands of bits per second. During the late 1970s, though, Prime began to sell their Ringnet and Datapoint their Attached Resource Computer (ARC) system, which were based on high-speed coaxial cable networks.

Though their origins are rather different, these approaches began, in 1981, to converge, as shown in Figure 1.3. There is now a general move to develop each technology to match the facilities of its competition, and this is leading to an increasingly competitive market.

CONCLUSION

The large and increasing variety of technologies and products places an increasing burden of choice on potential users. Unfortunately, the ingenuity of the developers prevents there being any simple answer to the question 'Which is the best local area network?'.

The principal purpose of this book is to present the technologies of local area networks and to indicate their value to the developers and users of data processing and office automation systems. In order to provide a coherent perspective, however, I use the first part of the book to lay some foundations. Part I therefore discusses the changes now affecting business communications, the reasons for believing that an enhanced PABX is an unsuitable vehicle for tomorrow's systems, and the general nature of LANs.

The second part deals with LAN technology in all its complexity and con-stitutes the core of the technical material. It may perhaps be omitted, at least at first reading, by those interested only in consequences and not in the technical detail.

The third part is also technical and explains how networks may be linked together and how they may provide useful services to terminals, computers, and other machines. It thus links LANs with more familiar concepts from the worlds of computers and telecommunications. (More technically, it deals with functions in the network and transport layers of the open systems architecture.)

The fourth part looks at the real value of LANs, both in strictly pragmatic terms and in terms of the new architectures that LANs make possible. These architectures will play a vital role in the information systems of the future.

The fifth part is the most practical and explains how an organization should select a local network to meet its particular needs. It brings together the broad generalizations of the first part, the technicalities of parts II and III, and the evaluations of part IV.

The book finishes with a discussion of future developments in this complex but fascinating field.

PART I

The Foundations

This part discusses the changes in business systems that require new communication systems. It discusses developments in digital PABXs and explains why they are an inadequate basis for future office systems. The final chapter defines LANs.

2. YESTERDAY'S SYSTEMS AND COMMUNICATIONS

At any given time organizations are mainly using clerical, computer, and communications systems that were installed at least a few years previously and designed earlier still. During the early 1980s, therefore, the systems in use will be predominantly systems that were installed in the late 1970s. In many cases these systems were designed much earlier, and often show signs of a need to remain compatible with systems developed in the 1960s.

Most of this book is concerned with the systems of the future. This chapter discusses those of the past, both for contrast and because of their longevity. To truly provide a 'data ring main' a local network must support yesterday's systems as well as tomorrow's.

YESTERDAY'S SYSTEMS

Paper-based systems have been used to store the large majority of business information, even in organizations that make (relatively) heavy use of computers. Paper is flexible—it can include text, diagrams, and pictures (both monochrome and colour), it is available in a variety of sizes, and it is very portable.

With only a few exceptions, offices have had separate systems for the principal forms of information—data, text, pictures, diagrams, speech, and video.

Speech has been the dominant form of office communication and much of it has taken place in meetings and without any mechanical assistance. The telephone has, however, been by far the commonest business machine. Table 2.1 shows figures for the penetration of various kinds of office machine, as collected by Butler, Cox and Partners Limited in 1980.

The penetration of telephones in companies has generally been between 20 per cent. and 100 per cent. of the number of people employed. In a few cases, hotels for example, the ratio has been much higher.

Where there have been more than a handful of phones on one site, they were normally connected to the Public Switched Telephone Network (PSTN) through a special switchboard. Where there have been more than a few dozen, a Private Automatic Branch Exchange (PABX) has often been used. A large PABX may support thousands of extensions and may itself be divided into a number of separate switching units in different places.

9

Table 2.1 Penetration of office communication equipment in the United Kingdom in 1980.

Device	Number of devices in the United Kingdom per thousand working population
Telephones	400
Data terminals	7
Telex terminals	4
Facsimile terminals	2
Communicating word processors	1

Telephones have almost invariably been attached to PABXs over unshielded twisted wire pairs, though multi-pair cables (also unshielded) have been used for certain special kinds of phone and for carrying signals from the PABX to a local distribution point. The distribution technology closely resembles that used in the PSTN.

PABX technology followed public switching technology up until the early 1970s when computer controlled PABXs (CBXs) were announced by Rolm in the United States and by IBM in Europe. Since then most of the main telecommunications companies have begun to offer CBXs of their own (often, in Europe, by adopting and modifying American products). More recently, of course, the PTTs have themselves began to use computer control in the public network.

The telephone system has mainly been used for communications between people, but with the use of a modem or acoustic coupler, it has also provided low-speed access to time-sharing computers. In addition, a small proportion of calls have been answered by telephone answering machines. More than half of all business calls have been to members of the same organization (Strassman, 1982).

The text of business documents has been generated in a variety of ways (often in manuscript or by dictation), but has usually been captured at some point by an electric typewriter. During the last years of the 1970s (earlier in the United States) European organizations began to install word processors on a limited scale, but by 1980 these still accounted for much less than 5 per cent. of all the business keyboards in use. Though many word processors offered communications facilities, by 1980 these were still little used.

The transmission of text has usually been by means of the physical transportation of paper. Telex and facsimile machines have been used to some extent, but have generally been restricted to cases of particular urgency. The use of facsimile machines has been restricted by the lack of common standards and by the absence of directories of users. The use of both telex and facsimile has been inhibited by their high fixed costs, and slowness and inconvenience in use. In only a few cases, the use of telexes in the international money market for instance, has either telex or facsimile become a standard part of business procedure.

Computers are a major source of paper in offices. Batch computer systems typically produce printed outputs for despatch to other businesses, as instructions for clerks within the company, reports on transactions and anomalies, and reference documents for clerks and managers. Commercial batch systems have been restricted for the most part to structured information of a conventional kind—orders, despatch notes, etc.

During the 1970s many organizations installed online transaction processing systems to supplement or replace their batch systems. These online systems have often done little to stem the rising tide of computer printouts (though they may have other advantages).

In many organizations, data processing (DP) systems have acquired a very poor reputation. They have been seen, often rightly, as being unreliable, difficult to use, and as meeting only part of the users' real needs. The reasons for this are partly technological, but the main cause is the slow and overcomplicated way in which large-scale DP systems have been developed. By the early 1980s, many organizations had found word processors and minicomputers easier to understand and to make productive.

Computer terminals became increasingly commonplace during the 1970s and were of three kinds:

1. Those used by clerks for transaction input and simple enquiries and connected to transaction processing systems. (These were often visual display units with synchronous communications, such as the IBM3270 or ICL7502.)
2. Those used by managers and professionals for their own processing on time-sharing computers. (These might be visual display units or printers but usually had asynchronous communications at lower speeds. They often needed to access several different time-sharing systems at different times.)
3. Those used by engineers for graphics. (These were typically expensive, required high-speed communications, and were used with a single processing system.)

Though the same hardware might be used, at least in the first two cases, particular terminals have usually been dedicated to one or other function.

Transaction processing (TP) terminals have handled structured data and a small amount of text. Time-sharing terminals have also mostly handled structured data but the structures were devised and revised by the user (rather than by the computer department). Graphics terminals have used structured data to create and manipulate images. The data may give characteristics of the object depicted that are not shown in the picture, such as the weight and strength of structural members or the inside diameter of pipes.

Graphics terminals have provided a sophisticated means of handling images and of relating the images to other systems. (For instance, the weight of a component may be calculated from its physical description and then used in a procurement system.) Facsimile transceivers have allowed images to be moved from place to place but they are not easily linked with other office systems. Basically they have provided a means of moving paper documents.

Television has been little used in European organizations. What use there has been is strictly limited to specific functions—typically site security, education, and management training.

Overall the pattern of office equipment has been characterized by a lack of functional linkage between machines and by the dominance of voice communications, with paper-related communication coming second.

Communications support for these machines has been correspondingly fragmented. Facsimile transceivers and telephones have used public or private voice networks. Telex machines have used the telex networks (or private networks built to similar standards). TP and graphics terminals have been either wired directly into a local computer or connected via specialized private networks that have usually included no switching facilities. Time-sharing terminals have used the PSTN or a private network to obtain access to host computers.

Because of the traditional high cost and batch orientation of commercial computers the terminal network has usually been developed as an adjunct of the computer rather than as a separate utility in its own right. (This point is seen particularly clearly in the dominant role of the host computer in IBM's SNA.)

YESTERDAY'S NEEDS FOR DATA COMMUNICATIONS

Communications in yesterday's systems may be described as follows:

1. The use of video systems has been both limited and specialized and, since analogue techniques were used exclusively (except within some broadcasting companies), video has been carried on its own coaxial cables.
2. Telephony has been very widely used, but its use of analogue techniques (except in some CBXs) has made it generally unsuitable for integration with data communications.
3. Many terminals have only been used in conjunction with a single computer and in these cases the terminals have been directly wired. Such direct lines have rarely operated at speeds above 9.6k bit/s.

During the 1970s organizations introduced a variety of data communications products to support time-sharing terminals and communications between sites.

By 1980, however, telecommunication managers were becoming concerned at the growth of *ad hoc* arrangements and were looking for unified solutions. They recognized that data terminals could be divided into four broad categories (see Table 2.2).

The requirements for a network were seen as follows:

1. Data communication was quite distinct from picture and voice communication, and did not need to be integrated with either. In Europe, integration

Table 2.2 Typical traffic parameters (1980).

Category / Device	Main use	Daily utilization (hrs)	Typical peak speed (bit/s)*	Peak/ average speed†	Notes
NON-DATA TERMINALS					
Television camera and monitor	Training courses	1	n/a (analogue transmission)	1	Uses own coax cables
	Surveillance	12–24		1	
Television monitor	Training courses	2		n/a	Driven from video tape
Telephone	Telesales	5	(n/a) (analogue)	2.5	Parties speak alternately with some pauses
	General	c3/4		2.5	
Facsimile transceiver	–			2	Half-duplex on full-duplex link
Group I	–	0.1	n/a (analogue)		
Group II	–	0.25			
Group III	–	0.5	4.8k (PSTN)		
Telex terminal	Message service	0.3	75	1	
DATA TERMINALS					
Teletype	Time sharing	2–4	150	10–15	After Martin (1981)
Screen mode VDU	Time sharing	2–4	1,200*	100	
	Transaction processing	3–8	2,400	200	
Graphics terminal	Computer aided design	4	200k	1,000	After Martin (1981)
HOST COMPUTERS					
Minicomputer	Interactive host	6–12	128k	400	After Bux et al. (1981)
Mainframe		8–24	1M	600	

* The devices could often benefit from the use of higher speeds, but it is typically too expensive to provide them.

† Traffic associated with polling has been ignored.

between data and text was also very limited, though in the United States and in overseas branches of some US multinationals such integration was a fully accepted requirement.

2. Reliability should be fairly high but, since the operation of the business rarely depended on it, and since the main computers were rarely available for more than 99 per cent of the time, very high reliability was not required.

3. Where more than one site was included in the network then at least all the long distance connections should be monitored and controlled from a central network management centre.

4. The main service required was a serial bit stream (a data circuit) connecting a terminal to a host computer. For time-sharing the terminals would usually be ASCII devices and the network should provide error correction over long distances and access to a time-sharing bureau over the PSTN or public data networks. For transaction processing, remote job entry (RJE), and file transfer, the terminals would normally implement their own synchronous error control protocol so that the network could provide a fully transparent service.

5. Time-sharing terminals would access ASCII services at speeds up to 2,400 bit/s. Transaction processing terminals would normally access synchronous services at speeds up to 4,800 bit/s. RJE, file transfer, and inter-computer traffic would benefit from rather higher speeds. Graphics terminals might use very high speeds but these would generally be provided by a direct connection to the graphics system.

6. Circuit switching under user control was required for time sharing, RJE, file transfer, and some graphics and TP terminals. Switching would be used both to gain access to various services and for reconfiguration following a failure in the network or of one of the hosts. Users should not have to be aware either of the network configuration or of which particular service port they were using at any particular time.

YESTERDAY'S NETWORK

These requirements could be very largely met by a circuit switched network providing transparent connections at up to 19.2k bit/s. It would also need a simple and user-friendly addressing system, error protection on trunk links, and centralized network management. By 1981 there were at least half a dozen systems available that could meet all these requirements through a combination of circuit switches, statistical multiplexors, and modems (see, for example, Spiegleman, 1982). These systems were usually able to accommodate a variety of speeds and protocols on each port. Some of the networks provided some protocol conversion, the commonest being that needed to allow ASCII terminals to access IBM 3270 host ports.

Though the restriction to 19.2k bit/s may seem a source of difficulty, actually few terminals were able to use speeds much higher, and fewer still were the organizations that could afford to lease the necessary PTT lines for data transmission. Those organizations that had real needs for higher transmission speeds could meet them by special engineering.

Though not intended for electronic mail or the support of personal computers, these networks proved able to accept electronic mail systems in the form of private telex switches or utility processes on time-sharing hosts. Personal computers could also be accommodated by loading programs that emulated suitable terminals. This technique could, of course, only be used when the cables of the network ran to the location of the personal computer. This was often not the case.

The Interface Problem

This approach still suffers from some problems. Figure 2.1 shows that four physical ports are needed for each connection:

on the terminal

on the network near the terminal } connected by a cable

on the computer

on the network near the computer } connected by a cable

Since only the terminal and computer ports would be needed for a physical connection, this approach increases the cost.

This is particularly absurd when the structure of a typical computer–network interface is considered in detail (Figure 2.2). The RS232 ports are provided through special boards connected to a bus. This may be the main bus of a minicomputer or the bus of a peripheral controller in the case of a mainframe.

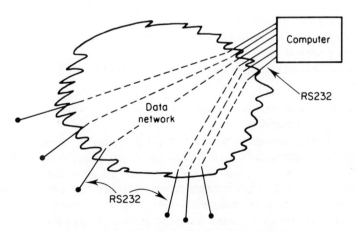

Figure 2.1   Virtual circuits in a data network.

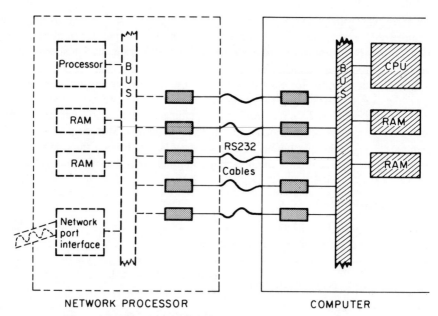

Figure 2.2   Host–network connections via low-speed circuits.

The port logic is then connected to a corresponding unit in the network processor. (The network processor may, depending on the network used, be referred to as a switch, multiplexor, multiplexing modem, or communications processor.) Being itself a specialized microcomputer, the network processor will, again, be based on a bus. Data from the computer port will pass across the bus to the network port interface through which it is relayed to the other parts of the network.

A much simpler, cheaper, faster, and more reliable interface is desirable and is shown in Figure 2.3. This requires the network controller to support the operations of the computer bus.

This is an ideal arrangement but several problems make it difficult to achieve in practice:

1. There is a wide variety of computer buses, each of which would require its own kind of controller.
2. The telecommunications software in the computer is usually orientated to driving the computer's own RS232 (or other) terminal ports. It may be difficult to modify it to interwork with the network controller.
3. Changes to the host telecommunications software may cause the computer supplier to withdraw or reduce his support for the machine. This will usually be unacceptable in a commercial environment, though research organizations often regard this price as acceptable.

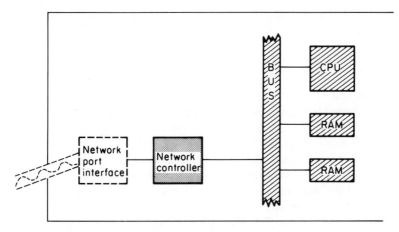

Figure 2.3 High-speed multiplex network interface.

4. The changes to the host software may have to be revised each time the supplier changes that software.

For all these reasons, a standard high-speed interface is needed that can carry several, interleaved, data circuits. This need had been recognized in the design of packet switching networks with the definition of CCITT Recommendation X.25. By the end of 1981 a number of computer manufacturers, including both IBM and DEC, had announced support for this recommendation, thus making the type of interface shown in Figure 2.4 practical. However, the X.25 protocol is not easy

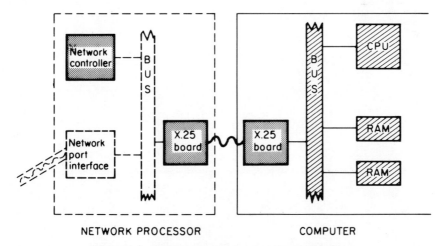

NETWORK PROCESSOR   COMPUTER

Figure 2.4 X.25 as a computer to network interface.

to relate to circuit switching and the suppliers have been slow to provide interfaces of this kind.

The Wiring Problem

In most cases these networks have been provided in order to support a quite small number of terminals. Each time a new terminal was installed, or an old one is moved, it is likely to be necessary to install extra cables or to allocate spare pairs on a main telephone cable, and these events will become increasingly common as the use of online computer systems expands.

In a large network, however, the costs may be less than those of pulling new cables from the host to the terminal. This advantage is encouraging users to attach even their dedicated terminals to the network. In some cases, users have installed network ports throughout their facilities to obtain some of the advantages of a data ring main.

CONCLUSION

A low-speed circuit-switched data network can conveniently meet the requirements of yesterday's systems. It can also meet some more advanced requirements, such as electronic mail and the connection of microcomputers.

The orientation to data circuits creates unnecessary complexity, and thus cost, in the computer interfaces used by these networks. In addition, if only a transparent circuit is provided such networks can do little to resolve incompatibilities.

3. THE CHANGING BUSINESS ENVIRONMENT

Organizations operate in a changing world—a fact brought home to many people very forcibly by the oil price rise of 1974. The rising price of oil has done more than change the economies of the energy-intensive industries—it has altered the political environment in which multinational companies, and even sovereign states, must operate.

But this is merely the most dramatic of many changes. The last three decades have seen technical, social, and political changes on an immense scale. Businesses and non-business organizations have been obliged to adapt more rapidly to a changing environment, not only in order to innovate but even to survive. To do this these organizations have increased their investment in scientific research, market research, and in computers—i.e. in the creation, acquisition and, manipulation of information.

Direct external pressures have also played a part. Increased government intervention in the economy has imposed new procedures and reporting require-ments on industry and commerce. These include drug safety tests, environmental impact statements, and equal opportunity procedures. In addition, companies and public utilities are increasingly liable to find their plans opposed in the courts and at public inquiries.

These trends are reflected in the composition of the workforce. Figure 3.1

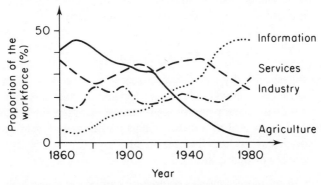

Figure 3.1   The changing composition of the US workforce.

19

shows the changing composition of the US workforce over the last century. Overall, and especially since 1950, the proportion of workers involved in manufacturing has fallen and the proportion in services and information handling has risen. Much the same is true within manufacturing companies; the proportion of staff, and especially of senior staff, in support rather than line posts has increased significantly (Strassman, 1979). The importance of information processing to the economy, and to the individual firms, is thus large and growing.

Yet, though computers have replaced clerks and machine operators in the performance of routine tasks, the overall productivity of office staff has increased only modestly. There is little doubt that the low productivity of office workers is associated with the low level of investment that supports such workers. Strassman (1982) has reported the following figures for the expenditure supporting US office workers in 1979:

Managers: $8,000—mainly secretarial and other office support
Professionals: $2,000
Clerks: $6,000—mainly computers and other technical aids

By way of comparison, widely quoted figures give the per capita investment for workers in agriculture, factories, and offices as $35,000, $25,000, and $2,000 respectively.

The lack of investment is, in turn, due to the lack of suitable support systems, difficulties in demonstrating an improvement in productivity due to the introduction of new support systems, as well as to organizational inertia.

New support systems are therefore needed to improve the productivity of the increasing numbers of information workers. The need for productivity is, of course, a management concern, but the information workers themselves are far from passive. In many major cities it is already almost impossible to find typists who will use manual typewriters. In the future, the advance of the word processor will make the electric typewriter equally unattractive.

Amongst professionals, computer programmers have long pressed their managers to obtain the latest hardware and languages. Professionals in other fields will doubtless soon expect their own personal micros.

INFORMATION TECHNOLOGY

Electronics—specifically digital electronics—is the key element in new systems. Figure 3.2 shows the improvement in the cost-effectiveness of processors, random access memory, and auxiliary storage since 1960. The cost-effectiveness has increased by a factor of about 10 every 6–8 years, and this trend is likely to continue for at least the next decade.

This has two main consequences:

1. Progressively more powerful computers can be made for a given price and the largest possible macines grow bigger continually.

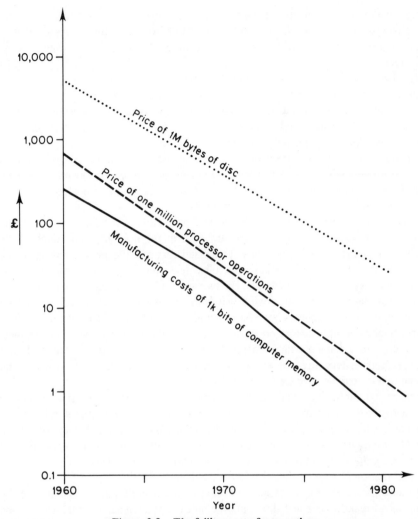

Figure 3.2   The falling cost of computing.

2. The cost of associating a computer with a disc store, printer, machine tool, domestic appliance, or telephone has fallen rapidly and it is no longer necessary to seek high utilization in order to justify such computers.

The first point implies that functions that require a lot of processing power become increasingly feasible. This has already happened in optical character recognition. Other functions that can be provided include encryption, inductive and deductive logic ('expert systems'), and associative searches of text and data archives.

The second point implies that sufficient intelligence can be added to electronic filing systems and to printers to allow them to operate autonomously, or nearly so. No longer must they be controlled in detail by the same processor that is executing the billing system, linear programming model, or word processing package.

It also means that many relatively small (though increasingly powerful) microcomputers may be placed in a single office. By 1981 the UK price of a business microcomputer had fallen to about half the salary of a secretary or, say, one-quarter of that of a middle manager or professional. In the United States, of course, this point was reached several years earlier.

In the factory, micros are now replacing an older generation of programmed logic controllers (PLCs) in controlling machine tools. Simple robots are also being introduced in increasing numbers, and will be replaced by more sophisticated robots with greater flexibility and functionality.

These micros serve a number of different purposes. In the case of robots and word processors the micro is an essential part of the machine, and much of the distinctive nature of the machine is expressed through the programming of the micro. In the case of numerically controlled tools, copiers, and transceivers, the micro provides extra convenience to the user and to the maintenance engineer.

There is clearly a general move towards having more digital machines on each site. Initially these machines have been installed in order to be used separately, but there are considerable attractions in being able to link them together. For instance, many copiers are used mainly to reproduce locally produced typescript. A link between typewriters and copiers would be useful, and, once typed, text may be stored in a central archive for future use.

On an assembly line, each machine receives its workpiece from the one before it. To regulate the overall speed and operation of the line requires either communication between computer-controlled machine tools or communication with a central computer. These communications can also allow successive workpieces to be treated differently, producing the 'flexible manufacturing systems' required for the automation of small batch production (Kilzer, 1982).

In addition, a central machine may monitor the overall state of the line. In the event of a breakdown it will direct maintenance engineers to the most urgent jobs and may, if the line is sufficiently flexible, reconfigure the line to bypass the failed machine.

In an analytical laboratory the final result may require data from several sources to be brought together and presented in a single report.

Micro-based machines may also communicate in order to share the use of single resources that are too expensive, bulky, fragile or in need of operator attention to be provided for each machine.

Data Processing Systems

During the 1960s it was usual to design data processing systems so as to minimize the use of online storage, since such storage was very expensive. The costs of such storage have already fallen sufficiently to allow large volumes of business data to be held online—in 1979 one British insurance company had more than two megabytes of online policy data for every head office clerk.

Text Systems

Most business data may be regarded as a compressed form of text in which single letters and digits represent standard phrases such as 'Overdrawn' or 'Pack in twelves', and longer codes identify goods or businesses.

Complete texts are therefore more expensive to store and process than data. From the mid-1960s word processors began to appear that stored text. Early machines used libraries of magnetic cards or fixed discs that were shared among a number of operators. Later machines used a library of floppy discs, or shared access to fixed discs. Prior to 1980 word processing systems were still organized so as to minimize the size of the online storage, but from that date an awareness began to grow that it could be cost-effective to hold material online permanently. Word processing and data processing have thus evolved similarly with regard to the use of storage (see Figure 3.3).

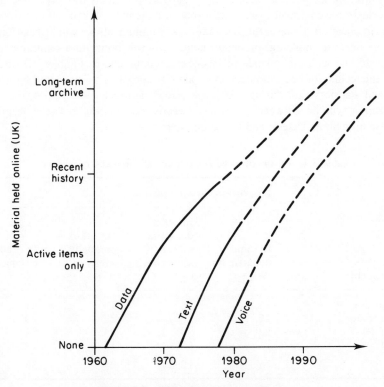

Figure 3.3   Changing storage patterns.

Voice Systems

This evolution has also begun in respect of digital voice. Initial voicegram systems assume that messages will be held online for only a few hours or days, but long-term storage will become reasonably economic in time and voice will provide a third instance of the same pattern.

Video Systems

Video communication requires much more storage and much higher transmission rates than speech. Digitization is, however, already used in such complex processes as conversion between US and European television standards, and video systems may also repeat the pattern in the future.

THE ROLE OF SUPPORT SYSTEMS

During the 1970s online systems usually served either specialist terminal operators or staff in 'back office' roles, rather than the executives with primary responsibility for the work of the office. The future tendency will be to cut out, or restructure, these specialist roles and to support principals directly. During the 1980s electronic equipment will be absorbed into the main flow of office work.

The implication of these trends is that data communications will increasingly be local to one site, building, or department. This will bring data communication more into line with other kinds of business communication. (Tables 3.1 and 3.2 show the locality of communications in one UK company as measured by Butler, Cox and Partners Ltd. during 1980. See also Strassman, 1982.) Also, the communication will be between machines directly rather than between terminals (representing human users) and host computers.

Table 3.1   Proportions of telephone calls in a UK company.

Department	Proportion to/from people			
	In same department (%)	In other department but on same site (%)	On other company sites (%)	In other companies (%)
Accounting	25	16	18	41
Retail trade	16	16	28	40
Personnel	12	30	34	24
Secretary	11	47	13	29
All	25	12	25	38

Table 3.2   Source and destination of mail in a UK company.

Department	Proportion to/from people			
	In same department (%)	In other department but on same site (%)	On other company sites (%)	In other companies (%)
Accounting	35	27	12	26
Retail trade	42	15	19	24
Personnel	11	27	32	30
Secretary	10	50	9	31
All	30	21	20	29

This will require a style of communications appropriate to the interaction of machines rather than of people.

OFFICE WORK

Office work may be analysed and described in many ways (see, for instance, the discussion in Mintzberg, 1973). One way that is frequently convenient is to divide it into:

1. Routine work, in which a defined procedure is applied to relatively large numbers of cases, usually by clerks, and
2. Executive work, in which individual decisions, projects, etc., are processed, usually by managers and professionals.

Data processing has successfully automated a good deal of routine clerical work in large organizations and is now expanding into smaller ones. For reasons of both economy and tradition, DP systems generally address only part of the information requirements of the users. System users therefore maintain additional paper and microfilm files to provide faster and/or more comprehensive records than are available through the computer. Furthermore, much clerical work involves contact with members of the public or with other businesses. This work is difficult to automate since machines still have very limited capacities for understanding speech and since, in any case, most people would rather deal with other people than with machines.

The automation of managerial and professional work is even more problematical. Where the tasks are rigidly defined and the relevant factors both quantifiable and well understood, then it may be possible. Computer programs can, for example, choose optimal locations for warehouses and optimal production mixes for oil refineries.

However, information in a more general sense is not well understood. Most business decisions depend on a mixture of objective and subjective considerations. Even the objective matters—the state of the law on redundancy for instance—may be very complex and subject to several interpretations. Most executive work has therefore resisted automation, and is likely to continue to do so for many years. The number of special cases in which decisions can be automated is likely to increase only slowly over the coming decade.

Where office work cannot be automated, however, it may be made easier. Managers and clerks may be assisted by systems that help them find information, prepare reports, perform calculations, and record notes. In short, it may be 'mechanized'. It is therefore particularly unfortunate that the term 'office automation' is generally used to describe the provision of tools for office workers.

TOOLS FOR OFFICE WORKERS

Electronics has already produced a number of tools that can make office work more effective and/or less time-consuming (Uhlig, Farber, and Bair, 1979). These tools may be used by secretaries and typists to support the work of others, by individual office workers for their personal work or by groups of workers to assist coordination and communication between them.

Word processing increases the productivity of typists when typing repetitive letters and when making successive changes to drafts of long reports. It also assists the author by ensuring that he need only check the parts that have changed or that vary between successive letters.

Secretaries and telephonists can be supported by systems that record the locations and future availability of their principals, indicate whether they can be interrupted, and allow messages to be recorded and delivered by an electronic mail system. (This allows good secretarial support to be provided to principals without secretaries of their own.)

The pocket or desk calculator simplifies the performance of complex calculations whilst increasing their accuracy. Office automation systems can improve on this by keeping records of the calculations done, indicating the limits of error, drawing source data from structured files or other documents, and filing the results. The system can also apply the same calculations to sets of similar data.

The mathematical power of the computer is applied in various financial and business modelling systems. A suitable model can rapidly show the effect on profits of an increased sales volume or a change in interest rates. It can thus allow planners to consider the implications of a range of options and market responses.

An engineering drawing may also be regarded as a kind of model of reality. Computer Aided Design (CAD) systems help the designer to lay out his drawing, and can then produce any consequent detailed drawings. A CAD system may be linked with Computer Aided Manufacturing (CAM) to produce an integrated CAD/CAM system. CAD and CAD/CAM systems really do automate the work of draughtsmen and other staff. They thus illustrate one direction in which other office support systems may eventually develop.

A data processing computer may be regarded, for many purposes, as a semi-intelligent filing system. In many organizations, unfortunately, the information filed is of uncertain quality and is inaccessible. Access may be improved by online query facilities and report generators, whilst quality and timeliness may be monitored through a data dictionary. Even when these problems have been solved users may still find tables and lists uninformative. A number of techniques may, depending on the circumstances, be used to increase intelligibility:

1. Summarization.
2. Exception reporting.
3. Calculation of key ratios, e.g. revenue per square foot in a retail store.
4. Graphs and histograms over time or some other significant variable.
5. Pie charts.
6. Time series analysis.
7. Animation to show changes over time.

In the past the use of these techniques has been hampered by the complexity of the tools, the difficulty of transferring data from one system to another, and the specialized hardware requirements of the various systems. These problems will become increasingly onerous as the use of data processing systems expands.

Office staff spend a great deal of time in generating and receiving communications. However, whilst senior managers spend a great deal of time dealing with the other people directly (Mintzberg, 1973) this is less true of more junior staff (Table

Table 3.3 Staff and office communications.

| Staff | Proportion of time spent (%) | | | | |
	In meetings	On telephone	Desk work	Other	Source
Five American chief executives	69	6	22	3	Mintzberg, 1968
Three presidents of small companies	36	17	35	12	Choran, 1969
Managers	52	6	31	11	Strassman, 1969
Technologists	64	5	32	0	Strassman, 1969
Staff planners	66	14	20	0	Strassman, 1969
Staff at head office of UK manufacturer	?	10	45	?	Butler, Cox research, 1980 (unpublished)

3.3). Such staff spend time in reading, writing, and thinking, rather than in interacting with other people, and are therefore well served by the tools discussed above. Data communication may be needed in order for the tools to work. Programs and data may be retrieved from a shared library; output may be sent to a central printer or plotter, or to a computer-controlled machine tool.

Many management and technical decisions depend upon arguments in which absolute, quantitative, and subjective elements are mixed. Though these arguments cannot be automated, they can be recorded. In a field such as medicine where the arguments may be complex, even contradictory, such a record may be used to reproduce the argument on a future occasion and to test the sensitivity of the conclusion to changes in the basic facts.

It is possible in some cases to express the general principles of an argument in the system. This has led to the production of 'expert systems' whose advice may be sought by people with corresponding needs. Expert systems have been largely restricted so far to technical areas such as tax law and plant diseases, but a gradual widening of the range of tractable topics is now likely.

INTERPERSONAL COMMUNICATIONS

Conventional systems for communicating with other people present a number of problems:

1. 'Telephone tag'. This is the name given to the problem of actually getting through to the required person. Between two busy people several days or more may elapse between the first attempt to make contact and ultimate success. Research shows that in the United States only 28 per cent. of business calls reach the intended person at the first attempt (Miller, 1979).
2. 'Hassle factor'. The interactive nature of telephony imposes a need for fast response that disrupts other work and may lead to an insufficiently considered response.
3. Impermanence. Telephone conversations are rarely recorded and have, therefore, often to be confirmed by a written letter or memorandum.
4. Information float. This occurs when the organization has the required information but it is in transit, usually by post.
5. Information pollution. This occurs when the recipient receives too much material or information of low or uncertain value.

The emerging office automation technology includes a number of technological solutions to these problems, including electronic mail, store and forward speech (voicegram), and telephone answering systems that keep secretaries and deputies informed of their principals' movements and intentions.

Use of the telephone may be eased by shortcode dialling, automatic retry, and 'camp on' facilities. If the required person cannot be reached, a telephone answering machine or service may take and deliver a message. The value of a telephone conversation is further limited by the impossibility of sharing access to a text or drawing. By the mid-1980s enhanced telephones will allow the parties to exchange documents or share access to a database.

Users of a Computer Based Message System (CBMS) may type messages for one another into the system. The CBMS will deliver the message in a manner appropriate to its urgency and confidentiality. The recipient can then reply to it or forward it to others. Both sender and recipient can file it electronically for future reference. Indeed, filing is a key feature of the CBMS. Research (Bair,1979) indicates that a CBMS can save substantial amounts of managerial and professional time.

Electronic filing systems may include externally published papers as well as internal correspondence. Structured data and text may both be included and may be retrieved through a common search mechanism (BCS Query Languages Group, 1981). As discussed above, the high costs of storage and lack of suitable terminals excluded images—except the crudest—from such systems during the 1970s. The falling cost of storage and increasing prevalence of raster-scan displays will change this during the early 1980s.

There would also be advantages in being able to speak a message into a CBMS and to annotate a document orally. Here again economics has been a constraint, but by 1981 several vendors had announced systems with one or both of these capabilities. Though initial systems allow speech to be held online for only a few hours or days, it is clear that speech will become fully integrated into electronic message and filing systems during the 1980s.

THE WORKSTATION

The work of office principals, whether managers, professionals, or junior executives such as salesmen, is varied, and usually involves all the main modes of communications—data, text, image, and voice. Within each mode the office worker will, in the future, typically have the need to access a number of databases, services, machines, and networks. To avoid the need to have as many terminals as there are modes and services, the concept of a 'workstation' has been introduced. The workstation provides the office principal with any computing power that he actually needs on his desk. It also provides him with a means of accessing a variety of services (Greenfeld, 1981).

Since the workstation is itself likely to be a computer, since it is able to call on the services of other computers, and since it is dedicated to meeting the needs of a single user, it will be able to provide an appropriate and high-quality interface. This may show itself in a number of ways:

1. The workstation will be able to react to every character typed by the user and this will enable the amount of typing he does to be reduced.
2. The processor will also be able to support the use of a graphics peripheral, such as a light-pen.

3. There will be enough processing power to transform received data into the forms preferred by the individual user.

4. The combination of screen and processor will allow various sophisticated visual effects to be exploited. These include multiple windows, so that the user may deal with several concurrent tasks, animations to imitate the turning of physical pages, and the more conventional graphs and histograms.

Many people, myself included, have difficulty in dealing with tabulated data unless they can plot it in some suitable form and also make considerable use of diagrams to clarify and present their ideas. The use of images in business communications is therefore likely to increase as workstations make these options more widely available.

It is, in practice, almost inevitable that the services will have been developed independently by a number of teams and based on a number of different ideas as to how to accomplish their tasks. Thus the style of interaction (I will follow Uhlig, Farber, and Bair 1979, and call it the 'grammar' of the interaction) will vary among services.

The user, however, wishes to see a single coherent interface to all the services he uses, and to exclude those features of the service that he does not use. The workstation can achieve this by translating the user's commands into the language required for the service. To do this the workstation needs to obtain details of the individual grammars from a special workstation support service. This is the concept shown in Figure 3.4.

To use service A the workstation transfers grammar A into its own local storage and uses this both to convert the user's commands into A's formats and to convert A's responses into terms that the user will understand. Since users vary, and since a single user may learn and then forget, the user's understanding and presentation preferences are stored in a user profile in the workstation. If, despite these precautions, the user still has problems, he can ask the workstation for help and the workstation will then retrieve appropriate explanations, or even programmed learning courses, from the support service.

In appropriate cases the workstation may need to interact with several of the supporting services in order to honour a single user request. In some cases the workstation may be called upon to perform substantial processing work. For instance, it may retrieve a file from one service, process it, and then use the records from the file to update files in another service.

This concept has been invented, more or less independently, several times. Figure 3.5 shows the architectural model for a query system developed by the British Computer Society's Query Language Working Group, and a similar model has been developed by the BCS's Job Control Language Working Group (Hopper, 1981). The implementation is, however, a very complex matter; implementations are largely restricted to the academic sector at present.

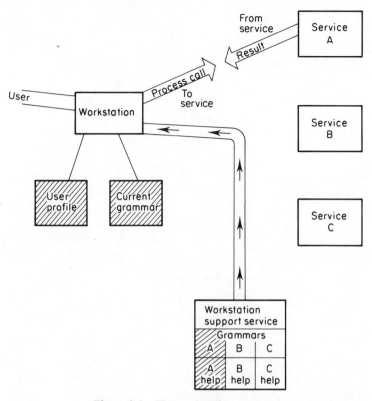

Figure 3.4   The workstation concept.

During 1981 vendors such as Xerox, Office Technology Limited, and Wang Labs. announced workstation products of their own. Initially these all concentrated on providing the user with a high-quality interface and access to services developed in parallel with the workstation.

These modes of working are only feasible if the workstation has high-speed communications with the shared services. Since its use of the services will be intermittent, the peak-to-average speed ratio will, as suggested in the last chapter, be especially high (Martin, 1981).

These workstations typically include a powerful microcomputer, a high-quality raster-scan display, and at least 128k of RAM. The screens have sufficient resolution to provide good graphics and a choice of typefaces for text. They are thus well suited to the preparation of complex documents and to modelling applications. Some workstations are able to go beyond this by providing animations as well as static graphics. These first-generation workstations are very attractive to professional workers in several fields, though their use seems likely to be restricted by their high prices.

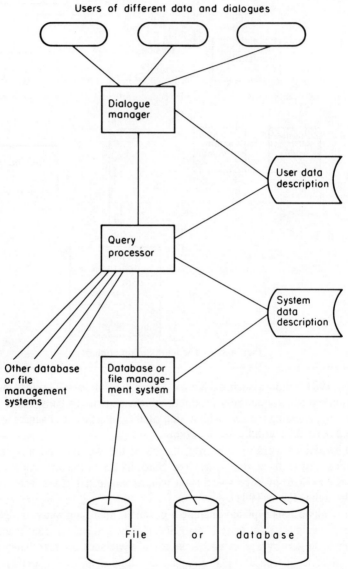

**Figure 3.5   Architecture of a query system (after BCS Query
Languages Group, 1981).**

It seems likely that a rather different, but hopefully compatible, approach will be necessary to support the general manager. He will require a very simple kind of interaction, so that any complex procedures must either be prepackaged for him or performed on his behalf by his secretary.

The workstation has a number of communications requirements that are rather different from those of simpler terminals:

1. It must be able to interact with several services concurrently (preferably without needing several network connections).
2. It must be able to load data and programs from the support service very quickly.
3. It does not require the screen control functions appropriate to simpler terminals as it will manage its own screen(s) or may not display the data at all.
4. It requires a high peak transmission speed.
5. It will exhibit a high peak-to-average ratio, perhaps as high as 1,000 to 1.
6. Interactions typically take the form of a request record in one direction followed by anything between a single response record and a file transfer in the other.

TOMORROW'S FACTORIES AND LABORATORIES

The 1970s saw the widespread use of numerically controlled machine tools and the introduction of some simple robots. During the 1980s the use of these machines will increase greatly, as will the degree to which they are linked together to form automated production lines. These developments are often known as Computer Aided Manufacturing (CAM).

Various 'office' functions are associated with any factory. These include production scheduling, progress chasing, production engineering, and time recording. As electronics enters both factory and office, new opportunities to link together the systems in these separate areas will appear.

At the time of writing (1982), only a few instances of such integration were known. At the Mini Metro plant in British Leyland's Longbridge works, for instance, an automatic warehouse is linked with the main assembly line. Supervisory computers determine the need for subassemblies from the warehouse, and these are then picked by automatic cranes. Other examples exist, especially in semiconductor plants, where the detailed design of the chip implies the manufacturing processes that must be used.

Electronics has been used in process control systems since the mid-1960s. The systems that will be installed during the 1980s will differ from those found previously in being more highly integrated and in using a much larger number of processors.

The control of the system is also passing from control rooms with large numbers of dials and buttons to intelligent interfaces similar to those discussed above in connection with workstations. The requirements for data communications for process control are broadly similar to those for offices. The main points of difference are that:

1. Distances may be large.
2. The environment may be electrically noisy, due to the operation of heavy electrical equipment such as spark welders and furnaces.
3. Some parts of the site may carry severe fire risks mandating the use of non-electrical signalling systems.
4. The maximum transit time may have to be guaranteed. The various subsystems on a plant being controlled are linked by the plant itself. An alarm at one point may therefore be associated with alarms elsewhere (Sloman and Prince, 1981), and the network must be sure to deliver them within some predictable period. Process control engineers are typically more concerned with worst cases than are the designers of office automation systems.
5. Uninterruptibility is important. Operation of the network must continue, even when part has failed catastrophically, and during routine changes and maintenance.
6. Error rates must be very low. Sloman and Prince indicate that bit error rates as low as 1 in 10^{15} may be needed in some cases.
7. Packet sizes may be small. In some parts of the process control environment the amount of data to be moved may be only a few bytes (Cain, Morling, and Stevens, 1974).

Laboratories now make extensive use of micro-controlled analytical machines. Initial uses were limited to providing consistent control of the apparatus and an appropriate presentation of the output, but more recent developments have included systems that can interpret their measurements. In some cases the computers can call on standard results and on rules of interpretation. These applications will clearly grow as the need for rapid results and the power of the machines both increase.

Like the factory, however, the laboratory exists in relationship with other functions that sponsor its work and use its results. These functions include hospitals, health and safety inspectors, factories, and chemical plants. Again, there will be benefits in linking the laboratory with its sponsors so as to provide rapid and error-free communication of test results.

4. THE ROLE OF THE NETWORK

Networks exist for four principal reasons:

1. To provide communications between organizations.
2. To support communications between people.
3. To provide access to shared data.
4. To allow expensive resources to be shared.

The telephone network is used for interpersonal communications much more than for any other purpose, but it is also used for communication between organizations and for gaining access to shared information (consider directory enquiries or the speaking clock). Message networks such as telex also serve these roles, with inter-business traffic predominating.

Computer networks have not usually been introduced for interpersonal communication but they have come increasingly to serve this purpose. IBM's internal file transfer network, VNET, for instance, was introduced in order to transfer data files and programs between mainframe computers. By 1980, however, 70 per cent. of all data transferred were textual (Gardner and Hartman, 1980) and those responsible expected this proportion to increase even further. The introduction of digital voice systems for office workers will allow data networks to carry speech as well as data, thus increasing further the use of data networks for interpersonal communication.

In the past all processing and data resources have been centralized and hence shared. This position is being seriously undermined by the growth of personal computing—to the extent, indeed, that some pundits believe that personal computers can replace all other kinds of computer. This is undoubtedly a mistake.

Much business data must be shared among the members of a single working group. The group may be a team of sales clerks, accountants, physicists, or programmers, but the principle is the same—some data, price lists, overdue accounts, bubble chamber tracks, or a data dictionary, need to be shared among them, and are not the particular property of any one user. Increasingly, however, users will have their own terminals and computers and will need networks to gain access to these shared data. In some cases it would be unsafe to leave the responsibility for the integrity of the data in the hands of a single user. In these cases shared storage shares with DP systems the advantage of allowing an independent guarantor of this integrity.

In any environment, some useful resources are too expensive, or too difficult or inconvenient to use, to be provided to all the possible users. These resources must be shared, and a network provides one means of doing this. Computer centres have traditionally provided their users with access to fast printers, tape drives, and microfilm equipment. As more users obtain their own computers, the network needs to provide those machines with the necessary supporting facilities. The resources that may usefully be shared are often electromechanical storage and input/output devices, but they might also be processors specialized for tasks such as modelling, fluid mechanics, compilation, and deductive logic.

The ability to share resources flexibly between users has a number of indirect benefits. Most organizations are obliged to expand their computing power progressively as limited funds allow. A shared storage unit will not only have a lower cost per character than a set of smaller stores but it will also enhance the value of all the machines that can gain access to it—some of which would not be able to justify their own extra local stores.

In the past the monolithic structure of computing systems has obliged users to locate all their shared equipment in physical proximity. A high-speed local network relaxes this constraint, making it possible to provide sufficiently important (or demanding) groups of users with their own printers, microfilm units, etc. These units may work better when removed from the 'mass production' environment of the computer centre.

Even within a computer centre there is often value in separating such functions as printing, network management, and microfilm production from each other and from the central computer. Noisy printers may be kept apart from delicate microfilm recorders, while the diagnosis and fixing of errors on transmission lines is best conducted in quieter surroundings.

TOMORROW'S NEEDS FOR DATA COMMUNICATIONS

Whatever the optimum shape for tomorrow's systems, it is certain that users will continue to use, and even expand, their existing systems. User investment in hardware and systems software for centralized systems is considerable, and the investment in application systems is much greater. Even where the benefits are clear (and often they are not) data processing managers will find that they have higher priorities than changing the basic architecture of their systems, and only enough staff to meet the most urgent needs.

Tomorrow's data communication needs, then, will include yesterday's (as given in Chapter 2) and the transparent, terminal-to-host, data circuit will be an important service for a future communications system to offer.

Tomorrow's office will, as we have seen, contain a variety of intelligent machines, many of them having high operating speeds. Appropriate communications for them must allow each to communicate with all the others with the minimum delay and interruption.

The New Functional Requirements

For the office machines of the future, however, yesterday's data circuit is too slow to establish, too cumbersome, and carries data at too low a speed.

Communication between computer programs characteristically takes the form of a short request (a CALL) followed, after a short time, by a reply (a RETURN). This contrasts with the prolonged association, lasting many seconds or minutes, found in telephony. Communication between computers will also show this pattern.

The 'bursty' (high peak-to-average ratio) characteristic of this traffic is best matched by a packet-switched communications system. Each packet may represent a request or a response and the communications system is free to serve other users while each computer is deciding its next action. Local communications facilities can operate with very low error rates, so that elaborate error control provisions are not required. For simplicity, then, the system should avoid the complexities required to manage a continuing association between communicating computers. It may use a datagram approach in which packets are processed singly (Sweetman, 1981).

A high transmission speed will be necessary to match the speed of the office computers. To match the speed of the computer's own internal bus is not necessary, since the overhead associated with constructing and receiving packets sets severe limits on the speed at which an external network can be driven (Balkovich and Soceanu, 1982). (This is fortunate as the cost of the communications system rises with the speed.)

The speed that is actually required may be estimated in a number of ways. I will consider, successively, disc sharing, program loading, and image transmission.

For shared access to discs the intervention of the network should cause only a small delay. In the case of a business microcomputer accessing a floppy disc this implies a speed of about 300k bit/s (Shirer, 1982). In the case of a minicomputer or office workstation accessing a fixed disc the speed implied is about 1M bit/s. For a high performance disc server in a mainframe environment a speed of 20M bit/s may be necessary (Bux et al., 1981).

When using the network to load a program from a shared program library it is desirable not to delay the user's work. The whole process should therefore be complete within, say, two seconds, of which the transmission may occupy one. To fill half the store of a 64k micro will require a transmission speed in excess of 300k bit/s. Again, higher speeds will be appropriate for bigger computers.

As indicated earlier, the use of images in office systems is likely to increase. In some cases the image will be generated locally by the workstation and there is in this case no corresponding communications requirement. In other cases, the image may be generated remotely, and the user may wish to 'flip' quickly through a succession of such images. The CCITT recommendation for facsimile implies the storage of up to 100k bytes per picture. This can be reduced by data compression, but even a tenfold reduction implies transmission speeds of around 1M bit/s.

It is clear that high transmission speeds will be needed for future communications systems. Approximately, these speeds might be:

For a microcomputer—300k bit/s
For a minicomputer or office workstation—1M bit/s
For a mainframe computer—20M bit/s

These speeds are required for resource sharing and distributed processing. I shall refer to the supporting communications system as providing wideband communications.

If speeds of this kind are available it is clear that the communication will be very bursty. The ratio of peak transmission speed to average transmission speed is likely to be at least 1,000 and may be even higher (Martin, 1981; Shoch and Hupp, 1980a).

Tomorrow's communications requirements can thus be met by a system that provides two basic services:

1. Low-speed data circuits, and
2. Wideband datagrams.

This two-level model of future communications requirements is shown, rather simplified, as it relates to office systems, in Figure 4.1.

The simplest part of the figure is that labelled 'data circuits'. The communications system here has the functions discussed in the last chapter. In fact, the data circuits may be supplied by direct cables, a terminal access network, a PABX, or as an additional service on the wideband network. Office machines communicate over an office wideband network which must meet the specifications developed in this chapter.

The figure also assumes the existence of a separate computer centre in which computers and peripherals are interconnected over a separate and very fast network. This network will have a functional specification similar to that developed in this chapter, but with a much higher maximum transmission speed. Since it is not the same as that installed in the office, the two are interconnected through a special processor called a gateway.

In practice, only a few organizations will have all these kinds of network, whilst some will have special networks in their laboratories, factories, and process plants. These, too, will communicate with the other local networks through gateways.

THE OTHER REQUIREMENTS

The most elegant and carefully thought out network will be unacceptable if it is too expensive or unreliable. We may therefore identify a number of other requirements for a real network.

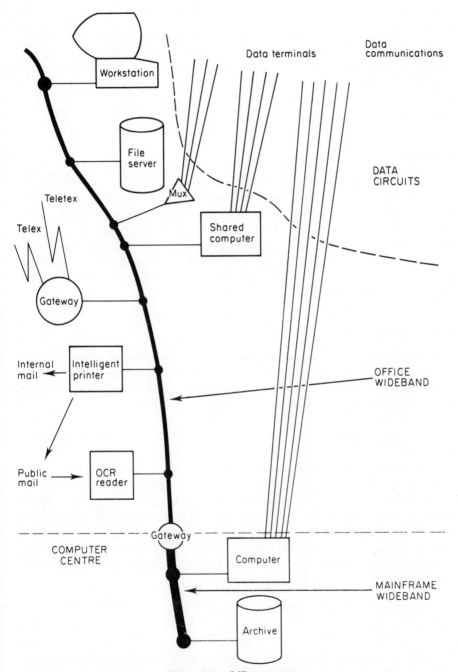

Figure 4.1   Office systems.

Cost

The cost of connecting to the network must be modest compared with the cost of the attached devices. For a 300 dollar educational micro 100 dollars may well seem excessive—after all, the network itself provides little value, only access to resources that also have their price. For a 10,000 dollar multi-function workstation even 1,000 dollars may be acceptable. It appears that 10–20 per cent. of the cost of the device will generally be acceptable.

Reliability

Future offices and factories will be as dependent on their data communications as present-day offices are on their telephones. Very high reliability is therefore essential, and this means both that system faults should be very rare and that users should have confidence that they will be fixed quickly. A reliability of 99.99 per cent. sounds excellent, but it implies one hour of lost time each year. If this hour falls, as Murphy's law* predicts, at the busiest time of the busiest day, then the business will lose an hour's work (and the manager responsible for the network will be very unpopular).

Ease of Installation

The network should be easy to install, modify, and extend. It will often be necessary for non-technical staff to move machines and to attach new ones, so these operations, at least, must not require technical skills. They should also have the least possible effect on other users.

Error Protection

The network should have a very low error rate and should detect a large majority of the errors that do occur. Most administrative computer systems require essentially perfect operation, but other applications are less fussy. In the cases of radar (Masterman, 1980) and facsimile transmission, for instance, it is not necessary to recover the lost data, whilst in the case of speech the attempt to do so may cause stuttering in the sound produced. If the inherent reliability is sufficiently high, the network itself need not correct detected errors—the decision may be left to the attached devices.

---

* Murphy's law exists in many forms, of which the shortest is 'If anything can go wrong, it will'. Humorous 'corollaries' abound, but the observation that 'Things always go wrong at the worst times' is more than a joke—it's the only reasonable basis for planning a reliable system.

Connectivity

Each attached computer should be able to interact directly with all other attached computers and, preferably, with all the attached terminals as well.

Delays

If the network is to carry interactive speech then it should offer a constant and low-delay service (probably at 64k bit/s, the PTT's standard speed for digital speech), and the maximum possible delay should be known. If the network is to be used for process control applications, it should provide a constant and low-delay service to small packets of data.

Interworking

Devices attached to a local network should be able to access wide area networks such as the public telephone network, public packet and circuit switched networks, networks of the teletex and videotex types, and those of service providers, such as time-sharing bureaux.

Special requirements

There are a number of characteristics that are not needed very widely but which are very important to some users. These include:

1. Wireless connection for mobile units.
2. Integration of video and other signals in the network.
3. Security of the network from accidental or deliberate penetration, possibly by very sophisticated means.
4. A means of broadcasting efficiently to all the stations on the network. (Though useful in network management this is rarely a user requirement. User requirements to send mail to a list of users are usually best implemented via separate calls to each, as it is difficult to manage the necessary low-level acknowledgements.)

5. CAN THE TELEPHONE SYSTEM MEET THE NEED?

The last two chapters have established the need for a data communications system in the office and factory of the future. But existing offices, and most laboratories, colleges, and factories, already have communication facilities in the shape of their telephone systems. The site telephone system is typically based on a central switch, known as a Private Automatic Branch Exchange (PABX), or on a manual switchboard on smaller sites. Telephones are found in all parts of the site and are connected to the central switch by pairs of copper wires twisted together ('twisted pairs'), as shown in Figure 5.1.

Existing PABXs have mostly been conceived and built to serve conventional telephones using analogue signalling methods. They are therefore limited to low data rates (9,600 bit/s is the usual maximum—and less over the public network) and long call setup times. Moreover, systems being installed at present are sized on the assumption that the typical telephone will be used for a score or so short calls each day, and that, especially during the busiest hour of the day, only a minority of phones will be in simultaneous use. Data terminals, by contrast, are typically connected to a single computer for hours at a time, and are often in use for most of the working day. During the busy hour they may all be in use.

Existing telephone systems are therefore both too inflexible and too expensive for data communication, leading to the installation of private communications networks by many organizations. But telephony, like data communications, is undergoing rapid and profound changes through the application of digital signalling and control techniques to speech transmission and switching. Some vendors (Hudson, 1981; Mackie, 1982) and independent commentators (Richer, 1980) have been so impressed by these advances that they see the digital PABX as the natural basis of all office communications.

A number of advantages are seen for the use of the digital PABX in this role. They include:

1. The use of a single set of wires, leading to economies in installation and maintenance.
2. The possibility of upgrading existing telephone systems in order to progressively meet future needs.
3. The integration of speech and data.
4. The inbuilt connection to the public switched telephone network (PSTN).

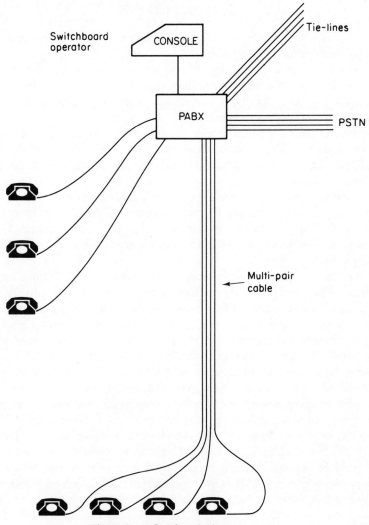

Figure 5.1   On-site telephone system.

5. Cheap switching units, due to the high production volumes made possible by the size of the telephone industry.
6. The simplicity, and hence reliability and cheapness, of the logic for circuit switching.

This chapter considers whether the arguments used in favour of basing business communications on the PABX are sound.

COMMON WIRING

The cost of wiring can be considerable, though it varies greatly with the nature of the particular building being wired.

In 1978, for instance, it cost about £100 per instrument to wire for telephony a modern office block in a British city. Three years later, however, a bank in the City of London paid over £400 per instrument to provide telephone-grade cables between a group of older office buildings.

The twisted pairs used in telephone systems are much cheaper than the multi-wire and coaxial cables used for data networks. This is of limited significance though, because the costs of physical installation are typically much greater than the cost of the cable.

An integrated network will avoid the cost of installing separate wires for data. If the existing telephone wires can be used for voice and data (which is not the case for all the systems proposed), the cost advantage will be even greater. However, these cost savings are balanced by extra costs in the telephone instruments and in the central PABX.

Where there are many data devices, or if moves are very frequent, it will be more convenient, and ultimately cheaper, to provide a data socket to every office than to install the necessary wiring each time the need changes. In this case, the use of existing wiring is a considerable convenience since it saves a great deal of disruption as well as expense. In modern practice, however, it is usual to install many more twisted pairs than are actually needed, precisely in order to cater for extensions and moves. In this case the pairs may be used as the basis of a separate data network at little more cost than an integrated network.

In older buildings there may be neither spare pairs nor spare duct space in which to lay new wires. In such cases a network based on existing wiring is a great advantage. Even here, however, alternatives exist. A data channel may be added to a telephone circuit by impressing the data on a carrier frequency outside the range used in telephony, and a collection of such circuits may be used for a separate network as in CASE's Grapevine system. By this means, a data network may be overlaid on wiring that is already fully utilized for telephony.

VOICE–DATA INTEGRATION

Voice–data integration in the workstation is desirable in order to minimize the number of machines on the worker's desk and to allow the workstation processor to assist the worker by finding numbers in directories, redialing failed calls, etc. (Naffah, 1982). These functions do not require integration in transmission and switching, since any data calls are made to shared machines, rather than to the other party to the telephone call.

There is currently very little experience of voice–data integrated applications, but what there is seems to divide into three classes:

1. Systems in which the computer sets up calls for a human operator and guides him or her in dealing with the called party. The most obvious example in this class is telesales.
2. Systems in which a spoken conversation is supplemented by the sharing of documents. This application has been most used in teleconferencing systems, but I prefer to use the more modest term 'hybrid call' to express the actual communications function.
3. Systems in which stored speech relates to a stored document. This facility is usually termed voice annotation, but it also offers the possibility of treating the speech, or other sound, as part of the finished document.

Of these, only the last (voice annotation) actually requires an integrated communications system, and this application also requires integration in the workstation and in data storage. The communications functions needed for applications in the first two classes can be provided by establishing independent calls in separate networks, provided that some control information can be passed between them. However, hybrid calls at least would probably be more easily and effectively achieved with an integrated network.

In principle, then, an integrated communications network is the best basis for future office communications. There are, however, a number of practical factors that tell against it.

Voice and data devices present very different interfaces to the communications system, and different kinds of data devices have different interfaces. The switch must therefore be able to accept calls over these various interfaces. This compatibility problem may be reduced by ignoring certain aspects of the interfaces, notably those associated with error control and addressing, but this reduces the value of the system, especially if calls have to be extended off-site over leased lines.

A modern computerized PABX (at CBX) has scores of features that help with the management of telephone calls. Such features include call forwarding, 'camp on busy', call transfer, and call distribution. Many fewer features are needed for data calls, though some extra features, such as the automatic determination of transmission rate, will be needed as well.

Where the features are nominally the same, there may in fact be differences. Thus, for statistical and accounting purposes, telephone traffic will be measured in call-seconds, or erlangs, whilst data traffic is better expressed as a number of messages or bits.

A major failure in an integrated network will paralyse all modes of communication, whereas independent data and speech networks can substitute for one another to some degree. An integrated network must therefore have a much higher reliability than the separate ones would need.

Because of these considerations, an integrated communications system will be more complex than a single-mode system, and possibly more complex than two single-mode systems serving the two purposes.

THE DEVELOPMENT OF COMPUTERIZED BRANCH
EXCHANGES (CBXs)

Until the 1970s, telephone circuits were completed at the exchange by the making of a physical contact between two conductors, a technique known as space division switching.

In 1974 IBM announced the 3750 CBX, a product typical of the first generation of CBXs. The CBX continued to make physical circuits but did so under computer control. This enabled IBM to offer a wide and expanding range of call management facilities. Users could divert their calls to other phones, and instruct the CBX to inform them when another phone became free. The 3750 has more recently been given the ability to collect data from telephone-compatible terminals for applications such as building security and time-recording. It also collects traffic statistics.

A second generation of CBXs may be defined by their use of digital time division switching as the basic technology. In this method, calls are digitized when they arrive at the switch and a number of them are multiplexed onto a high-speed bus. Calls are then removed from the common highway by units connected to the outgoing lines for which the calls are intended. Time division switching alone is adequate for small CBXs, but there is a limit to the number of calls that can be multiplexed onto a single highway. Above this limit, a mixture of space and time division switching is generally used. Both kinds of switching are implemented by LSI digital electronics rather than by physical contacts, so second-generation CBXs are fully digital machines.

Despite their digital technology, second-generation CBXs do not offer much support to data transmission. Telephone calls are digitized at the interface to the switch, limiting data transmission rates to what can be sent over one or two twisted pairs (usually 9,600 bit/s). Data and voice calls cannot usually be multiplexed over the wires to the phone; nor can a data device gain access to the digital paths within the switch (which operate at 64k bit/s or more).

The year 1980 saw the announcement of the first of the third-generation CBXs, the Intecom Integrated Business Exchange (IBX), and this was followed in 1981 by comparable announcements from a number of other US vendors. To match this, the suppliers of second-generation CBXs have announced enhancements to provide their products with third-generation facilities.

The IBX is typical of these new products and has, in fact, set the standard. A schematic diagram is shown in Figure 5.2. Each telephone has an RS232 data socket into which a terminal or other data device may be plugged.

All telephones are connected to the nearest switching partition over four-wire cables. The cable carries digital data at 128,000 bit/s, divided as follows:

64,000 bit/s for digital speech
56,000 bit/s for data transmission over an independent data circuit
 8,000 bit/s for signalling

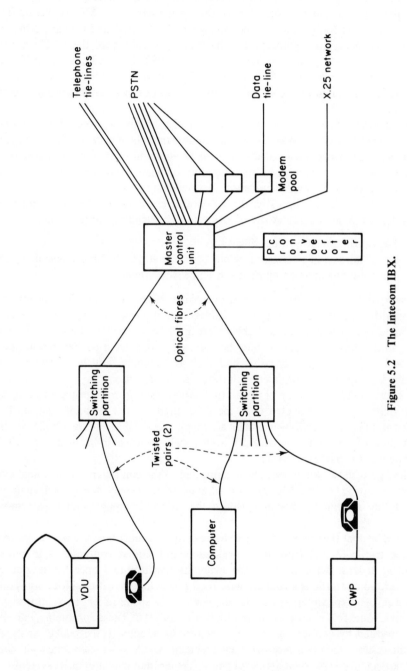

Figure 5.2   The Intecom IBX.

Each switching partition can accept cables from up to 256 telephones.

Switching partitions are connected to the main control unit (MCU) over optical fibre cables. The MCU contains the intelligence of the IBX and is responsible for call management, user features, and the routing of calls onto the PSTN or tie-lines. In addition to placing voice calls over the PSTN or tie-lines, the IBX can extend data calls over the PSTN or leased lines using one modem taken from a pool. It can also multiplex data calls onto an X.25 or other suitable network connection.

During 1981 Intecom announced the first of a family of protocol convertors. This first product allows ASCII asynchronous terminals to access IBM3270 computer ports, allowing users to save substantial sums in their terminal purchases. Intecom has also announced its intention of supporting certain local area networks, presumably by attachment to the switching partitions.

The IBX, despite its impressive design parameters, is still limited in a number of ways, ways that are characteristic of its origin as a telephony circuit switch:

1. The maximum data rate is 56k bit/s.
2. Each station can establish only one data call at a time. This makes it unsuitable for connecting computers and office workstations.

These problems can, of course, be overcome. Higher transmission speeds can be provided by the use of special cables and drivers, and by using several switching points within the switching partition. To support multiple concurrent calls, all the devices concerned may be required to observe a packet multiplexing protocol (CCITT X.25 perhaps), and their bit streams may be analysed into packets by extra logic associated with the switching partition.

Figure 5.3 shows the kind of design that would result from pursuing these ideas. Terminals are still connected over the data channel of a telephone cable. The workstation is connected over a dedicated high-speed cable and uses X.25, whilst the shared computer also uses X.25 over a high-speed cable but has been wired directly into the packet analyser.

The figure shows the workstation connected to the computer, one terminal and a remote device (via the MCU), with all calls going through the packet analyser first. Other terminals are connected to the shared computer and to a remote device.

It is clear that the 'packet analyser' has exactly the functions of a packet switch. All the traffic to and from the workstation and shared computer is therefore switched at least twice, once by the switching partition and once by the packet analyser. Some traffic is switched twice by the switching partition. Not only is this wasteful of (expensive) switching capacity, it also requires two addressing schemes, one for circuits and another for packets. These problems can be circumvented by connecting all the workstations directly to the packet analyser but the result is then two essentially independent switches—a telephone switching partition and a packet switching exchange—rather than one integrated system.

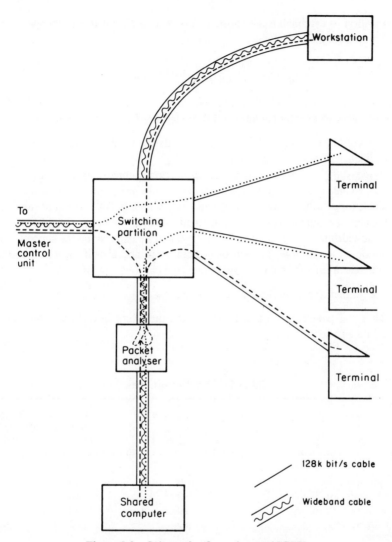

Figure 5.3   Schematic of an advanced ICBX.

One manufacturer, GTE, is proposing to link its PABX and packet switching products in an 'integrated' switching system rather similar to that suggested here. Other vendors are proposing to support a local area network, i.e. a distributed packet switching system, in conjunction with their CBXs (Mackie, 1982).

Hybrid schemes of this sort are likely to be successful if they follow the model developed in the previous chapter. The key features are that the CBX should be used for telephony and low-speed data circuits, and the LAN for wideband data communications. Communications channels between the two systems may allow a workstation to establish a telephone call or a data circuit to be extended across the LAN to a suitable machine.

THE CBX AS OFFICE CONTROLLER

The argument in favour of basing the future office controller on a CBX has been given very clearly by Richer (1980). Stated briefly, his argument is:

1. The volume of voice traffic greatly exceeds the volume of data traffic. (Some of Richer's figures are given in Table 5.1.)
2. Voice–data integration is desirable in the communications system.
3. Since voice predominates, 'the network should be optimized for voice'.
4. The shape of the network should be a star with a (CBX) switch at the centre.
5. Circuit switching (or an equivalent method which allocates a fixed bandwidth for the duration of a call) should be used, since the central switch accounts for a large fraction of system costs and circuit switching requires simpler circuits than packet switching (the obvious alternative).

This argument turns on three assumptions:

1. That the penetration of terminals and other data devices will remain low relative to speech devices.

Table 5.1   Traffic volumes.

	Hypothetical future office	Bolt, Beranek, and Newman office, c. 1980
No. of		
Telephones	500	500
Word processors	50	40
Data entry terminals	50	0
Fax transceiver	10	2
Copiers	10	?
Printers	10	7
Busy hour utilization (erlangs)		
Voice	125	—
Data	102	—
(bit/s)		
Voice	8M	4.5M
Data	161k	33k
Number of 64k bit/s duplex channels		
Voice	144	70
Data	12	6

2. That a 64k bit/s switched channel in the CBX can be divided amongst many data circuits, provided only that the sum of their transmission speeds is less than 48k bit/s (the balance being multiplexing overheads).
3. That data and voice traffic can sensibly be compared in terms of bits transmitted alone.

Terminal penetration in Europe is low but rising. Some US sites already have as many terminals as telephones, whilst some European organizations are already planning ratios of 1:2 or more. Although terminal penetration will remain low on many sites, it is the more innovative users who will set the pattern for new systems.

Multiplexing of the sort assumed is quite possible; indeed, by the use of sophisticated data compression techniques and statistical multiplexing, one commercial multiplexor is able to carry a load of up to 150 per cent. of the nominal capacity, rather than the 75 per cent. assumed by Richer.

If this is done, however, the CBX will be unable to discriminate between the data circuits in order to switch them. Since this switching is an essential requirement, the switch must either dedicate the whole of the channel to each data circuit or be given extra logic so that it can switch within the channel. Either approach (both have been taken in commercial products) must add to the complexity and cost of the CBX.

Telephony traffic conforms to certain widely accepted technical standards and is thus easily measured and compared. Data traffic, by contrast, is much more varied. The discussion in the last chapter indicated that data devices require speeds from a few tens of bits per second to a million or more. The requirements for a data circuit are fairly similar to those for a speech circuit, but those for wideband data are quite different. In addition, if one measures the number of logical connections made and broken per day, rather than the number of bits transmitted, one finds that there are either a fairly small number of connections of long duration or a large number of very short duration (see, for instance, Torp, 1980). Neither profile is close to that assumed by the designers of CBXs and for which they have designed their switches.

The previous section showed how CBX designs could evolve so as to meet the full requirements for future business communications. It also showed that the resulting designs would be remarkably complex, and hence expensive. This may be seen in another way. A CBX that connects 100 terminals or workstations to computers, using 56k bit/s circuits, will need to switch 5.6M bit/s.

ASCII terminals may send about one character per second (1 c.p.s.) and receive up to 60 c.p.s., giving an average rate of about 340 bit/s. Synchronous terminals may operate at up to 9,600 bit/s but do so only for a few seconds in each minute. Workstations may be able to exploit the full 56k bit/s speed of the line but will do so only intermittently. Of this 5.6M bit/s, then, only about 1 per cent. is useful data and an ideal network would only need to carry about 56k bit/s. A packet switching network might, allowing for overheads, need to carry as much as

100k bit/s and a total speed of twice that would be desirable to prevent queues from forming.

Relative to an ideal network, then, a packet switching system is about 25 per cent. efficient whilst a CBX is about 1 per cent. efficient. This inefficiency will, inevitably, be reflected in the price to the user.

Ultimately, it is this inefficiency, together with the need to support instantaneous speeds in excess of 64k bit/s and to interwork with several other devices concurrently, that makes the CBX a poor basis for future office communications.

6. TAKE A BUS!

Circuit switching is limited by the transmission capacity of a single circuit, yet modern electronics makes it fairly inexpensive to send and receive digital signals at speeds of 1M bit/s and above. To exploit this, it is possible to arrange for all the data devices to be connected to a single bus.

Buses were first introduced to the computer world by minicomputers. Prior to their introduction in the mid-1960s, the various parts of a computer had usually been connected by direct channels, as shown in Figure 6.1. (Indeed, this arrangement is still usual in mainframes.) In a bus-based architecture (shown in Figure 6.2) each module is connected to the common bus and can send messages addressed to other modules. In a minicomputer the bus is usually a number of wires in parallel.

The use of a bus reduces the number of interfaces needed by the CPU. It also enforces a common interconnection standard for the various modules, and allows some of those modules to access the memory directly, thus offloading the CPU. The common interconnection standard has the advantage of encouraging suppliers other than that of the CPU to develop compatible modules for attachment to the bus. Though this development has been important for minis it has been very much more important in the case of micros—which have also used bus structures. One popular micro—the Apple—is built with an easily removable top so as to encourage the addition of compatible boards, many not built by Apple itself. A bus also requires less physical cable than the direct circuits.

A bus is particularly appropriate to communications of high peak-to-average ratio. If, for instance, there are 10 modules each requiring a maximum transmission speed of 1M bit/s but presenting, on the average, only 10k bit/s, they will occupy just 10 per cent. of the capacity of a 1M bit/s bus. This occupancy is sufficiently low to ensure that most attempts to use the bus will be immediately successful. Thus each module is able, on most occasions, to use the full speed of the common bus.

When several modules have simultaneous needs to use the bus, some set of rules must be applied to arrange that each gets access in turn. In a minicomputer the rules are generally implemented by a central adjudicator which decides the order in which modules may transmit.

A bus provides high reliability. Because the only common elements, the

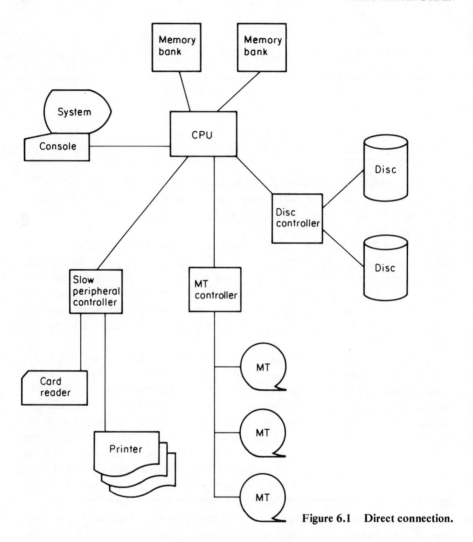

Figure 6.1   Direct connection.

common wires and the adjudicator, are rather simple, they are more reliable than a CPU.

A bus also provides universal connectivity. Any module can use the bus to send data to any other device. In addition the bus provides the possibility of broadcasting data from one module to all the others, a capability that has proved valuable in some situations (Dalal, 1977).

THE SITE BUS

Communication between the devices on one site presents many of the same characteristics as the communication between the modules of a computer system.

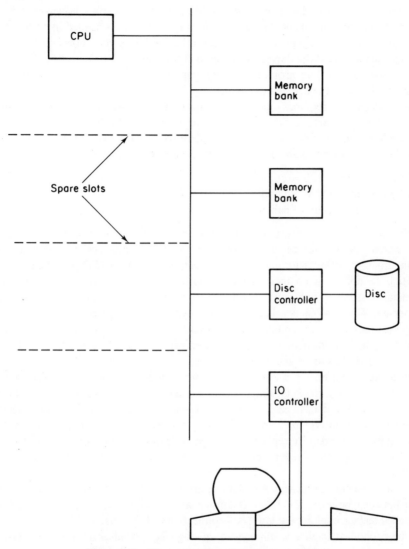

Figure 6.2   Bus connection of computer modules.

Traffic is bursty, the pattern of flow changes frequently, and individual devices can benefit from high transmission speeds. The main differences are that speeds can be lower and bursts are typically longer.

Site communications may therefore be provided by giving all the devices access to a common bus carried round the site. *The provision of a high-speed shared channel is common to all the new local area networks (LANs) and constitutes their most distinctive common characteristic.*

Of course, the issues in local network design are rather different from those in the design of mini- and microcomputers. Many of the principles, however, are the same. Thus some means of sharing the capacity of the bus is needed in both cases, though this is generally provided by a central adjudicator on a computer bus but is dispersed amongst the devices in the case of a LAN.

In both cases a bus provides reduced wiring costs, high reliability, universal connectivity, and a broadcast capability.

A physical bus requires much less wiring than an equivalent number of direct connections. Research by the Mitre Corporation (Everett, 1975) showed that, if the US Tactical Air Force's AN/TSQ-91 Control and Reporting Centre had been based on a bus rather than direct wires, it would have required:

28 rather than 2,800 circuits
13 cables rather than 95 and
two tons less weight of cables

These features have attracted military planners, especially of airborne systems (Czaplicki, 1981), but are also attractive to office managers whose ducts are beginning to overflow with power cables, computer cables, CCTV cables, etc.

High reliability is an increasingly important consideration in business communications, but it is difficult to achieve when the components of the system are dispersed. Where a bus is used, two devices will be able to communicate provided only that they are functioning, that the bus adjudicator is functioning, and that the bus is intact. It is not necessary that any central unit, such as a mainframe, CBX, or packet switch, should also be functioning.

Because of the bursty nature of data communications, the bus usually carries data in the form of packets. Each packet includes the addresses of the destination and the source, the data and, usually, a checksum (see Figure 6.3). Each device removes the packets that are addressed to itself, validates the data via the checksum and sends any reply to the originating device. Since one device may be receiving packets from several others, the source address is an essential part of the format.

Where the communications system keeps no record of any continuing association between devices, the LAN is known as a datagram network. This simple packet interface exploits the universal connectivity of the bus.

The broadcast facility is obtained by giving one special desination address the meaning 'ALL'. All devices will then be expected to act on these packets.

The effect of a digital bus of this kind is to extend the internal buses of the connected computers round the site, whilst restricting traffic within a single computer

Destination address	Source address	Data	Checksum

Figure 6.3   LAN packet format.

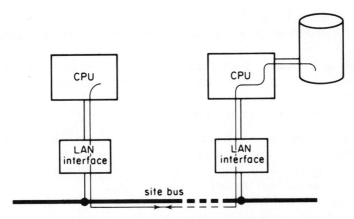

Figure 6.4   Inter-computer communication.

to that computer alone. The bus therefore allows a CPU to access peripherals, memories, or other processors that are physically remote but connected to the bus, as shown in Figure 6.4.

This approach is clearly very appropriate for inter-computer communication which, I argued earlier, will come increasingly to dominate business communications during the 1980s. But whilst 'dumb' terminals remain in use, a situation that will continue well into the decade, it will be desirable for a LAN to support them.

Terminals are generally connected to the bus through an intelligent interface unit. The unit consists of two parts (see Figure 6.5), one of which, the network controller, manages the use of the bus, whilst the other, the call processor, manages the interface with the terminal(s). The call processor is responsible for establishing a virtual circuit across the network to a computer port, and for clearing this circuit when the terminal session is over. During the session it receives data from the terminal, constructs packets for the LAN, and then passes the

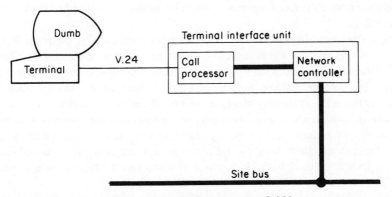

Figure 6.5   Terminal support on a LAN.

packets to the network controller. The network controller is responsible for passing the packets across the bus. Data for the terminal goes through the reverse process.

Where, as is usual on Unix[tm] and similar systems, the computer may react individually to each input character, a packet must be created and received for each character input.

The bus has several characteristic disadvantages:

1. Every station must be able to send and receive at the full speed of the bus, which may be much greater than it would otherwise require.
2. Every station must be able to recognize data for itself in a time less than the transmission time of the data.
3. Every station must apply enough signal power to the bus to reach the most distant station on it.
4. Since all stations see all the traffic, a bus is inherently insecure and, if some data are sensitive, it must be protected by encryption (and possibly by other means as well).

Network designers have sought to minimize these problems by, for instance, restricting the size of the LAN.

THE LOCAL AREA NETWORK—A DEFINITION

These considerations suggest a more formal definition of a LAN than was possible earlier. I offer the following:

A LAN is a communications system that carries one or more high-speed digital channels round a building or other facility in such a manner that many devices may obtain brief exclusive use of the channel from time to time.

This definition clearly excludes circuit switches and the older style of packet switched networks, since the only common channel is restricted to the internals of the switch.

The size of facility covered by a LAN varies considerably. Some are limited to 1,000 metres or less; others can serve the whole of a metropolitan area. This book will focus on those intended to serve more than a computer room and less than a town, but with occasional excursions outside those limits. The facilities served may be factories, ships, and planes as well as offices and colleges.

The term 'high speed' is fairly imprecise. Several manufacturers have developed networks for terminals in which the common channel is run at speeds as low as 20k bit/s; indeed there is no clear distinction between these products and the older multi-drop lines used with block-mode synchronous terminals such as the IBM 3270.

The speed must therefore be judged in relation to the devices being supported.

Chapter 4 discussed the peak transmission speeds required by various kinds of computer. To be sure of providing these speeds to a large population of dispersed computers, and to allow for overheads, the LAN is generally run at a higher speed than that required by a single machine.

As Table 6.1 shows, a speed of 50k bit/s may suffice for a LAN that supports only terminals, whilst 5M bit/s will be needed for minicomputers.

Table 6.1 Devices and LAN speeds.

Device	Speed required of a LAN bus (bit/s)
Mainframe computer (communicating with peripherals and slave processors)	50M
Minicomputers and intelligent workstations	5M
Microcomputers	500k
Terminals	50k
Calculators	5k

Figure 6.6 shows how LANs relate, in speed and range, to other kinds of communication network:

1. Computer buses provide high speeds over very short ranges.
2. The IEEE 488 standard (sometimes known as the Hewlett-Packard bus) provides high-speed local communications for laboratory instruments.
3. CCITT Recommendation V.24 defines cables, etc., for a terminal to modem interface and is rather limited in both speed and range.
4. Line drivers allow terminals to access computers over twisted pairs for distances up to a few miles, but are limited in speed.
5. Trunk networks, including both public networks such as Transpac and Tymnet and private networks implemented under SNA and similar systems, can girdle the earth but support speeds little higher than those needed for terminals.

One consequence of their speed and distance characteristics are their short data transit times. A packet will typically cross a LAN in a few milliseconds or less. To cross a trunk network may take a significant fraction of a second.

Though the idea of a single shared channel is basic to the concept of a LAN, there are a number of products that provide, at least optionally, multiple shared channels, and these should not be excluded. These products are known as 'broadband' networks and will be dealt with fully in Chapter 15.

For most purposes it is convenient to treat these systems as a number of separate and independent LANs that happen to share a single cable, and this is the approach taken here.

The concept of the shared channel is a logical one rather than a physical one.

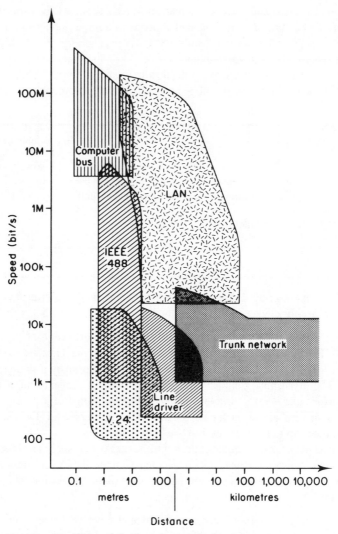

Figure 6.6   Local networks in context.

That is, it defines the services offered by the LAN rather than its physical shape. Of course, a physical bus is the most direct way to implement a logical bus, but it is not the only one—stars, rings, and other shapes have also been used.

A great variety of LANs have been developed differing in their shape, speed, resilience, price, and in the nature of the devices that can be attached. This variety forms the substance of the second part of this book. Before considering the technologies, it is useful to consider the requirements that a LAN should meet.

THE REQUIREMENTS FOR A LOCAL AREA NETWORK

A good LAN must meet a number of requirements concerning the number and kinds of device it should support, the effectiveness of its capacity sharing algorithms, reliability, etc.

Though some requirements—high reliability, for instance—are common to all LANs (and to other systems, for that matter), others depend critically on the way in which the LAN is to be used. An example of this is the cross-network delay, which must be small and constant if speech is to be carried, but which may fluctuate widely if only terminal support is intended.

The requirements for a *data* LAN have been studied by the Local Area Network Standards Committee (project 802) of the US IEEE (Clancy, 1981) and published by the IEEE as a draft standard (IEEE, 1981).

The discussion that follows draws heavily on the IEEE work. For clarity the requirements identified by them are shown in *italics* (though they are not usually stated in the words of the draft standard, as these are excessively precise and lengthy for my purpose).

Applicability

The LAN should support a variety of data communications functions, including file transfer, terminal support (including support for high-speed graphics terminals), electronic mail, paging from auxiliary storage, transaction processing, file and database access, and voicegrams.

An ideal LAN would cater for real-time speech—i.e. telephony—and video services as well.

The LAN should allow a wide variety of types and of particular devices to be attached to it. These include:

Computers
Terminals
Mass storage devices
Printers
Plotters
Photocopiers
Facsimile transceivers
Monitoring and control equipment
Bridges to other LANs and gateways to other networks
Telephones
Television cameras and monitors

The LAN should support a range of standard interfaces as well as any devices that are built especially to work with it.

The LAN should be cheap. Although the IEEE standard makes no mention of cost, all standards activity is intended, in part, to reduce costs by increasing the market for conforming devices. The cost of connecting a device to the network should be small compared with the cost of the device.

General

1. *The LAN should deliver packets to the indicated destinations with high probability (but not absolute certainty). It should provide both data circuit and datagram facilities.*

    For some limited purposes, notably communications between similar machines, the data circuit facility may be dispensed with. If the LAN is intended to support only terminal-to-host operation, only the data circuit is needed.

2. *The LAN should conform with existing standards so far as possible.*

Physical Characteristics

1. *The LAN should provide a transparent service; it should accept and convey all possible bit patterns.*

2. *Communications between attached devices should be direct on the bus and should not require intermediate storage in any third device. Traffic may go via intermediaries if they are to perform a protocol conversion or traffic recording function.*

3. *One LAN should support at least 200 devices and should be able to span at least 2 kilometres.*

    This requirement is really not critical, provided that LANs can be linked to provide service over a larger area. This is in any case a necessary requirement, since some sites are larger than 2 kilometres.

4. *The transmission rate shall lie between 1M and 20M bit/s.* As indicated above, higher speeds may be needed to interconnect certain larger computers, whilst speeds below 1M bit/s may suffice for small machines.

5. *It must be easy to add or remove devices. Such changes may cause a transient fault lasting no more than one second.* Moving devices may involve informing other devices of the change, and this should also be easy.

6. *When devices need to share LAN facilities, especially the bandwidth of the bus, this sharing must be fair to all devices*—even in overload conditions.

7. *If access to the bus is via a 'medium access unit'* (usually a modem or transceiver), *that is separate from the attached device then the device should be able to be placed at least 50 metres from the bus.* (In some LANs the bus can easily be carried to the device and this requirement is then unnecessary.)

8. *The LAN should provide protection from lightning and galvanic effects.*

9. Installation and extension of the LAN should not require skilled staff.

Link Characteristics

1. *Devices should be able to address packets to individual devices, to groups of devices, or to all connected devices.*

2. *The LAN should allow some users to allocate and change their own addresses* (within the limits set by network integrity).

3. The LAN should support a variety of word and character lengths, not all of which will be multiples of eight. (This requirement goes counter to the IEEE position which specifies that *'data units shall be . . . an integral number of octets'*. Though widely acceptable, this is inconvenient in some circumstances—radar data, for instance, is not always structured in octets.)
4. *The LAN should allow a variety of network management and other network processes to coexist.*
5. The total throughput of the LAN should not fall significantly as the total load presented to the LAN approaches or even exceeds its actual capacity. (A collapse in throughput can lead to a permanent lockup in which no data can flow.)
6. The maximum delay before a packet can be transmitted over the LAN should be deterministic - that is, calculable in advance.

Errors, Failures, and Maintenance

1. *There should be no more than one packet per year containing an undetected error. For a 5M bit/s network this implies a bit error rate of 10^{-14}. The rate of detected bit errors may be as high as 10^{-8}.* This residual error rate is sufficient for most process control applications, but it may be excessively stringent (and hence expensive) for some speech and text applications.
2. *The error detection functions should detect* all *packets containing up to four bit errors.*
3. *Failure or loss of power to a connected device should cause no more than a transient error.*
4. The LAN should be highly reliable. It should not be inoperative, for whatever reason, for more than 0.02 per cent. of the total time. (This permits about 20 minutes of downtime per year for a system that is used during office hours only, or nearly two hours for a system in continuous service.)
5. *The LAN should have features to aid in maintenance and fault location.*
6. The LAN should be able to detect and report any attempt to use two devices with the same network address. (This is an optional requirement in the IEEE standard.)

Miscellaneous

1. *The LAN should conform to local safety rules, telecommunications licensing provisions, etc.*
2. *The LAN should be easily connected to other telecommunications facilities, including lines leased from a common carrier and switched voice and data networks, both public and private.*
3. *The interface between the LAN and the attached devices should be simple.*
4. Data exchanges on the bus should be secure. If tapping is possible it must be

made uninformative by encryption. (This requirement is really only important for military and other security-conscious sites—those in the nuclear industry, for instance.)

Meeting the Requirements

To meet all the functional requirements given above would imply both great complexity and high cost. Complexity would tend to undermine the reliability requirements, whilst the high cost would make it unacceptable to many prospective purchasers.

This point was mentioned earlier with regard to telephony; the difficulties posed by telephony have caused the IEEE to exclude this from their proposals. It also arises in relation to reliability and recovery from faults; error management logic and redundant components cost money.

Essentially all LAN design work so far has aimed at meeting a sufficiently large proportion of the requirements whilst avoiding the worst consequences of failing to meet the remainder. The perfect LAN has yet to be designed!

PART II

LAN Technology

This part presents the technology of local area networks in some detail. It includes descriptions of some of the more important commercial products and experimental systems.

Since LANs form a complex field of study, Chapter 7 starts by developing a classifications scheme that is used in the rest of this part.

CHAPTER

LAN Technology

7. THE CLASSIFICATION OF LOCAL AREA NETWORKS

In 1978 there were, depending on the exact definition chosen, about five LAN products. By 1982 there were over 70 different, commercially available, LANs and some, notably Ethernet were available from more than one supplier. In addition, at least as many experimental systems had been developed in industrial and academic laboratories.

It is not the job of a book such as this to give a comprehensive treatment, or even a list, of the products. Comprehensive reports on commercial products have been produced by 3Com (1982), Architecture Technology Corporation (Thurber, 1982), Frost and Sullivan Inc. (1981), Urwick-Nexos (1981), the Yankee Group and others, and doubtless these works will be brought up to date periodically. The variety of technical options (for cable or topology, for instance) is too great to make a comprehensive treatment feasible, and the reader would soon weary of the recital of minor differences. In any case some suppliers are extremely secretive about their interfaces and protocols, making it impossible to include them in the coverage.

I have therefore chosen to discuss general principles and widely applied techniques, and to illustrate the discussion by reference to products and experimental systems. To help the reader to pursue such references, Appendix 1 lists all the commercial products referred to in the text, together with the names of the developers.

To put these systems into the wider context, it is helpful to have some system of classification (sometimes known as a taxonomy).

A variety of taxonomies have already been proposed by various authors. Thurber and Freeman (1981), for example, have defined seven categories by considering successively the context in which the LAN was developed, the reasons for the development, and some aspects of the communications technology. Their scheme is shown, with some examples, in Figure 7.1.

This scheme has the disadvantage of classifying apart systems that are similar in important respects. Ethernet, Fibrenet, Mitrenet, and HYPERchannel, for example, all use contention for a logical bus, yet they are placed into four categories. In other cases the scheme brings together systems that are rather dissimilar. Thus Aloha—a low-speed terminal support radio network—and

67

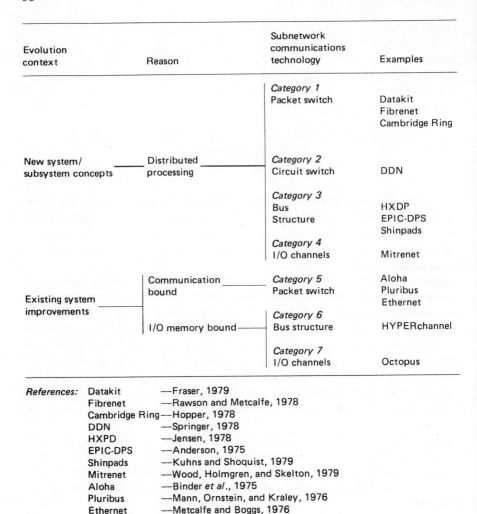

Evolution context	Reason	Subnetwork communications technology	Examples
New system/ subsystem concepts	Distributed processing	*Category 1* Packet switch	Datakit Fibrenet Cambridge Ring
		Category 2 Circuit switch	DDN
		Category 3 Bus Structure	HXDP EPIC-DPS Shinpads
		Category 4 I/O channels	Mitrenet
Existing system improvements	Communication bound	*Category 5* Packet switch	Aloha Pluribus Ethernet
	I/O memory bound	*Category 6* Bus structure	HYPERchannel
		Category 7 I/O channels	Octopus

References:
Datakit	—Fraser, 1979
Fibrenet	—Rawson and Metcalfe, 1978
Cambridge Ring	—Hopper, 1978
DDN	—Springer, 1978
HXPD	—Jensen, 1978
EPIC-DPS	—Anderson, 1975
Shinpads	—Kuhns and Shoquist, 1979
Mitrenet	—Wood, Holmgren, and Skelton, 1979
Aloha	—Binder *et al.*, 1975
Pluribus	—Mann, Ornstein, and Kraley, 1976
Ethernet	—Metcalfe and Boggs, 1976
HYPERchannel	—Thornton, Christensen, and Jones, 1975
Octopus	—Fletcher, 1975

Figure 7.1   The Thurber and Freeman taxonomy.

Pluribus—a high-speed packet switching exchange—are both placed in category 5.

The Thurber and Freeman taxonomy breaks down because it attempts to place every LAN into just one category. Similar objections may be made to the classifications used by Shoch (1980), Cotton (1980) and Way (1981).

The classification of LANs has become more difficult in recent years as the range of media and interfaces has expanded and as particular design principles have been applied in a wider range of contexts. The various hardware and software options can be combined in a wide variety of ways, rather like choosing a Chinese meal. It will be convenient, however, if we can find a suitable structure for the 'menu' (Clark, Pogran, and Reed, 1978).

Without some taxonomy, however, this book would be in danger of degenerating into a recital of uninformative technical detail.

THE REFERENCE MODEL FOR OPEN SYSTEMS INTERCONNECTION

During the 1970s, awareness grew of the great complexity of communications technology and of the importance, for both implementation and for the specification of standards, of dividing the subject matter into parts that could be discussed independently. In 1977, therefore, the Computers and Information Processing Committee of the International Standards Organisation set up a new subcommittee to develop a model of the communications process within which new standards could be developed (Jacobsen, 1980). The intention was to define, through the model, the scope of further standards which would be developed over the following decade.

The subcommittee (known as ISO/TC97/SC16) produced a report (ISO/TC97/SC16/N227) in June 1979 in which it laid down the Reference Model for Open Systems Interconnection (OSI), usually known as 'the seven-layer model'. The model was subsequently published in a draft proposal (ISO, 1980).

The OSI model provides both a framework through which existing systems can be analysed (as by Martin (1981)), and a prescription for the definition of new systems and standards.

The OSI model is shown in Figure 7.2. The layers are all involved in any actual communication and are arranged in a strict hierarchy; i.e. each layer provides services to the layer above it and uses services from the layer below (Scantlebury and Wilkinson, 1971). The interfaces between the layers were not intended to be standardized—standardization was intended to control the protocols that exist between corresponding layers in communicating devices.

ISO intends to develop an Open Systems Architecture (OSA) consisting of one or more protocols at each level.

Once the full set of protocols is defined, it will be possible for any two conforming devices to communicate despite differences in construction, processing power, place of manufacture, business function or internal interfaces. In this way, communication will be made open to a wide range of machines, rather than being restricted, as is currently more common, to a few machines from a single supplier.

Before any communication can take place, however, there must be some physical connection between the machines. It has been suggested by Scholfield

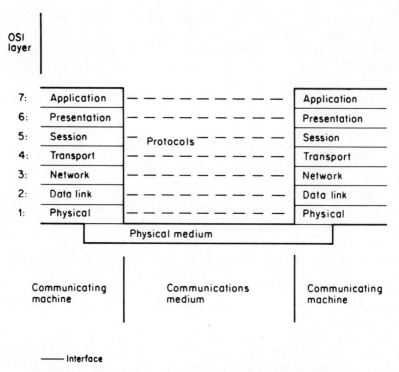

Figure 7.2   **The reference model for open systems interconnection.**

(1981) that the physical medium should be regarded as layer 0 of the model and I shall adopt this view (which is also held by the IEEE LAN Standards Committee; see Elden, 1981).

The physical layer (1) *provides the interface between the communicating machine and the (digital) physical medium. It controls the flow of bits across this interface. Standards at this level include CCITT Recommendation V.24 (EIA RS232).*

The data link layer (2) *groups the bits provided by level 1 into 'frames' or sequences of frames. This layer will also control access to the medium where it is shared by several machines, and may provide error detection and correction. The best known standard at this level is ISO's High Level Data Link Control (HDLC).*

The network layer (3) *adds extra routing functions to enable level 2 frames, now usually called packets, to be passed over a succession of data links within one or more networks. This usually requires the inclusion of a network address in the packets, and network addresses relate to attached machines rather than to communications nodes. This layer may also provide error control, multiplexing, and flow control. The best-known standard at this level is CCITT Recommendation X.25 (for public packet switching networks).*

The transport layer (4) *provides for communication between processes in the attached machines. It provides end-to-end control of the movement of data packets between these processes.*

These first four levels are generally thought to complete the specification of data *communications* functions. The remaining layers are better thought of as data *processing* functions.

The session layer (5) *is responsible for the management of the dialogue between processes of a particular type. There may be several distinct session layers (and associated protocols) for such different kinds of process as digital speech and interactive computing.*

The presentation layer (6) *is concerned with the interpretation of the data exchanged during a dialogue. It therefore includes character, page layout, and graphics codes, together with any encryption rules. In the case of the control of a screen-mode terminal this layer also includes functions for clearing the screen, locking the user out of some parts of the screen, and drawing attention to certain fields (possibly by flashing).*

The application layer (7) *is the least well-defined layer since it collects all the functions that are not proper to the lower layers. These functions include network management, job control, and protocols for the exchange of specific kinds of data—for instance, invoices. So disparate are these functions that it will probably prove necessary to identify further layers in order to clarify them. (See, for instance, Flint, 1982b, and Naffah, 1980.)*

Some recent developments have regrettably violated the clarity of the original model and have led to some dispute and confusion. For this reason, as well as because of its complexity, anything said about the model is to some degree a matter of interpretation. Progress on the development of the OSI model has been discussed by Zimmermann (1981) and by Mier (1982).

The layers may, in actual systems, be collected together in various ways. In a microcomputer, for instance (Figure 7.3a), all the functions may be provided by a single program. In a large mainframe, by contrast (Figure 7.3b), the functions may be divided between a number of programs and processors. CCITT has defined a terminal access protocol (Recommendation X.28) which allows terminals to be used on packet switched public networks (Figure 7.3c).

In adapting the OSI model for their own work, the Local Area Networks Committee of the US Institute of Electrical and Electronics Engineers (IEEE Project 802) has made a further decomposition of layers 1 and 2. Their revised model is shown in Figure 7.4 (IEEE, 1982).

The data link layer is divided into two sublayers, logical link control (LLC) and medium access control (MAC). LLC deals with the flow of frames between stations, including error recovery. LLC is independent, except for timing considerations, of the capacity sharing algorithm. MAC deals with the capacity sharing

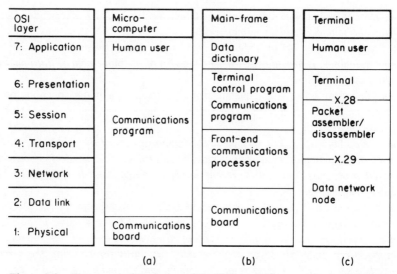

Figure 7.3   Placement of the layers of the OSI model in several practical cases.

algorithm and with station addressing. The IEEE model differs from that of ISO in including explicit provision for broadcast operation.

The physical layer is divided into a physical signalling (PS) sublayer, access-unit interface (AUI), and physical medium attachment (PMA). PS is separated in order to facilitate integration, on silicon, with the data link layer. The PMA matches signals from PS to the requirements of the medium, allowing for the possible use of a particular PS with several different media. The AUI includes a cable, thus allowing the PS (and its attached device) to be placed some distance from the medium where appropriate.

THE CHARACTERISTICS OF LOCAL NETWORKS

I will now consider the characteristics of LANs in the light of the IEEE model.

Physical Medium and Medium Attachment

A LAN may use a number of physical media: metal conductors (in various configurations), optical fibres, and even radiation. The nature of the medium dictates the general nature of the device used to place signals on it—the physical medium attachment (PMA).

The physical medium may be arranged in a number of ways. The overall shape—the topology—is of considerable importance in LAN design.

The topology also influences the design of the PMA. Thus a transceiver (PMA) for a 1 kilometre bus will need to transmit a more powerful signal than one intended to reach 100 metres to the next station on a ring.

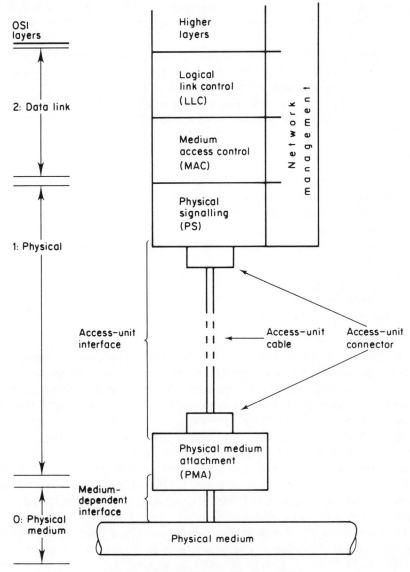

Figure 7.4   IEEE 802 reference model.

Physical Signalling

A number of means exist for encoding digits on the physical medium, but the most significant distinction is that between baseband and broadband systems. A baseband PMA applies the signal directly to the medium. A broadband PMA uses the digits to modulate a carrier signal which is then applied to the medium. In reception a baseband PMA obtains the signal directly, whilst in a broadband PMA a filter selects the required frequency and extracts the digital signal by demodulation.

It is convenient in practice to minimize the complexity of the PMA. For this reason the encoding and decoding of the signal is allocated to a physical signalling (PS) sublayer that may be incorporated in the data link control logic.

Medium, topology, and signalling are in practice so closely interlinked that it is necessary to consider them together. They are discussed in the next chapter.

Medium Access Control

The MAC sublayer of the model consists principally of the algorithm for sharing the capacity of the logical bus. Since this is the function that gives LANs most of their most distinctive properties, it is used as the framework for most of the detailed discussion of LANs.

Following Luczak (1978) capacity sharing techniques may be divided into four main classes:

Selection methods
Contention methods
Reservation methods
Ring methods

In selection methods each station is only allowed to transmit when it has received permission from elsewhere. If the permission is conferred on each station in turn by a central controller, the network is said to be polled. Polled LANs are discussed in Chapter 9. Networks in which permission is passed round the stations are known as 'token passing' networks and are discussed in Chapter 10.

In a contention system, each station that wishes to transmit may claim the physical medium for itself, subject to some discipline to minimize the effects of interference between stations. These methods all descend from the ALOHA radio network and include products such as HYPERchannel and Net/One, and published specifications such as Ethernet. Contention systems form the subject of Chapter 11.

In reservation systems each station transmits only in a time slot that was previously reserved for it. Reservations may be made during the generation of the system, at the start of a datacall, or from moment to moment. Reservation systems are discussed in Chapter 12.

All the above methods may be used in ring systems but there are two techniques which are restricted to rings.

In slotted rings, the subject of Chapter 13, a fixed number of slots circulate continuously round the ring for stations to empty and fill as appropriate. In register insertion rings, dealt with in Chapter 14, any station may insert a packet, or 'register', between any two adjacent packets on the ring.

OSI layer	Characteristic	Main possibilities
0	Physical medium	Twisted pair
		Multi-core cable
		Coaxial cable
		Optic fibre
		Power cables
		Radio
		Infrared
1	Signalling	Baseband
		Carrier modulation (broadband)
1	Topology	Bus
		Tree
		Daisy chain
		Ring
		Star
		Snowflake
		Mesh
2 (MAC)	Capacity-sharing algorithm	Polling
		Token passing
		Contention
		Reservation
		Empty slot
		Register insertion

Figure 7.5   Classification 'menu'.

Some local networks use the principles of frequency or time division multiplexing to partition the capacity of the bus rigidly over an extended period. Since these networks do not provide individual stations with access to the full capacity of the bus, they do not satisfy the definition of a LAN given in the last chapter, and this book does not deal with them.

In some cases, however, the developer has used modulation of radio-frequency transmission on coaxial cable as the basis of a shared digital bus. Indeed, with these techniques a single cable may support several independent LANs or a mixture of LANs and other digital services. These systems are known as broadband networks and are discussed in Chapter 15.

Figure 7.5 shows our 'menu' of the technical factors that characterize a LAN.

Logical Link Control

The logical link control (LLC) provides addressing, error control, and flow control functions. Those chosen by IEEE are closely related to HDLC and, indeed, it is often convenient for LLC functions to be based on those found in wide area networks.

Some logical link issues are mentioned in Chapters 9 to 15 and others are dealt with in Chapter 16.

Higher Layers

As indicated by the OSI model a LAN needs network and high-level protocols in order to function. These, together with a number of other technical issues, are discussed in Part III of this book.

LANs IN THE MARKET

So far we have discussed LANs in terms of their internal characteristics. It is also helpful, especially when considering commercial products, to consider the devices they are intended to support.

Since many LANs are able to support a wide range of devices, it is necessary to focus on the most powerful device that can be fully supported. A device is fully supported when the LAN provides an interface that does not unduly inhibit the operation of the device. A 9.6k bit/s V.24 socket will suffice for a data terminal, for instance, whilst a minicomputer requires a high-speed interface across which several independent connections can operate concurrently. Figure 7.6 shows a set of categories derived in this way (Flint, 1982a). In order to enable a number of attached devices to exploit the speed of their network interfaces, the network itself must have a higher speed than that required by any single device. The categories of LAN thus differ most obviously in their internal speeds.

Terminal support networks (TSNs) provide point-to-point or, sometimes, multi-point circuits. They provide a means of connecting a population of terminals to a computer whilst saving on cabling costs. They compete with conventional data networks and with enhanced digital telephone exchanges. Baseband TSNs such as Clearway are very competitive in price. Broadband TSNs like LocalNet System 20 (Biba, 1981b) and the terminal support features on faster LANs, like Net/One (Bass, Kennedy, and Davidson, 1980), are much more expensive.

Micronets and minicomputer networks both provide message passing, file access, and file transfer between a population of computers of the appropriate kinds. Since most early office automation machines—word processors for instance—were based on microcomputers, micronets form a possible basis for office automation systems (Yeomans, 1982). Micronets and minicomputer

Device	Network category	Internal speed (bit/s)
Data terminal	Terminal support network	20k –300k
Microcomputer	Micronet	100k –1.5M
Minicomputer	Minicomputer network	2M–10M
Minicomputer and telephone	Integrated office network	2M–10M
Mainframe computer	Mainframe LAN	50M–500M

Figure 7.6   LAN categories.

Table 7.1 Some commercially available LANs.

Category	Product	Physical medium	Capacity sharing method	Transmission speed (bit/s)	Notes
Terminal support network	Clearway	Coax ring	Register insertion	50k	
	LocalNet System 20	Coax tree	Contention	128k	A broadband system
	Net/One	Coax bus	Contention	10M	Virtual call on top of Ethernet
Micronet	Econet	Four-wire cable bus	Contention	210k	For Acorn Atom and Proton
	Z-Net	Coax bus	Contention	800k	For Zilog micros
Minicomputer network	Ethernet	Coax bus	Contention	10M	Device interfaces available from several vendors
	ARCNet	Linked coax stars	Token passing	2.5M	Interfaces available from Datapoint and Tandy
	Cambridge ring	Four-wire cable, coax or optic fibre	Empty slot	10M	Interfaces from several vendors
Integrated office network	SILK	Coax ring	Register insertion	16.896M	Ring is highly redundant
	Ubits	Multi-wire bus	Contention	140M	
Mainframe LAN	HYPERchannel	Coax bus(es)	Contention with priority	50–200M	

networks blend into one another in much the same way that big micros and small minis do. It is therefore impractical to draw a sharp dividing line.

Commercially available micronets include Z-Net and Econet whilst minicomputer networks include Ethernet (Metcalfe and Boggs, 1976), ARCNet, and the Cambridge Ring (Wilkes and Wheeler, 1979).

The integrated office network (ION) is different from the others since it is intended to provide communication for the whole range of office machines including word processors, copiers, and telephones. By early 1982 several manufacturers had announced their intentions to offer IONs, but only two products were actually available—Hasler's SILK and Litton's Ubits. Both were expensive and offered only limited ranges of computer interfaces.

Mainframe LANs provide similar services to the minicomputer LANs but with higher speed and at higher prices. They are usually limited in range to a few hundred metres. The best-known example is Network Systems Corporation's HYPERchannel (Thornton, 1979).

By way of illustration, the technical characteristics of the products mentioned are listed in Table 7.1. Commercial information on these products is given in Appendix 1.

'OPEN' NETWORKS

It has become increasingly common to claim that a LAN is 'open' or in conformity with the OSI model. It is difficult to attach any very clear meaning to these claims. It may be sufficient to note that many LANs are quite definitely 'closed'. Networks which allow the attachment of the products of only one vendor, or in which the interface specifications are closely guarded secrets, cannot be classed as anything else. The 'openness' of a LAN is not a technical characteristic but rather a function of marketing and support policies.

CONCLUSION

This chapter has developed a number of categories that may be useful in discussing either products or LAN designs in the literature. It will form the basis of the rest of the book.

8. TOPOLOGY AND TRANSMISSION

The physical layer of the OSI model provides for the transfer of bits between devices attached to the LAN. The physical layer also provides information on the state of the physical medium for the benefit of the medium access control.

In the IEEE model the physical layer is divided into four parts (as shown in Figure 7.4):

The physical signalling sublayer (PSS)
The interface cable
The physical medium attachment (PMA)
The physical medium

The division allows the most complex part of the layer, the PSS, to be physically combined with the station logic in an attached device or network controller and to benefit from the economies of large-scale integration. The IEEE draft standard for signalling on the interface cable is compatible with differential emitter coupled logic (ECL), allowing the cable to be directly connected to such logic.

Since PMAs may sometimes be installed in ceilings or other inaccessible places, it is desirable to minimize their complexity so as to increase their reliability.

The general nature of a PMA is determined by the topology and signalling conventions of the LAN. The detailed construction of the PMA will, however, also reflect the environment in which the network is intended to operate. In a military environment, for instance, it is important that network components should neither emit nor be affected by electromagnetic radiation and PMAs for such environments will need extra shielding.

The ideal physical layer would be easily installed and extended, capable of carrying high data rates with few errors, immune to electrical, chemical, mechanical, and radiological interference, non-radiating, reliable, and cheap. None of the many technologies used so far meets all these needs in full. Instead, designers have had to trade high performance in one area for weaknesses in others.

The remainder of this chapter discusses topology, physical media, and signalling conventions separately.

TOPOLOGY

Topology, the overall shape of the LAN, is probably the feature that has attracted the most public attention.

Topologies may be divided into two main classes, broadcast and sequential. In a broadcast configuration each PSS transmits enough signal to reach all the others. Broadcast configurations include buses, trees, and stars with passive centres (Figure 8.1).

Broadcast configurations require relatively powerful transmitters and receivers that can tolerate a wide range of signal levels. This problem is usually ameliorated by setting limits on the length of a cable segment and on the number of taps. Where the network needs to exceed these limits, conforming cable sections may be linked through (analogue) amplifiers or (digital) repeaters. They also require a method of tapping the physical medium that does not greatly reduce the signals reaching the other taps.

Broadcast configurations are vulnerable to 'streaming' (the condition where one station transmits continuously), and it is therefore desirable for the PMA to be able to detect this condition and to suppress the transmission.

Since only one station can use a broadcast LAN at one time a control overhead is associated with the establishment of control by a station. This overhead is

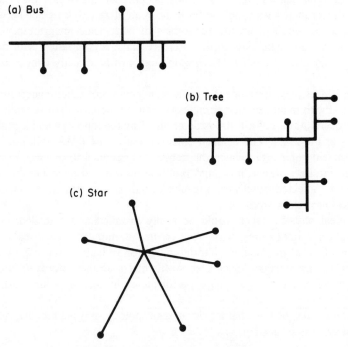

Figure 8.1   Broadcast topologies.

related to the time taken for a signal to propagate across the network, affect a remote station, and be returned. This time is known as the 'slot-time', a term reflecting its use in contention networks.

Since electrical signals travel over wires at roughly two-thirds the speed of light *in vacuo*, the slot-time cannot be less than 10 *l* microseconds, where *l* is the span of the network in kilometres. The actual slot-time will exceed this by the time needed to:

1. Transmit any control message.
2. Affect a remote station.
3. Pass the signal through any repeaters.

A two kilometre 10M bit/s network with a 5-byte control message will have a slot-time of about 30 microseconds—time for 300 bits.

Since this overhead is present on each transmission, it is desirable that the average transmission should last much longer than this time. Broadcast LANs are therefore usually designed to carry fairly long packets. In most broadcast LANs the recipient of a packet can only acknowledge it by sending back a complete packet. Since the useful data are only a few bits this process is very inefficient and is generally avoided (or, at least, minimized) by the protocols used.

In a sequential configuration each PSS transmits to just one other PSS. Sequential configurations include the ring, daisy chain, star with an intelligent centre, snowflake, and mesh (Figure 8.2).

Sequential configurations place less stringent requirements on the PSS transmitters and receivers than broadcast configurations, and allow different physical media to be used in the various inter-PSS segments.

Rings and daisy chains require the constant operation of all the PMAs for correct functioning. To reduce the dependence on correct PSS functioning, it is now common to include a relay in the PMA. Figure 8.3 shows the arrangement used by INRIA in their TARO ring (Scheurer, 1980). The relay is open in normal operation but closes if the PSS loses power or malfunctions (Saltzer and Pogran, 1979). The PMA may be passive or it may have its power needs met from the ring itself. In the Cambridge Ring, for instance, PMA station logic are powered by 50 V of direct current on the ring wires (Wilkes and Wheeler, 1979). The arrangement ensures that the ring continues to operate when power is switched off locally.

Broadcast configurations and daisy chains require each segment to be able to carry signals in both directions. This may be achieved by:

1. Using a single cable alternately for transmission in both directions.
2. Using two one-way cables.
3. Using, in a broadband system, different carrier frequencies for the two directions.

The use of a single cable imposes an overhead on the system due to the turnround time for the cable. In large systems or at high speeds this may become

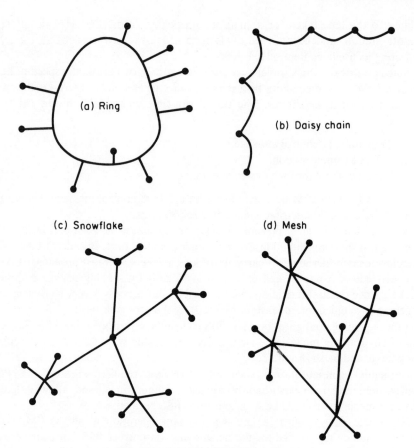

Figure 8.2   Sequential configuration.

substantial. A two-way cable must have similar transmission properties in both directions and this may create engineering difficulties. CATV amplifiers and optic fibre couplers, for example, generally work in only one direction.

Multiple cables have sometimes been deliberately installed in the interests of resilience. The SHINPADS bus network (Andersen, 1979; Kuhns and Shoquist, 1979), intended for use on naval vessels, can support up to six cables. Damsker (1982) has described a LAN using up to four cables and intended for use in nuclear power stations.

Individual Topologies

The most basic topology for a LAN is the **bus**. To the advantages of the logical bus, discussed in Chapter 6, we may add the fact that it minimizes the requirement for cable. Being, usually, passive, the bus has excellent inherent reliability (though this may be compromised if the medium access control is centralized).

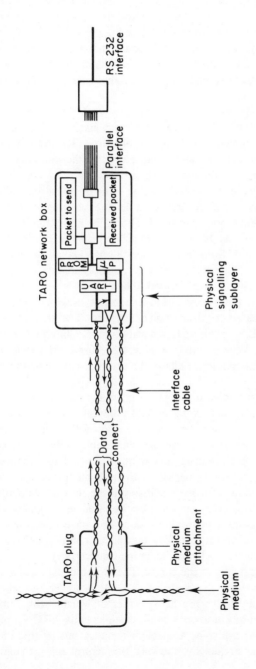

Figure 8.3   The TARO ring station. (After Scheurer, 1980. Courtesy of Kayak.)

A cable bus will often be installed over a corridor with drop cables to the LAN stations (such a configuration may also be described as a tree). It is desirable that the connection between the main bus and the drop cable should be passive to reduce the need for physical access to the main bus.

Contention networks such as Ethernet require active transceivers that must be installed within a few centimetres of the cable. This implies either the installation of transceivers in ducts, false ceilings, etc., or the extension of the bus to reach each station.

A bus is, however, vulnerable to physical damage. A single break may partition the bus into two functioning half buses; it is more likely, in practice, to produce two parts, neither of which can function properly. To guard against this, a duplicate cable may be installed at the same time as the main one, and stations switched to the backup cable following a failure.

On most sites the backup cable will use the same ducts as the main cable, as a result of which physical interference, such as the severing of the ducts by a bulldozer, will often break both cables. (It should be noted that the reliability of passive cables is sufficiently high as to make improbable events of this sort a major contributor to LAN downtime—see Binns, Dallas, and Spratt, 1982; Crane and Taft, 1980.) This problem may be ameliorated in various ways; so far commercial users have mainly just decided to live with it.

The **tree** configuration is an extension of the bus in which several buses are joined by active repeaters or by passive splitters. The tree provides needed flexibility to carry the LAN services to several floors of a building or to the several buildings on one site. Where active repeaters are used, failure of one segment leaves the others still functioning. Failure of a repeater partitions the tree into two trees or buses.

The trees used with broadband LANs are generally *rooted*. That is, they have a unique control point at which some critical components are placed. Baseband trees, such as Ethernet, are more commonly *unrooted*, though exceptions to both these generalizations exist. Rooted trees are vulnerable to the failure of the equipment at the root and, being active, this is much less reliable than the physical medium itself. It may therefore be necessary to duplicate this equipment.

The **star** may be seen as a further extension of the rooted tree configuration in which a branch extends to every attached device. Star networks are very familiar from traditional data communications practice and have been operated at high speed for local communications (see, for example, Christman, 1973, for a description of the network at the Los Alamos Scientific Laboratory).

Stars usually have a switch at the centre. The switch constitutes a unique point of failure and may have to be duplicated. In a LAN, however, the centre may be a passive connector or an active repeater—either of which, being simple, will be very reliable. Datapoint has used both configurations in its ARCNet products.

A star LAN will, generally, be less reliable than a bus or tree but it may be made resilient to cable breaks by allowing the central relay to ignore broken cables. A problem that cannot easily be avoided is its need for cable. A star will need more, and sometimes much more, cable than a bus or ring.

The **snowflake** needs less cable than the star but introduces more components that may fail.

In a **ring** each station takes an active part in transmission, receiving, scanning, and regenerating signals on the ring. To simplify the design of the PMA and PSS, signals generally flow round the ring in only one direction.

The storage included in the ring at each station may be anything from a couple of bits to a complete packet. The existence of this storage impedes the movement of data on the ring, causing a delay that depends upon the number of stations.

Where the packet traverses the whole ring to return to its station of origin the receiving station may set an acknowledgement indicator as it relays the packet. This indicator may be used for flow control and/or configuration of delivery, and has the merit of being returned to the source in a short time. (For example, in a 50 station Cambridge Ring of two kilometres circumference, the acknowledgement would return in about 25 μs.)

The ring requires that packets should be actively removed, either by the recipient or, on their return, by the source. (In broadcast and some sequential topologies packets will 'fall off' the ends of the network.) Since stations may fail, a 'garbage collector' is generally necessary to identify and suppress these stray packets.

As a sequential configuration, the ring is especially vulnerable to faults. Failure of any segment or PMA prevents service to all users, and ring designers have gone to some trouble to ameliorate this problem.

In the **star-shaped ring** (Figure 8.4; see Saltzer and Pogran, 1979) the gross topology is a star, each limb of which comprises two circuits. Each station com-

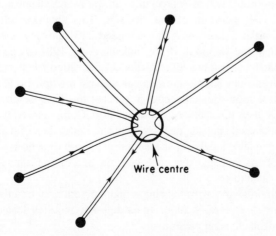

Figure 8.4   The star-shaped ring.

municates with the next ring station via a central 'wire centre' which is passive in normal operation. When a fault occurs the wire centre may be used to isolate the failed unit permanently or as part of an empirical process for locating the fault. Operation of the wire centre may be manual, but it may be controlled by a suitably programmed microprocessor if service must be restored especially quickly.

The star-shaped ring gains its ease of maintenance at the cost of:

1. Much more cable than in a simple ring.
2. The need to run a new cable for each new machine that is to be supported.

The Saltzer and Pogran ring has been marketed under the name Pronet and star-shaped rings are also used in the token-passing system developed by IBM's Zurich Research Laboratory (Müller, Keller, and Meyr, 1982).

It is possible to obtain protection from failures whilst retaining the overall ring layout. Consider, in Figure 8.5a, a break in the ring between stations 2 and 3. Deprived of its normal route, station 2 may close the ring by using an alternative forward route (Figure 8.5b), a backward route that circles the ring (Figure 8.5c), or a route that bypasses the broken segment (Figure 8.5d). Alternatively, the stations may be switched to a duplicate ring (Figure 8.5e).

Options b and e are the most straightforward but share a practical disadvantage. In most buildings there will only be one physical route from 2 to 3 so that whatever condition broke the first route may also have broken the second. Option e is used in the Xionics XiNet.

The second option (c) avoids this problem, though it changes the size of the ring and will probably require it to be re-initialized. Option c is used in the IBM R-loop with manual switching and in Racal's Planet with automatic switching under the control of the monitor station.

The third option (d) will also probably require re-initialization and, in addition, it complicates the operation of the repeater. This arrangement is basic to the design of the Hasler SILK which has extended it by allowing selective triplication of routes (Hafner and Nenadal, 1976; Jackson et al., 1981). A possible SILK configuration is shown in Figure 8.6. In this configuration there are generally three routes between stations so that the ring can survive multiple breaks.

An even more sophisticated recovery scheme has been described by Wolf and Liu (1978) for their Distributed Double-Loop Computer Network (DDLCN). This allows individual ring segments to be used, under the control of a distributed routing algorithm, alternately for transmission in both directions.

All these options involve extra cabling costs, and option d may also require the installation of extra ducts.

The **daisy chain** shares with the ring a high vulnerability and the requirement to regenerate signals at each station. In addition it requires transmission in both directions over the physical medium.

The **mesh** has been used in wide area networks because of its high resilience

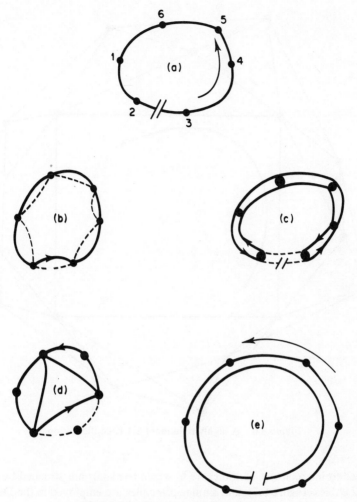

Figure 8.5   Recovery in ring networks.

and because the flexibility in the placement of transmission paths can be exploited to minimize communications cost. These advantages are much less useful in LANs where the physical environment is typically benign and bandwidth is cheap. The complex routing logic needed to provide its flexibility is therefore a wasted expense.

Meshes may, in the future, have some part to play in providing resilient communications between LANs in different buildings on single large sites.

A variety of **hybrid topologies** are also important in current practice. In Net/One, NBS Net (Carpeter and Sokol, 1979), and LocalNet, for instance, trees

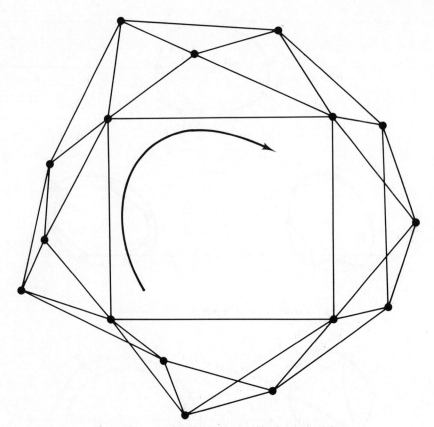

Figure 8.6   A highly redundant SILK configuration.

are used to interconnect multiplexors to which terminals are attached by a star of
RS232 cables (Figure 8.7), and similar principles are employed in the Data Ring,
in ARCNet, and in Wangnet. These hybrids serve to spread the cost of the LAN
interface, initially several thousand dollars, over a number of terminals. As the
cost of LAN interfaces falls this will become less significant, and simpler
topologies will be preferred.

THE PHYSICAL MEDIUM

Multi-core cables have been used in a number of networks for microcomputers.
The cables are readily available and are familiar to both engineers and users. The
several lines of the cable may be used separately for various functions. In the
ClusterBus cable used in Nestar's Cluster One, for instance, eight wires carry

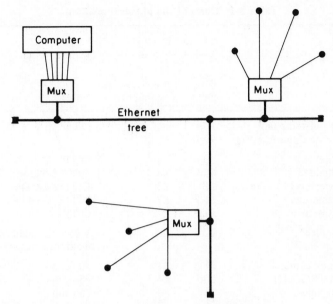

Figure 8.7   Net/One hybrid configuration.

data, a ninth indicates that the bus is active, whilst two more are used for hand-shaking protocols between sending and receiving micros (Thurber and Freeman, 1981).

The use of multiple lines for data multiplies the capacity of the bus. Thus ClusterBus carries data at 240k bit/s whilst needing a signalling rate of only 30k baud.* In addition the control lines free more of the data channel for useful information. The low signalling rate reduces the cost and complexity of the interface circuits, whilst increasing their number, and also avoids the reflection and impedance matching problems that are found at higher speeds.

Multi-core cable is generally used in point-to-point configurations, such as rings and stars, rather than in buses. The main disadvantages of multi-core cable are:

1. Poor immunity to electrical noise unless shielded.
2. High cost (see Table 8.1)

Twisted pairs avoid the problem of high cost, both through the low cost of the material and because many sites have spare pairs in the telephone wiring that can

---

* One baud is sometimes said to be one bit per second. It is, in fact, one signal per second, and the signal may encode any number of bits. In the case of a cable with 16 wires for data the signalling rate might be variously stated as 50k baud, 800k bit/s, or 100k bytes/s.

Table 8.1   Costs of the physical medium.

| Medium | UK cost in 1981 | | Notes |
	Per metre	Per physical connector	
Unshielded twisted pair	10p	—	Phone wire
Shielded twisted pair (2 pair)	90p	—	
4-wire unshielded	50p	£6 ⎫	⎧ CCITT V.24
7-wire unshielded	65p	£6 ⎭	⎩ (50ft maximum range)
Nestar Clusterbus (16 wire)	£1	£3	For Cluster One
16-wire unshielded	£1.3	£7	CCITT V.24
25-wire unshielded	£1.8	£7	CCITT V.24
25-wire shielded	£2.3	£8	V.24 (extended 500ft maximum range)
Ethernet coax cable	£1.5	£12	50 ohm
CATV coax (RG62U)	20p	£4.5	75 ohm
CATV semi-rigid	75p	—	75 ohm
Optical fibre	50p	£30	Bandwidth > 200 MHz
Polynet	45p	—	

be allocated to data transmission. Twisted pairs also are mainly used in point-to-point links but they may be tapped either by splicing or inductively.

The main disadvantages of twisted pairs are:

Poor immunity to electrical noise unless shielded
Easily tapped by intruders
Severely limited in range and signalling speed

Twisted pairs are used in some versions of the Cambridge Ring (Wilkes and Wheeler, 1979).

Coaxial cable has probably been the most popular medium for LANs to date. It combines robust construction, light weight, and modest cost with good electrical isolation, reasonable range, and the capacity for high data rates. These characteristics are found to different degrees in the various grades of coaxial cable however, as is shown by the trade-off between range and speed shown in Figure 8.8 (Moran and Starkson, 1975).

The various grades of coax used in CATV and CCTV systems are well proven in practice and both the cable and the associated equipment are reliable and inexpensive.

The heavier coax cables specified for Ethernet and similar systems can be readily tapped without cutting the cable, an advantage where a new device has to

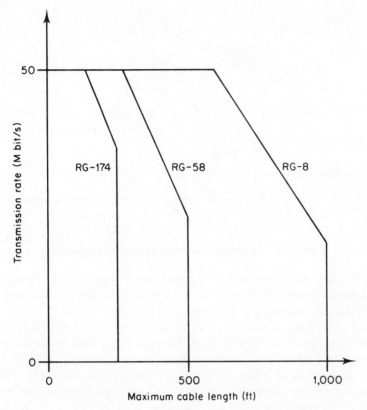

Figure 8.8 The trade-off between speed and range for three coax cables.

be added to a cable during working hours. Figures 8.9 and 8.10 show the construction of a typical pressure tap. (The figures are taken from the draft IEEE standard, described further in Chapter 20, but the construction is not part of the standard.)

For operation at high speeds, care must be taken in the installation, termination, and tapping of coaxial cables and suitably skilled staff will be required (Crane and Taft, 1980; DIX, 1980; Roman, 1979).

Twinax and triax cables have electrical properties that are rather better than those of coax and have been used in some systems (for instance, in the IBM Series 1 Ring (CM/1) and in the SHINPADS bus (Kuhns and Shoquist, 1979) respectively).

Power cables have been used in some experimental systems, in domestic products, e.g. for remote control of lights, and their use is envisaged in building management systems (Sterling, Williams, and Kirtley, 1982). They are recom-

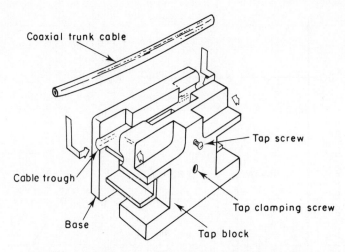

Figure 8.9   Typical coaxial tap connector configuration.

mended by their ready availability; but low speed, regulatory concerns, safety worries, and the possibility of interference from other similar systems seem likely to inhibit their use in commercial systems.

Optical fibres have a number of advantages that recommend them in some particular circumstances. They are light, capable of very high transmission rates (certainly over 1,000M bit/s), immune to electrical interference, difficult to tap, and free of any risk of starting a fire or explosion (Polishuk, 1980). They are therefore particularly attractive in military, airborne, and chemical plant applications.

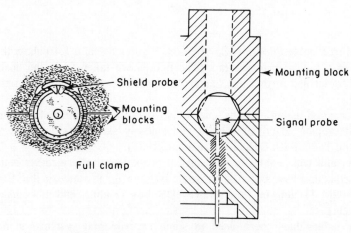

Figure 8.10   Typical coaxial tap connector.

They have, equally, some disadvantages:

1. They are unfamiliar to site engineers and require special splicing techniques.
2. They cannot carry electrical power for repeaters or other devices.
3. Tapping generally introduces a substantial attenuation of the signal, restricting fibres to sequential configurations.
4. They can usually carry light in one direction only.
5. Their high-speed modems are expensive.

Some of these problems are likely to be overcome by advances in fibre technology. Increases in transmission power and improvements in tapping techniques (Dunphy, 1982; Kawasaki and Hill, 1977) may make bus configurations practical within a few years. In addition, the costs will be reduced as the applications for fibres grow.

Fibres have been used in ring and star networks and in a number of innovative experimental systems, of which Xerox's Fibrenet is probably the best known (Rawson, 1979; Rawson and Metcalfe, 1978). In Fibrenet the fibres form a star and are joined at the centre by a passive transmissive coupler as shown in Figure 8.11. Light from one host enters the coupler on the inward fibre and is then divided amongst all the outward fibres. The logical effect is thus that of a bus and the capacity is shared by the Ethernet contention protocols. Operating at 100M bit/s over a distance of 1.1 kilometres Fibrenet exhibited a bit error rate of 10^{-9}.

Optical fibre stars have been described by Yajima *et al* (1977); Mesiva, Miller, and Pinnow (1982); Chipman (1982); and Kunikyo and Ozeki (1982), and an optical fibre bus exhibiting high efficiency at speeds up to 100M bit/s by Limb (1982). Rings have been reported by Yada *et al* (1981); Favre (1982), and others.

Optical fibre is now the obvious physical medium for systems, such as those used to interconnect the components of mainframe computers, that require very high rates (Kearns and Basch, 1982). At lower speeds, however, they are not yet the obvious choice.

Radio has been little used in LANs due to the shielding effects of buildings, shortage in many countries of available frequencies (Fox, 1982), legal restrictions, and the low data rates that have been possible until recent years. It was, however, used in the pioneering ALOHA network, in which contention protocols were first developed (Binder *et al.*, 1975).

The chief advantages of radio are, of course, the absence of any need for cables and the consequent ability to support mobile stations. These advantages have made radio an essential part of military communications since Hitler used it to coordinate the blitzkrieg, and it has been developed for battlefield LANs (Nilsson, Chou, and Graff, 1980). Some low-speed civilian uses have been reported by Albright (1982).

Infrared light is already used in controlling televisions and children's toys, and has been demonstrated for cordless telephones. In 1982 its use in LANs was a

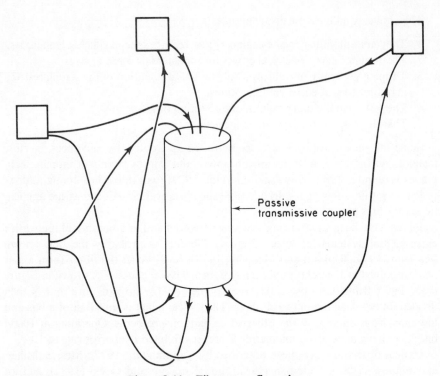

Figure 8.11   Fibrenet configuration.

laboratory curiosity but it may find applications in the future for distributing digital signals within a single room. A ceiling-mounted 'intelligent lightbulb' could provide an interface to a building network and might also control signals on the local 'IR bus' (Fox, 1979).

IR shares with radio the advantage of not needing cables between the devices connected, and could therefore be used for battery-powered enhanced calculators and pagers. Unlike radio it is limited to very short distances but, most importantly in Europe, it falls outside PTT regulations.

The potential of a physical medium for data transmission may be indicated roughly by multiplying the maximum data rate by the range. For the main options this gives the following results:

Twisted pair   1G metre-bit/s*
Coax   15G metre-bit/s
Optical fibre   400G metre-bit/s

* 1G metre-bit/s is a capacity of 10^9 metre-bit/s; for instance, 1M bit/s over 1 kilometre.

These figures show very clearly the vast capacity of optical fibres relative to the alternatives.

SIGNALLING

The signalling used in LANs is largely determined by the physical medium used. The maximum rate at which data can be transmitted over a physical medium is shown by information theory to depend on the bandwidth and on the signal-to-noise ratio. Both these factors depend on the medium chosen whilst the latter also depends on the environment in which it is installed. Both factors fall as distances are increased.

It is rarely sensible to actually work at, or even close to, this limiting rate since the high-performance drivers and receivers required are, typically, unreasonably expensive. Practical systems are, therefore, run below this rate. In the case of optical fibres, for instance, the operating speed is typically less than one-thousandth of the maximum.

LANs are generally designed to achieve very low error rates. This is possible because of the short distances involved, because all the various components can be specifically designed to work together and because each actual network is under the control of a single management. Actual error rates are typically better than 1 in $10''$ bits.

The signals applied to the physical medium inevitably weaken and become distorted as they travel. In a sequential configuration it will usually be possible to increase the gain of the receiver to compensate for this, and amplifiers may also be used to extend the range. It is also possible to choose a physical medium to match the distance; twisted pairs for 50 metres, coax cable for 500 metres, and optical fibre for 5,000 metres, for instance. Amplifiers, however, also amplify the noise so it is often preferable to use a digital repeater which decodes the received signal and transmits a clean, freshly created, signal.

In broadcast configurations, the variety of distances separating senders and receivers means that every receiver must be able to accept a range of signal strengths. In the case of Ethernet, for example a maximum length cable (500 metres) may introduce an attenuation of 8.5 dB at 10M Hz. Thus receivers must be able to tolerate a sevenfold variation in signal levels. Clearly the designer of a broadcast LAN must strike a balance between the cost of extra repeaters and the cost of receivers with a wide dynamic range.

For coaxial cables, two rather different signalling techniques are available. In a baseband LAN, signalling voltages from the digital electronics are applied directly to the cable. In a broadband LAN, the digital data modulates (i.e. varies) a radio frequency carrier signal generated by an oscillator.

The range of a baseband system can be extended by a repeater or regenerator which identifies the bits being transmitted and then transmits a clean signal. Since digital repeaters suppress noise they may be cascaded without limit. For this reason baseband signalling has the potential for very large distances, though existing systems do not exploit this advantage. Baseband systems are also generally cheaper (for any given speed), though less flexible.

The range of a broadband system is usually extended by the use of analogue amplifiers, since these can cope with the arbitrary mixture of analogue (e.g. television) and digital services that may be found on a broadband cable. Since amplifiers amplify noise as well as signal the maximum range of broadband systems is limited by signal quality (though at low speeds this limit may be 20 kilometres or more).

In practice the ranges of both baseband and broadband systems are limited by the capacity sharing algorithm rather than the transmission technology. In broadcast systems, the size of the network determines the time necessary for control to pass successfully between stations. It is often desirable to limit this overhead by restricting the size of the network.

In addition to carrying data, the signal must usually include enough synchronization information to keep the receiver in step with the sender. This may be done by timing signals on a separate channel, as in the case of the Cambridge Ring, or by embedding the timing in the data signal.

In baseband systems this is often done by Manchester (Müller, Keller, and Meyr, 1982), differential Manchester, or Miller encoding. These schemes are shown in Figure 8.12.

In both Manchester and differential Manchester a transition occurs at least once for each bit, in the middle of the time reserved for the transmission of that bit (the 'bit time'). With Manchester encoding the transition is always up for a 1 and down for a 0. With differential Manchester it is the same as in the previous bit time for a 0 and opposite for a 1. The high density of transitions eases synchronization and also allows the omission of occasional transitions to be used as a control signal. Manchester and differential Manchester are therefore generally preferred to Miller coding.

Where radio frequency modulation is used the synchronization may be taken directly from the carried signal in appropriate cases. The signal may be encoded by variations in the amplitude, frequency, or phase of the carrier.

In broadcast systems it is likely that successive packets will be sent by different stations, and inevitable that, because of the different locations of those stations, such packets will appear unsynchronized. In these systems it is necessary to send an initial signal to warn of the imminent arrival of a packet and to allow synchronization to be established. Since receivers may achieve synchronization at different times, this initial signal must be terminated by a distinctive pattern to indicate the start of useful data.

In Ethernet (DIX, 1980) the warning signal is 31 repetitions of '10' terminated by '11'—64 bits in all. Due to the use of Manchester encoding this resembles a squared-off wave with a frequency of 5M Hz, half the transmission rate of the system.

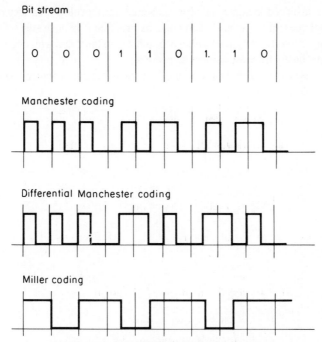

Figure 8.12　Encoding in baseband systems.

COMBINATIONS

Chapter 7 suggested that topology, physical medium, and signalling could be chosen independently in designing a LAN, but this is not in fact strictly true. Some combinations are impractical:

1. The lack of suitable taps makes it difficult to use optical fibres in broadcast configurations.
2. The broadcast nature of radio makes it difficult to use it in sequential configurations.
3. The high cost of the necessary electronics makes it impractical to use broadband cables in sequential configurations.

CONCLUSION

For most commercial purposes one of two main possibilities is likely to be best: the cable tree or the ring.

An unrooted tree constructed from coaxial cable combines low cable costs with considerable bandwidth. The choice between baseband and broadband signalling will depend on the needs of the particular installation.

A ring, reinforced in some way for resilience, may exploit a variety of transmission technologies in its several segments. In practice it is desirable to standardize on just one or two for any particular product or installation, and coax and optical fibres are probably the best choices at present.

In both cases it is likely that optical fibres will become rapidly more attractive as the technology improves.

9. POLLED NETWORKS

Polling is the capacity-sharing technique that is most familiar in data processing, due to its use on multi-dropped lines in wide area networks (Figure 9.1). The essence of polling is that a central unit successively invites other devices to use the common channel. On receipt of such an invitation (a poll), a device with data to transmit will respond by transmitting the data. A device with no data to transmit will usually transmit a short 'no data' packet (though silence may be acceptable in some systems).

The commonest arrangement is for the polling unit to poll each device on a

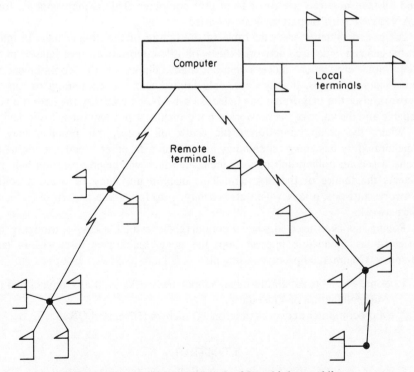

Figure 9.1   A wide area network with multi-dropped lines.

fixed rotation, the order of polling being held in a polling list. The polling unit completes a cycle by polling each device in turn.

A number of variants of this procedure have been developed for specific cases:

1. Very active devices may be polled several times within a single cycle.
2. Inactive devices may be polled only, say, every fifth cycle.
3. The frequency with which individual devices are polled may be varied dynamically to reflect their current activity level.

These options may all be referred to as 'roll-call' polling and are discussed in more detail by Puzman and Porizek (1980).

In 'hub' polling the central unit polls the furthest device on each multi-drop line and the poll is passed back between successive devices on the line until it reaches the centre. This technique reduces the delay due to the propagation of polls from the centre to the individual devices (Knight, 1972) at the cost of extra complexity, especially in the fault recovery logic.

All polling systems suffer from the disadvantage that a device with data to send must wait until other devices have indicated that they do not have any data to transmit.

In most polling systems the polling unit is associated with a central computer and all transmissions are to or from that computer. This is inappropriate for a LAN since the traffic pattern is more varied.

All polled systems are vulnerable to the failure of the polling unit. In mainframe-centred wide area networks this is of little importance, since failures of the mainframe are much more common than failures of the communications processors. There is, in any case, only limited value in continuing to run the network after the mainframe has failed. In a LAN, by contrast, the lines are very reliable and the value of the network is not critically dependent on any one device.

Where the polling unit forms the centre of a star, this problem may be ameliorated by designing redundancy into the unit. In other broadcast configurations, a second polling unit may be included which will begin operation only if it detects the failure of the first unit. This backup unit may be used to collect network statistics, a task which also requires it to follow the pattern of traffic on the network.

Polling has been used in several commercially available LANs, though it has received less academic interest than the novel techniques discussed in later chapters. Commercial products using polling fall into two main groups:

1. Some older broadband terminal support networks such as Comtrol and the Autopoll feature of Videodata.
2. Microcomputer networks (micronets) such as HiNet and QNet.

COMTROL

Comtrol is a family of computer controllers and remote multiplexors. Each remote multiplexor supports up to 28 terminals, printers, and other devices over a variety of interfaces, whilst the computer controller provides a high-speed interface to one of a variety of computers (including the PDP-11, Data General Eclipse, and IBM 370). These products share a channel operating at speeds up to 1M bit/s provided on up to 50,000 feet of coaxial cable.

The computer controller implements roll-call polling using the IBM's SDLC

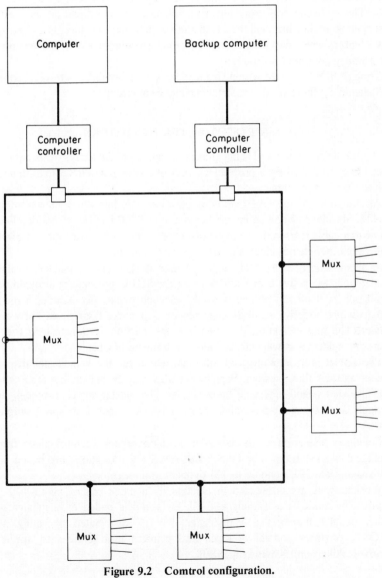

Figure 9.2   Comtrol configuration.

protocol. The controller can issue up to 4,250 polls per second and may be programmed to depart from a simple sequence where appropriate.

The problem of performance is particularly onerous where there are many stations but a low average utilization—conditions that are common on LANs. If, for instance, 100 devices share a 1M bit/s bus then half the capacity of the bus must be dedicated to polls and responses to ensure 50 polls/s at each device. As the load increases the effective polling rate will fall of course.

In order to provide resilience the cable may be installed in a ring (see Figure 9.2). The controller will normally transmit in only one direction, but is able to detect cable breaks and will then transmit to both parts of the cable. Comtrol also has a feature which can pass control to a backup computer on a spare controller if the primary computer should fail.

Though SDLC is used within Comtrol, it is not available to attached computers and terminals; these see a completely transparent circuit.

MICROCOMPUTER NETWORKS

Digital Microsystems (DMS) makes a range of Z80-based business micros which may be linked by a proprietary network known as HiNet to gain access to shared files and printers.

As shown in Figure 9.3 HiNet is based on a cable bus which must comply with RS422. Standard ribbon cable can be used up to 200 feet but a shielded two-pair-plus-earth cable is used over longer distances. One pair carries data at 500k bit/s whilst the other carries clock signals for synchronization.

A network may consist of up to 32 user micros plus a master station. The master polls the active user stations using the SDLC protocol at a maximum rate of 60 polls/s. Roll-call polling is used, but each cycle also includes a broadcast poll to which inactive stations may respond to make themselves known to the master. The master station will then instruct the user station to load the HiNet operating system and will enter its address in the polling list.

The HiNet is invisible to user stations, which see the Winchester disc on the master as their filing system. Winchester files may be bigger and faster than the disc files that would otherwise be available. The master station provides security through the locking of files, and groups of files. It can also spool output to a printer.

Polling is also used as the basis of the Convergent Technologies[tm] family of intelligent workstations. The IWS[tm] and AWS[tm] workstations are based on Intel 8086 and 8088 CPUs and up to 1M bytes of main memory.

Workstations are connected in clusters by a cable bus of up to 400 metres length. The bus carries signals at 307k bit/s and is polled by a master station, which usually manages a Winchester disc. A distributed operating system, CTOS[tm], provides control of discs and printers and services to applications (Garrow, Alker, and Rosenfeld, 1980).

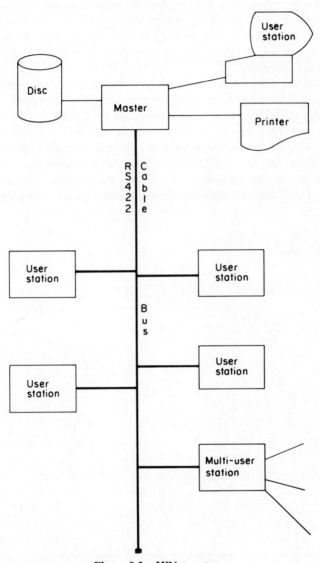

Figure 9.3   HiNet system.

CONCLUSION

The characteristic advantages of polling include simplicity, familiarity, the availability of cheap chips that implement suitable protocols, and fairness as among all the stations except the polling station itself. That is, it provides all but that station with equal access to the transmission capacity. It also provides a response with a known upper limit—a valuable feature where highly time-critical processes are concerned.

Its disadvantages include vulnerability to the failure of the polling unit, high overheads, and (relatively) long delays to gain access to the channel.

The vulnerability problem may be mitigated by duplication. The performance problems may be mitigated by restricting the number of devices that may be attached, or by increasing the speed of the channel. Though its performance may be acceptable in small LANs, its centralized philosophy makes polling inappropriate in the distributed environments characteristic of local area networks. The distributed algorithm closest to polling is token passing.

10. TOKEN PASSING

Token passing may be seen as a fully distributed polling system. It resembles hub polling in that the poll (or token) is passed among the devices, but differs in that:

1. Packets may flow between any pair (or greater number) of devices rather than just to and from the central unit.
2. Control of the LAN is distributed amongst the stations.
3. Although one device may have a special responsibility for network management, it has no special privileges in normal operation.

In a token-passing LAN, the token is a distinctive bit pattern that is passed between the stations in a fixed sequence. A station may only transmit when it holds the token and must pass it on within a short time.

A token-passing LAN always, therefore, has a logical ring which is defined by the order in which stations receive the token. This mechanism was originally devised for use on a physical ring (Farmer and Newhall, 1969) and this has clear advantages. The logical ring can be taken to be the physical ring and, with unidirectional working, there is no doubt as to where the token should be passed after a station has finished with it. A 'bare' token can be passed directly in a ring, rather than having to be included in a packet and addressed to the next station, thus reducing the associated overhead.

Physical rings are used in commercial products such as Ringnet and Domain, and star-shaped rings (explained in Chapter 8) are used in Pronet and the IBM experimental LAN.

Amongst broadcast configurations the star and snowflake are found in ARCNet and the bus and tree in Modway.

All token-passing networks have to deal with two key problems: lost tokens and duplicate tokens. Either may result from the failure either of the physical medium or of a station. Both must be remedied quickly because the loss of a token means that no station can transmit, whilst duplication of the token generally leads to mutual jamming by two or more stations. The need to deal with these conditions introduces significant complexities into what is otherwise a rather simple system.

105

RINGNET

Ringnet is a LAN developed by Prime Computer Inc. to connect a number of Prime minis on a single site. It forms part of Prime's more comprehensive network architecture, Primenet^tm (Gordon, Farr, and Levine, 1979).

The physical medium is a ring of coaxial cable in which the distance between adjacent attachment points is not normally greater than 250 metres. (Larger distances may be obtained by including an amplifier or repeater in the ring.)

The ring is operated at a speed of 10M bit/s but uses a coding system in which only four out of five bits are available for general use (the fifth bit is used to guarantee the uniqueness of the token and other special patterns, and to ease their recognition).

Figure 10.1 shows how a Prime mini is connected to the ring. The junction box

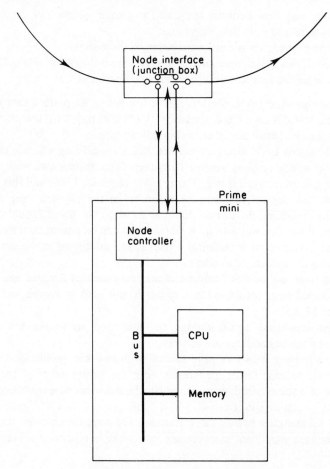

Figure 10.1   Ringnet connection.

(or PMA in IEEE terminology) includes a relay which may be used to exclude the computer from the ring or to extend the ring up the cable to the node controller. The node controller implements the data link protocol and sits within the computer cabinet, with direct access to the computer's internal bus.

Figure 10.2 shows the format of data on the ring. At the bottom the physical layer (layer 1) is concerned with the flow of bits on the ring. The data link layer is concerned with control of the token whilst the network layer is X.25 level 3, and provides a virtual call service between computers.

During normal operation the node controller scans the incoming data for the special pattern F1, whilst continuing to transmit the received data. (The node hardware introduces a delay of about 3 bit times between receipt and transmission of a bit.)

Receipt of F1 causes the node controller to compare the destination address field with its own address, and to capture any packet that is addressed to itself. The controller hardware acknowledges receipt using the Ack/Check field. The controller also scans for a token. When it sees a token the controller will claim it if it has data to send and pass it on otherwise.

While it holds the token, the controller will not copy any received data to the

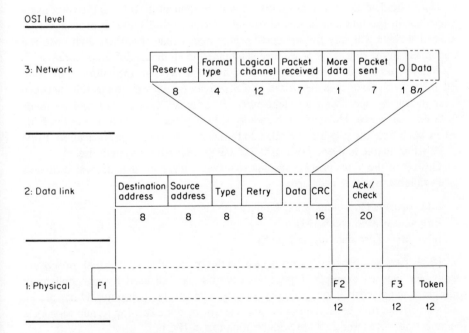

CRC = cyclic redundancy check
(Field lengths are in bits.)

Figure 10.2   Ringnet protocol hierarchy—packet structure.

output line. It will, instead, transmit its own data whilst monitoring the ring for the return of its own traffic. The controller will also inspect the Ack/Check fields of returned packets to determine whether they have been accepted by the destination.

The node may send one packet of up to 2,048 bytes and must then pass the token to the next station on the ring.

The controller will then be expecting to see the end of its own packet before it sees another token. If a token is detected prematurely it will be suppressed and the packet treated as having not been delivered. The associated token is thereby lost.

The loss of the token is detected by a finding that there has been no traffic on the ring for an excessive period. This diagnosis may be made by any controller—token management is fully distributed. This condition is normally detected during an unsuccessful attempt to transmit a packet and, if this occurs, the controller will create a new token and retransmit the packet. If two hosts execute this procedure concurrently, they may introduce two tokens to the network, though the likelihood of this happening is minimized by the fact that the hosts will wait different periods before creating a new token. If it does happen, however, the duplicate tokens will be identified and suppressed by the process described previously.

If a node detects persistent failures it will disconnect itself from the ring, using the relay in the junction box, and execute various self-diagnostic procedures. A defective node will stay disconnected whilst nodes that pass their own tests will reconnect to the ring. This procedure is intended to eliminate defective nodes.

Ringnet uses X.25 level 3 as its own network layer in the interests of compatibility with wide area networks. X.25 provides a virtual connection between computers. By specifying an eight-bit 'port' address, connections can be made between processes. However, the relationship between port and process is fixed anew each time the process is loaded so that care is needed in port selection. Ports 1-99 are available to users, ports 100-255 being reserved for system use.

On top of the 'inter-process transport service', three main high-level protocols are available to users. They are:

Inter-process Communication Facility (IPCF)
File Access Method (FAM)
Interactive Terminal Support (ITS)

IPCF provides programs with access to the transport layer through procedure calls. By way of example, Figure 10.3 shows the call used by an application program to establish a connection to a process on another computer. Other procedures provide for the transmission and receipt of data and for termination of a connection. FAM and ITS are both built on top of IPCF.

Port 255 on every host is used to provide access to the local file access manager. This program provides remote processes with access to local files and local processes with access to remote files. In both cases the two programs cooperate to provide what the user sees as a single service. The Manager also

PORT:=17	The port currently being used by the required process
ADR:='ENG.3'	The name of the remote computer
ADRL:=5	The length of that name (in bytes)
CALL X%CONN(VCID, PORT, ADR, ADRL, VC-STAT)	
VCID	Identity of the completed call, to be used during subsequent data transmission
VC-STAT	Status of the remote process

Figure 10.3   Primenet procedure call for connection to a remote process.

provides, as part of the file access method, necessary security controls and file locking during updates.

A similar system provides Interactive Terminal Support (ITS), whereby user terminals may become connected to processes on remote computers. Port 0 is used in this case.

These three high-level protocols can also be used between Prime computers that are connected by low-speed leased lines or by a public data network. The total set of communications protocols and their supporting products is known as Primenet and is shown in Figure 10.4.

OSI layer			
7: Application			
6: Presentation	Port allocation conventions, file access manager, and interactive terminal support		
5: Session			
4: Transport	Inter-process communication facility		
3: Network	CCITT X.25 level 3		
2: Data link	CCITT X.25 level 2	Token passing	CCITT X.25 level 2
1: Physical	Various	Ring integrity	CCITT X.25 level 1
0: Physical medium		Coaxial ring	Leased lines with modems
	Public data network	Ringnet	Leased lines

Figure 10.4   Primenet[tm].

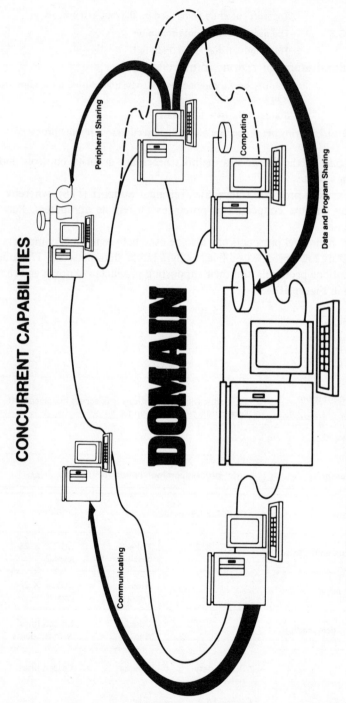

Figure 10.5   The capabilities of the Apollo Domain. (By courtesy of Apollo Computers (UK)).

A LAN very like Ringnet forms the basis of the Apollo Domain range of very powerful personal computers. Being more recently designed and being orientated towards locally distributed computing, Domain is able to make more and more original use of the LAN than is Primenet. Thus Domain allows the Apollo 'computational nodes', which are 32-bit personal computers based on the M68000 chip, to access one another's files and peripherals. This is especially useful in allowing Winchester discs to be shared between a number of nodes. The capabilities of Domain are shown in Figure 10.5.

THE IBM RING

In the work of IEEE project 802, IBM has taken a leading role in the definition of standards for a token ring. Details of IBM's own experimental ring, which has been the basis of their standards proposals, were given to the IFIP International Symposium in April 1982 (Bux et al.; Müller, Keller, and Meyr).

The IBM ring consists of a number of 4M bit/s rings interconnected by high-speed 'block switches'. Each ring consists of a cable backbone linking distribution panels. A local lobe will usually descend from a panel to each station (see Figure 10.6). As in the star-shaped ring (Saltzer and Pogran, 1979) the distribution panel can be used to isolate individual stations and their drop cables.

The ring carries data in the form of packets with the format shown in Figure 10.7. Delimiters are formed by violations of Manchester coding. Addresses are in two parts. The first two bytes identify the ring whilst the second two designate the station on a ring.

The control byte contains a number of fields used in maintaining the integrity of the ring and also indicators to distinguish between asynchronous and synchronous traffic.

The ring has two modes of operation. The asychronous mode is similar to Ringnet and will not be described further. Periodically, however, the ring monitor will declare a period of synchronous operation. During this period the ring can only be used by stations that have already requested and received permission from the monitor. (The monitor will refuse permission for a new synchronous call if insufficient spare bandwidth is available.)

In synchronous operation each 'calling' station is able to send one packet to the 'called' station and can receive a reply in the returned packet.

Synchronous operation may be used for both telephony and for transparent circuits for arbitrary communicating devices. (If the ring were installed commercially this might include non-IBM devices.)

Asynchronous operation can be used to support a conventional data link protocol such as SDLC, and this seems certain to be part of IBM's plans. Since SDLC contains various complexities that are inappropriate in a high-speed low-error LAN environment, it is also possible that IBM will define a simplified form of SDLC for such use. Figure 10.8 shows how a ring might support a hierarchy of alternative protocols.

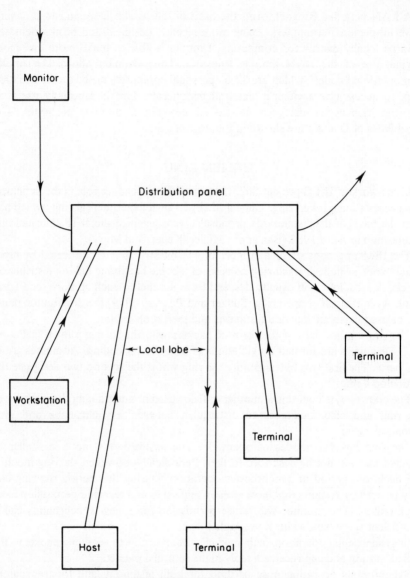

Figure 10.6   IBM token ring configuration.

It can be seen that the IBM ring does not integrate voice and data communications, except in the sense of using the same wires for both.

During the autumn of 1982 IBM and Texas Instruments announced their intention to collaborate on the development of controller chips for a token-passing ring.

Both the capabilities of the technology and IBM's own product needs indicate

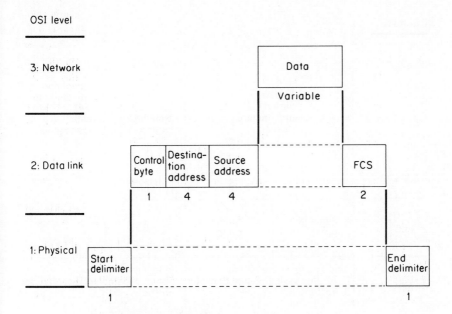

Field lengths are in bytes.

Figure 10.7   IBM ring packet format.

that the IBM ring will find its first commercial applications in terminal support and as a basis of office automation systems. In the longer term, IBM seems certain to exploit the synchronous mode to provide telephony services. The consequences of this, for IBM's products, customers and competitors, will clearly be substantial.

A TOKEN-PASSING BUS

A token-passing bus is one of the options identified for standardization by the IEEE 802 committee. The proposed standard was described by Miller and Thompson (1982).

Two physical topologies are proposed, both constructed from CATV cable. One topology uses trunk cables to carry the signal along the main routes of the site and drop cables, attached via passive taps, to connect the trunk cables to the devices. The other topology carries the trunk cable to every individual device, thus reducing the dynamic range required of the modems.

In normal operation the token passes round a logical ring which is defined by the addresses of the stations. The token passes in the direction of decreasing addresses until it reaches the lowest address, at which point it is passed back to the highest. A station may only transmit when it holds the token and must pass on

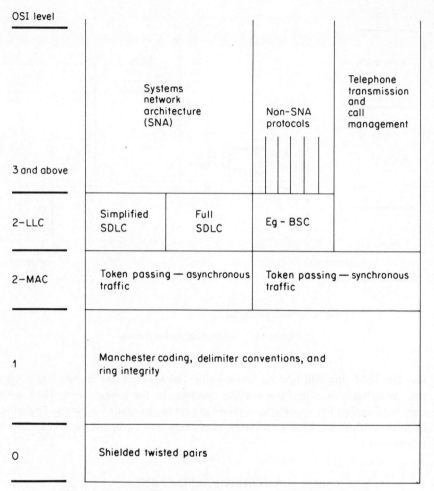

Figure 10.8   Possible protocol hierarchy on the IBM token ring.

the token after making a transmission. When it holds the token a station may remove itself by instructing its predecessor to link with its successor on subsequent cycles. This is done with a 'set next node' frame (shown in Figure 10.9).

The existence of a logical rather than a physical ring creates a need for logical ring maintenance. The main routine functions are:

1. Reconfiguration of the ring.
2. Adjustments of the parameters that govern the algorithm (for instance, the maximum time for which one station can hold the token).
3. Accepting requests to join the ring from previously silent stations.

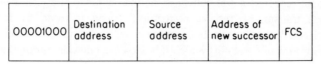

Figure 10.9   Set next node frame.

One or more stations must be designated to perform these functions and any designated station may perform maintenance when it receives the token.

The first two functions are accomplished by transmitting appropriate instruction frames; in the first case 'set next node' frames are again used. The third function presents a problem, since stations may not transmit unless they hold the token, whilst stations not on the ring will never receive the token.

To resolve this deadlock a process called 'controlled contention' is used to accept new stations into the ring. An extended form of the same process is used to initialize the system following a failure during operation.

Each station with ring maintenance responsibility initiates controlled contention each n'th time it receives the token (where n is set by the system). To start the process the maintenance station transmits a 'solicit successor' frame (see Figure 10.10) with one or two demand windows (two windows are used when the maintenance station is the station with the lowest address). Stations wishing to join the ring transmit 'set next node' frames in the appropriate window.

Loss of the token will be detected by an extended period of silence on the bus. At the end of this period stations will conclude that the token has been lost and will contend in a manner analogous to that given above for control of the token. The winner will then reestablish the logical ring as given above.

If the maintenance station hears one response it will add that station to the ring.

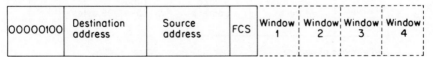

Figure 10.10   Ring management frame formats.

If it hears no response it will conclude the maintenance phase. If it hears a collision it will transmit a 'resolve contention' frame followed by four demand windows. Each demander selects one slot according to the first two bits of its own address and transmits 'set next node'. If it detects a collision during that window it drops its demand.

If the controlling station hears a collision it repeats the 'resolve contention' frame but, in this case, demanders respond according to the third and fourth bits of their addresses. This procedure continues until the controlling station hears a valid 'set next node', until there are no further demanders, or until a maximum retry count has been exceeded.

Transferring Data

During normal operation stations may not transmit until they receive the token in the form of an 'explicit token frame' (see Figure 10.11). On receiving the token a station may transmit data transfer frames for a period not exceeding a limit characteristic of the network.

Frames for transmission may be assigned to one of four classes of service:

Synchronous
Urgent asynchronous
Normal asynchronous
Time available

The system will then clear all the frames on the system in priority order ('synchronous' first and 'time available' last). This system allows traffic of several kinds to coexist on a single bus.

There was, by 1982, no practical experience of the IEEE token-passing bus, but

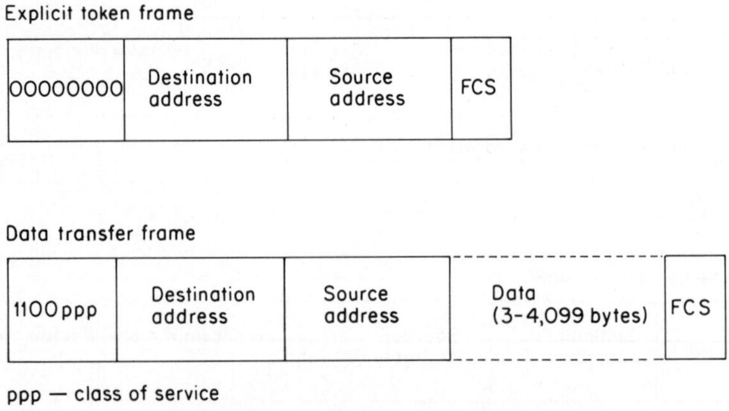

Explicit token frame

00000000	Destination address	Source address	FCS

Data transfer frame

1100ppp	Destination address	Source address	Data (3-4,099 bytes)	FCS

ppp — class of service

Figure 10.11   Ring operation frame formats.

the largest selling LAN, the Datapoint ARCNet, worked by token passing on a physical star that is treated as a broadcast bus. ARCNet provides communications between Datapoint minicomputers and also allows some specialization of function between those computers—'application processors', each with a few terminals, may share files held on a 'file processor' (as shown in Figure 10.12).

Datapoint also offers an IBM gateway, the DCIO. This product connects ARC

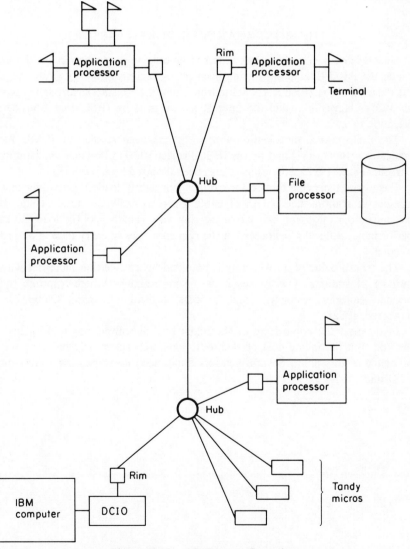

Figure 10.12   ARCNet configuration.

to an IBM byte-multiplexor channel and appears to the IBM computer as a group of unit-record devices, such as card readers and printers. ARC, however, sees the DCIO as another 'application processor' and thus extends the corresponding facilities to IBM programs.

During 1981 Datapoint and Tandy announced an agreement under which Tandy micros would be able to gain access to ARCNet. 1982 saw further announcements in which Datapoint added graphics and facsimile interfaces to ARCNet.

THE SIGNIFICANCE OF TOKEN PASSING

Until 1981 token passing was little known outside academic circles, despite its use in the ARC (Datapoint having been rather secretive about its system). Then the decision of the IEEE LAN Standards Committee to standardize token passing as well as contention, and the interest shown in it by IBM, drew considerable attention to it.

The performance of token-passing rings has been studied at IBM's Zurich laboratory (Bux, 1981) and by the IEEE Project 802 Traffic Handling Committee (Arthurs *et al.*, 1982). Studies have also been reported by Liu (1978).

Token rings provide fair performance when lightly loaded, providing that the number of stations and length of cable are reasonably restricted. Under these circumstances the token will circle the ring very rapidly. As the load increases, performance naturally degrades but the ring continues to carry data in an orderly manner.

The transit delay of a token ring is bounded by a value that increases with the number of stations. This makes it usable in situations where response time is critical—notably telephony and process control (Ansaldi, Olobardi, and Trauerso, 1982).

In the past the complexity of the token bus algorithms has told against this method. But the falling cost of electronic logic is progressively reducing the significance of this point. Several vendors announced token-passing LANs during 1981 and 1982.

11. CONTENTION BUSES

In all LANs the attached devices operate independently and therefore develop needs to communicate across the network at unpredictable times. In polled and token-passing systems, each station is required to defer transmission until it is authorized to begin. Contention LANs take a simpler approach—the station may try to transmit immediately.

Since this may lead to interference between transmissions, some scheme has to be introduced either to avoid such interference or to minimize its effect. A number of such schemes have been implemented.

Contention systems are simple to implement and provide rapid access to the bus (at least when the load is small). They allow stations to be attached and removed readily. They are resilient, since most faults present themselves as silence or as collisions—both conditions that must be handled anyway—and since there need be no central controller. The main disadvantages arise when the bus is heavily used: waiting times for the bus become large and vary erratically.

Contention has been used in a number of commercial and experimental networks, of which the best known is Xerox's Ethernet.

DEVELOPMENT AND PERFORMANCE

The contention principle was used first in ALOHA, a radio network used in Hawaii to provide a dispersed population of terminals with access to a time-sharing computer (Binder *et al.*, 1975). ALOHA terminals were allowed to transmit at any time, and could therefore interfere with one another.

To avoid the use of erroneous data, each packet included a checksum which was checked by the receiving station. Only correct packets were acknowledged, packets with incorrect checksums being simply ignored. To avoid the permanent loss of data, ALOHA required an acknowledgement for every packet. Because of the loss of data due to collisions between packets, the throughput that ALOHA could provide was restricted to 19 per cent. of the channel capacity.

The throughput of an ALOHA system can be improved in a number of ways. In 'slotted ALOHA' a central clock defines a series of successive slots, and packet transmission must start at the beginning of a slot. In consequence, collisions can only occur in the early part of the slot and a packet that survives this without a

119

collision will certainly be able to complete without interference. This doubles the throughput to 37 per cent. of the channel capacity.

An alternative to this fixed slotting is for each station to listen to the bus before starting to transmit ('listen before talk' or LBT). It should refrain from transmitting until it ceases to hear transmission from any other station. In a radio system this is done by listening for the presence of the carrier frequency, rather than of data, and the technique is known as Carrier Sense Multiple Access (CSMA). CSMA may be applied in systems where there is no carrier *per se*, in which case the station may listen for the data itself. An alternative (employed, for instance, in Ethernet) is for the transmitted signal to include an unbalanced d.c. component which can be very easily detected by rectifying the signal on the cable.

If each station with traffic attempts to use the medium as soon as it falls silent, we have 'persistent CSMA'. This gives rapid access to the channel at low utilization, but leads to an excessive number of collisions when many stations have traffic to send. Throughput may be up to 53 per cent. of the channel capacity.

If, instead, the contending stations defer transmission for a randomly determined time, we have 'non-persistent CSMA', and the throughput may then rise above 80 per cent.

A further sophistication is for the sending station to detect collisions and to retransmit packets that suffer collisions. An Ethernet station detects collisions as they occur by the presence of an excessive d.c. component on the cable and can therefore immediately abort its transmission. In two-channel systems, such as are usual on broadband cables, interference may be detected via the checksum at the end of the packet. (The Ethernet form of collision detection is not available in broadband systems since there is no d.c. component to the signal.) This technique is generally known as CSMA with collision detection (CSMA/CD), and allows the throughput to rise to over 90 per cent. of channel capacity.

Collisions may also be detected by requiring immediate acknowledgement of packets, for which purpose all stations except that addressed must leave the channel quiet after the end of a transmission (Luczak, 1978).

After a collision all the stations involved will try to retransmit their packets but, if they do so at the same time, they will simply produce a new collision. They must therefore defer for different periods of time; and this is usually achieved by having each station generate a pseudo-random number, and determine its delay from that. In some systems, HYPERchannel[tm] for instance (Thornton, Christensen, and Jones, 1975), the delays are fixed for each station and provide a priority system under which devices with critical response needs may gain preferential access to the network.

Figure 11.1 shows how the throughput of some contention systems varies with the load presented to the system (Tobagi and Hunt, 1979). In each case a sufficiently great load causes an excessive level of collisions and a fall in throughput. In the case of CSMA/CD, however, throughput remains substantial up to very high loads.

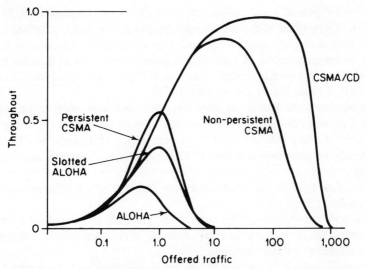

Figure 11.1   Throughput versus offered load for several contention
systems.

Several teams have developed contention systems that attempt to avoid this collapse of throughput:

1. In Ethernet, attempts to transmit a packet are abandoned after the sixteenth.
2. In acknowledging Ethernet (Tokoro and Tamaru, 1977), there are low-level acknowledgements.
3. In FB/CSMA/CD, feedback from the state of the medium causes further deferment (Gable and Sherman, 1981).

The performance of contention systems has been studied extensively (Arthurs and Stuck, 1982; Tobagi and Hunt, 1979; and Vo-Dai, 1982; amongst others.) This work shows the more advanced systems to show excellent performance at low load, but that the waiting times worsen rapidly as the presented load increases.

Most studies published to date have been concerned with the medium access control level alone. However, research at the Lawrence Livermore Laboratories (Donnelley and Yeh, 1979) has shown that an inappropriate link layer control protocol can greatly restrict the performance of a contention LAN.

ETHERNET

The original Ethernet (Metcalfe and Boggs, 1976) was implemented at the Xerox Palo Alto Research Center (PARC) during 1975. That system was intended to provide communication between Alto personal minicomputers (Thacker et al., 1979) and various shared facilities. It operated at 2.96M bit/s.

The project proved a success and by 1980 Xerox had installed over 30 Ethernets in the United States and elsewhere supporting over 1,000 attached devices. Most of these Ethernets were within the Xerox Corporation, and neither Ethernet nor the Alto was marketed as a product. A number of studies of installed systems were published by those involved (for instance, Crane and Taft, 1980; Shoch and Hupp, 1979, 1980a; Shoch and Stewart, 1979).

In September 1980 Xerox, together with DEC and Intel, published a specification for a revised Ethernet operating at 10M bit/s (DIX, 1980). The specification covers only the physical and data link layers of the OSI model and is given in some detail; the document amounts to 92 pages of text, diagrams, and PASCAL programs.

At the same time Xerox announced its willingness to sell Ethernet licences at $1,000 each.

The specification declared the goal of the Ethernet to have been a low-cost, high-speed, digital communications channel with guaranteed compatibility between conforming implementations.

Ethernet is defined in terms of both an architecture and the interfaces in a typical implementation, both of which are shown in Figure 11.2. The architecture comprises two layers (or three if the physical medium is counted as a separate layer), and each layer being further subdivided thus:

2: *Data link layer*   Data encapsulation, the recognition of packets for this station and the detection (but not correction) of errors.
Link management, the capacity-sharing algorithm for the bus.

1: *Physical layer*   Encode and decode, the generation/removal of the frame preamble and conversion between binary and Manchester encodings.
Transmit and receive, the matching of data signals to the bus and the detection of other transmissions and of collisions.

0: *Physical medium*   Coaxial cable and repeaters.
Transceiver cable.

These layers and sublayers correspond fairly closely to the layers of the IEEE Reference Model, thus:

Ethernet:	IEEE
Data Encapsulation	Link layer control
Link management	Medium access control
Encode & decode	Physical signalling
Transmit & receive	Physical medium attachment

In each case it is expected that the PMA will usually be implemented in the

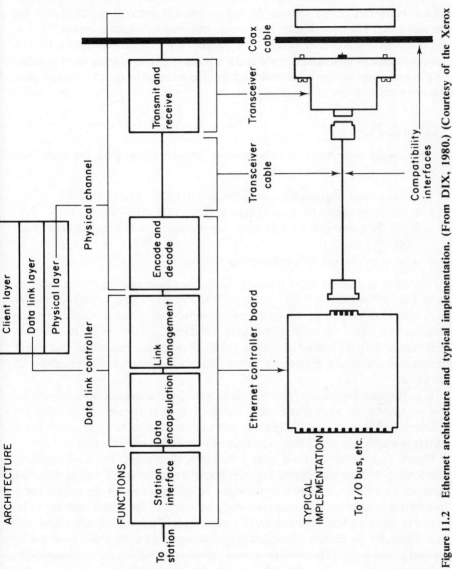

Figure 11.2 Ethernet architecture and typical implementation. (From DIX, 1980.) (Courtesy of the Xerox Corporation.)

form of a separate component, a component which the Ethernet specification calls a transceiver.

The specification requires strict compatibility between implementations in the logical behaviour of the station, defined by the architectural model, and in the coaxial cable. The specification also invites, but does not require, compatibility at the transceiver–transceiver cable and transceiver cable–controller interfaces. This further degree of compatibility will allow a number of transceivers to be installed at the same time as the cable and later to be connected to controllers and other devices from a variety of suppliers.

The Physical Layer

The coaxial cable that forms the basis of Ethernet differs from the commoner CATV cable in a number of respects:

1. It has a lower characteristic impedance—50 rather than 75 Ω.
2. It will allow signals to travel at least at 0.77 c (2.3×10^{10} cm/s).
3. It can be penetrated by a pressure tap without introducing excessive losses or distortions.
4. It must be marked with bands every 2.5 metres.

The cable is installed most typically in ducts or false ceilings, in segments no more than 500 metres in length. A single Ethernet may comprise any number of such segments connected by repeaters, provided that there is only one route between every pair of stations and that this route includes no more than two repeaters and 1,500 metres of coaxial cable. To minimize reflections that might imitate collisions, each segment is terminated in the characteristic impedance of the cable.

Ethernet repeaters detect 'carrier', data signals, and collisions from either side, and regenerate the appropriate cable condition or data stream on the other. In addition, an Ethernet may include one point-to-point cable, not more than 1,000 metres in length. Up to 1,024 devices may be attached to one Ethernet.

Figure 11.3 shows a typical large Ethernet configuration. The high signalling speed used in Ethernet imposes a number of restrictions on actual Ethernet installations which are needed to minimize reflective losses on the cable. These restrictions include considerable care in the selection of the cables that are to be joined to make a single segment, and the placement of taps at 2.5 metre intervals. In addition, for the collision detection system to work, the cable shield must not be earthed at any point. (These restrictions are given more fully in the specification.)

Transceivers are placed immediately adjacent to their taps, which in practice means that they will usually be placed within the ducts or false ceilings. The usual configuration is shown (following Crane and Taft, 1980) in Figure 11.4. The transceiver matches signals to the coaxial cables, isolates the drop cable from the

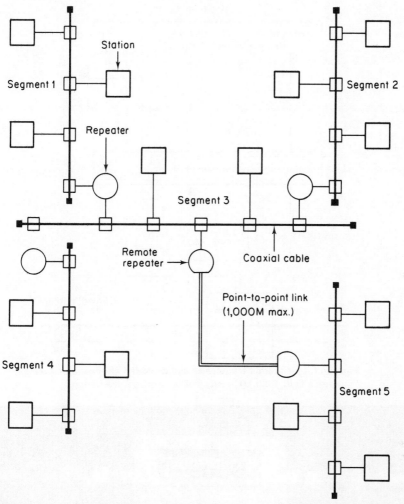

Figure 11.3   A typical large-scale configuration. (Courtesy of the Xerox
Corporation.)

common bus cable, and detects collisions. In addition, the guard circuit can detect
certain errors in the transmitted signal and will interrupt the transmitter if it does
find errors.

The transceiver may be connected to the station electronics by up to 50 metres
of drop cable. The cable contains four twisted pairs—transmit data, receive data,
collision detect and power—in an overall shield. A transceiver is shown in Figure
11.5.

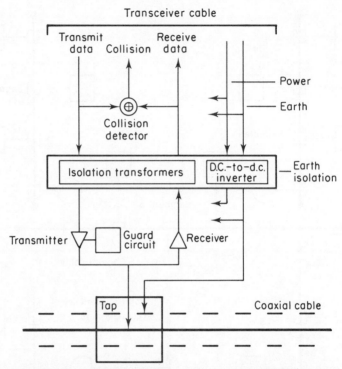

Figure 11.4   Ethernet transceiver and cable tap. (Following Crane and Taft, 1980.) (Courtesy of the Xerox Corporation.)

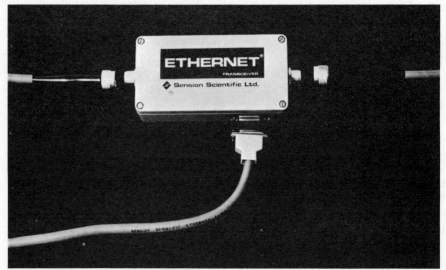

Figure 11.5   An Ethernet transceiver. (Illustration by courtesy of Sension Scientific Ltd.)

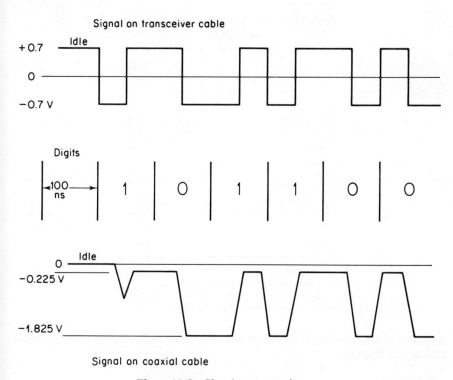

Figure 11.6   Signals at transceiver.

Figure 11.6 shows a typical signal as received from the transceiver and as presented to the coaxial cable. The roles of the signals are reversed in the case of a received signal. Received signals will be weaker and will have a rounder shape than that shown in the figure, due to losses and distortions on the cable.

The encoding of data in Manchester code is the responsibility of the encode and decode sublayer which is physically located in the controller logic rather than in the transceiver.

The maximum size of an Ethernet is determined by the time taken to detect a collision between two packets. In the worst case a station at one end of the network will begin transmitting just as it receives a packet from a station at the far end of the cable. The time taken for that packet to cross the network and for the collision to propagate back to the sending station is the round-trip delay for the network. Table 11.1 shows the worst-case delay to be 45 μs; i.e. sufficient time for 450 bits to be transmitted.

Proper operation of a contention LAN requires that all stations agree as to whether a collision has occurred. To ensure this, Ethernet specifies a minimum length for data packets such that the transmitting station will, even in the worst

Table 11.1 Worst-case round-trip delay in Ethernet.

Element	Delay (μs)
Encode and decode	2.40
Transceiver cable	3.08
Transceiver	4.65
Coaxial cable	13.00
Point-to-point cable link	10.26
Repeaters	2.00
Detector delays	1.20
Signal rise-time*	0.30
Collision rise-time†	8.10
Total	44.99

* The signal must reach 70 per cent. of its final value to be detected as 'carrier'.
† The signal must reach 94 per cent. of its final value to be detected as a collision.

case, still be transmitting the same packet when it hears the collision. The smallest packet is defined as:

Preamble	64 bits
Header	14 octets
Data (artificially padded if necessary)	46 octets
Frame check sequence	4 octets
Total	72 octets = 576 bits

This restriction applies to all contention LANs, however implemented. It may be relaxed by reducing the signalling speed or the size of the network. It can be seen from Table 11.1, however, that the restriction of Ethernet to a single segment would only take about 13 octets off the minimum packet length. Halving the speed would halve this minimum and a reduction to 3.75M bit/s would remove any need to pad the data field.

The Data Link Layer

The data link layer receives packets from the attached device, assembles frames for the physical layer, and calculates the frame check sequence. (Frame and packet formats are shown in Figure 11.7.)

The data link layer is informed of activity on the coaxial cable by the physical layer. It will not seek to transmit a packet until that activity ceases; even then it waits for at least 9.6 μs for the channel to recover its idle state. If the data link

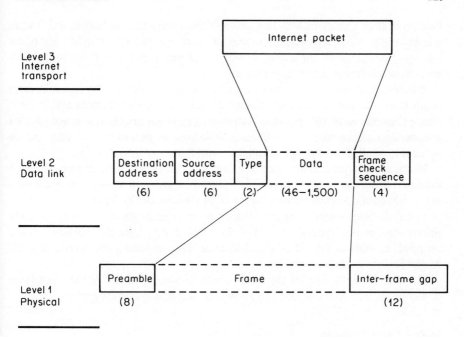

Figure 11.7   Ethernet formats. (Lengths are in octets.)

layer is informed of a collision during its attempt to transmit, it aborts its own transmission after transmitting a jam signal. (The jam signal is undefined but serves to ensure that all stations affected are aware of the collision.)

Following a collision all stations enter a process known as 'truncated binary exponential backoff'. Each station generates a random number which determines for how long it should pause before making a retry. The delay is always a multiple of 51.2 µs (a period known as the slot-time, and rather longer than the worst-case round-trip delay discussed above). Because of this, any single station which 'throws' the lowest random number is assured of being able to complete its transmission without a collision. Stations with random numbers even one unit higher will detect carrier in less than 51.2 µs and will defer to it. If two or more stations have the same lowest number, the process is repeated with a wider range of possible numbers.

During the first 10 retries the range increases exponentially from 0–1 to 0–1023 (implying a maximum delay of 65 millisecs), and up to five more retries may be made with the same range. If the sixteenth attempt fails, the data link layer will abandon all attempts to transmit the packet and will so inform its client. Such catastrophic failure is unlikely to happen in normal operation, and usually indicates a break in the coaxial cable or other gross interference with its electrical properties.

The physical layer passes all received frames to the data link layer. The data link layer then rejects frames that are less than 64 octets in length and frames whose length is not an integral number of octets (since these should only occur following collisions on the cable). It will accept any frame that is addressed to it and pass such frames to the client layer.

Ethernet addresses are of two kinds, physical and multicast. Physical addresses begin with a 0 and are unique amongst all stations on all Ethernets everywhere. (Since there are over 10^{14} possible addresses, this is not unduly restrictive.) Xerox proposes to assign blocks of addresses to interested parties so that they can be wired into controllers during manufacture and thus guaranteed unique.

Multicast addresses start with a 1 and are themselves also of two kinds. A multicast-group address defines, by convention, a group of stations on one Ethernet. A broadcast address defines the set of all stations on one Ethernet.

The type field is used to specify the client layer protocol that is to process the packet and is not processed by the data link layer. Like the address, Xerox proposes to control the use of this field itself, at least until some standards body can be found to take over the job.

The data link also verifies the frame check sequence, informing the client layer of any error. The data link does not, however, attempt to correct errors.

Higher Level Protocols

Both the experimental and commercial Ethernets require a variety of higher levels protocols, of which the most basic is that at the network level. Xerox's own network level protocol is described in Chapter 17.

Like the bottom two layers of Ethernet, this protocol is based on two major principles:

1. Operation is fully distributed—there is no need for any central controller or switch.
2. Packet delivery is not guaranteed but undertaken on the 'best efforts' principle.

Accordingly Ethernets may occasionally discard packets without notice. Non-Xerox Ethernets need not employ Xerox's higher level protocols and most do not do so.

Though designed for data transmission it would clearly be useful if Ethernet could also carry speech. Protocols that can provide speech capacity on Ethernet have been developed by Xerox PARC (Shoch, 1981), Intel (Melvin, 1981), and Olivetti (Ravasio, Marcogliese, and Novarese, 1982).

COMMERCIAL DEVELOPMENTS

The first Ethernet products were not produced by any of the three original companies but by small independents. The first products were transceivers (3Com and TCL Inc.), software (3Com), and terminal support units (Ungermann-Bass).

3Com's Unet package provides communications between Unix systems. It is not restricted to Ethernet and has been adopted by Zilog as the basis of Z-Net II.

Ungermann-Bass's Net/One is a terminal support network in which clusters of terminals gain access to Ethernet via network interface units (Figure 11.8). The original product provided transparent circuits to ASCII terminals only, but

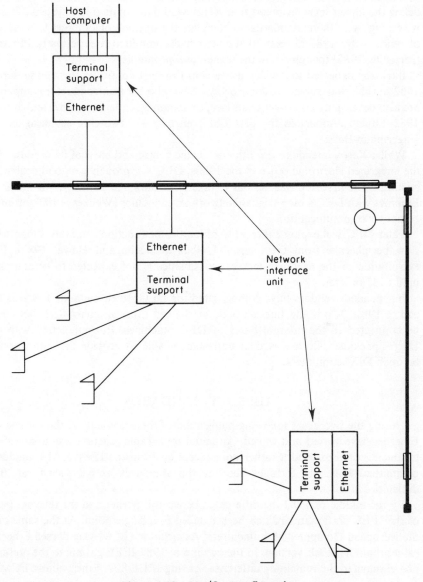

Figure 11.8   Net/One configuration.

enhancements have added support for other kinds of terminals, high-speed parallel interfaces for computers, and a datagram service.

Xerox's first Ethernet products appeared in 1981 and were the 8010 Star workstation (a descendant of the Alto), and file and print servers to support the 8010. Xerox later added interfaces for its word processors, intelligent typewriters, and facsimile machines. During 1981 Xerox also published the first two Xerox Systems Integration Standards (XSISs) (Xerox, 1981a, 1981b). These began to define the higher level protocols that Xerox would use in its office systems. Xerox is seeking, with these standards, to complete the opening of Ethernet to a variety of vendors. By 1982 at least 30 suppliers had committed themselves to Ethernet (Metcalfe, 1982) though not to the higher level protocols.

Intel was expected to develop a one-chip Ethernet controller for release during 1982 but this was subject to some delays. Several other semiconductor companies are also developing controller chips (see, for example, Coleman, 1982) and in June 1982 Fujitsu announced the first LSI controller—a two-chip set designed by Ungermann-Bass.

Whilst Xerox intends to use Ethernet as the centre and basis of its products for the integrated electronic office of the 1980s, DEC's approach is a good deal more cautious. The first step was not due to take place until mid-1983 and will integrate Ethernet with DEC's own Digital Network Architecture (Wecker, 1980) for intercomputer communication.

Later DEC will exploit Ethernet to offload some functions, notably support for slow peripherals, from the internal Unibus (Marathe and Hawe, 1982). Full exploitation of the new architectural possibilities is not expected to be complete until 1985 or later.

Independent vendors have compensated for DEC's own caution. Towards the end of 1981, 3Com and Interlan both announced Ethernet controllers that could be connected to the internal buses of DEC machines. In conjunction with the Unet™ package 3Com was then immediately able to provide full interworking between DEC computers.

ETHERNET STANDARDS

During the two years following publication of the specification, the fortunes of Ethernet have waxed and waned. An initial favourable reaction was followed by technical criticisms and a rather poor reception from the IEEE LAN standards committee. Later its fortunes rose as the standards activity itself ran into difficulties.

By the middle of 1982 the differences between Ethernet and the relevant parts of the IEEE draft standard had been reduced to a single point. At the same time the European Computer Manufacturers' Association (ECMA) endorsed Ethernet rather than the IEEE version. In the autumn of 1982 IEEE gave in to the pressure and eliminated the remaining difference, leaving IEEE 802, Ethernet and ECMA-

82 'substantially' the same. This will at least allow systems built in accordance with the three specifications to share a single cable. (Standards activity is discussed further in Chapter 20.)

OTHER DEVELOPMENTS

Contention has been used in a variety of other LANs including 'home-built' LANs such as NBS Net (Carpenter and Sokol, 1979) and Mitrenet (Hopkins, 1981) and commercial products like LocalNet[tm], HYPERchannel[tm], HYPERbus[tm], Ubits (Casteuil, Giovachino, and Lengyel, 1981), Z-Net[tm], Cluster One, and Econet. These networks all use bus or tree topologies. Two of them, LocalNet[tm] and Mitrenet, use broadband techniques whilst the others are baseband systems.

LocalNet[tm] (Biba, 1981a,b) supports terminals over a number of 128k bit/s common channels. Collisions are detected by examining the frame check sequences of packets that are re-broadcast from the head-end. (LocalNet[tm] is described further in Chapter 15.)

HYPERbus[tm] (Binney, 1981) is a direct competitor to Ethernet-based products such as Net/One. At 6.3M bit/s it is rather slower than Ethernet but quite fast enough to support the intended terminals and computers. The vendor, Network Systems Corporation (NSC), has extensive LAN experience through HYPERchannel[tm].

HYPERchannel[tm] (Thornton, Christensen, and Jones, 1975) uses a prioritized CSMA/CD system to provide communications between mainframes, large minis, and specialized peripherals such as mass stores. HYPERchannel[tm] uses up to four cables, each operating at 50M bit/s, and is limited in range to a large computer room. Adaptors for a wide range of computers are available, and high-speed terrestrial and satellite links can be used to interconnect HYPERchannel centres. By 1982 several hundred systems had been installed.

Cluster One (Malone, 1981) supports a population of Apple micros over a bus operating at 240k bit/s. The Apples share the use of disc files, printers, and communications gateways.

Z-Net[tm] provides communication at 800k bit/s between Zilog computers. It uses coax cable which may be Ethernet-compatible, allowing for a subsequent upgrade to Ethernet.

CONCLUSION

Contention is a simple and robust technique that can be used in a variety of LANs. Its principal disadvantages are that:

1. Response is statistical. There is always some probability of an arbitrarily long response time.
2. Fast collision detection is difficult in baseband systems since the collision must be heard whilst the station is itself broadcasting.

3. Installed systems cannot generally be upgraded to higher speed because a fixed relationship exists among speed, range, and minimum packet size.

Despite these limitations, the initial success of several products and developing standards ensure a continuing place for contention networks.

12. RESERVATION SYSTEMS

Reservation LANs divide the time on the bus into slots. Each active station is allocated one or more slots and transmits, if it has data, in the time slot(s) reserved to it. There must, in general, be a process by which slots are allocated to stations, and we may distinguish four main cases:

1. Allocation during system construction or configuration (static allocation).
2. Allocation for the duration of a call—typically minutes to hours (call allocation).
3. Dynamic allocation.
4. Allocation by a hybrid of call and dynamic methods.

STATIC ALLOCATION

This approach may be used when the patterns of traffic are both constant and predictable. It can give high efficiency in these circumstances because no capacity is wasted in passing control between stations.

One static system, the Vector-Driven Proportional Access (VDPA) method was developed by Honeywell in the early 1970s for use in a military avionics system, the Distributed Processor/Memory (Anderson, 1973). It was later used in the Modular Computer System (Jensen, 1976), in the Honeywell Experimental Distributed Processor (HXDP; see Jensen, 1978), and in the Modular Missile-Bourne Computer (Arnold *et al*, 1981), a high performance multi-processing system intended for use on antimissile missiles.

The HXDP was, as the name suggests, a system intended to support research in distributed systems, especially those in which the distributed computers were to exercise real-time control over some external, and typically non-computer, process. In HXDP a number of minicomputers were connected by a high-speed bus built with a shielded twisted pair and operating at 1.25M bit/s.

VDPA is based on a slot vector and index in each bus interface unit (BIU). At the end of each transmission, the transmitting station issues an 'increment index' signal that causes each BIU to increment its local index. For protection against

135

lost signals the signal contains the index value currently held by the transmitter and other BIUs set their indexes by this.

The BIUs thus step their way together through their vectors. At each step just one BIU will find permission to transmit in its slot vector and that BIU will either transmit a packet or issue the 'increment index' signal. Packets are addressed to names, rather than to BIUs, and each BIU can support up to eight names. Names may be interpreted as defining processes, message types or priorities at the discretion of the programer.

Though static allocation can give high efficiencies, it requires both the ability to foresee traffic patterns accurately and stability in the patterns themselves. These conditions may be met in a real-time control system or, by extension, within a general-purpose computer system (since the operating system is itself a real-time control system), but are not likely to be met for LANs in a more flexible environment.

CALL ALLOCATION

A LAN may reserve slots for a call between two stations for the duration of a call. This will require a separate reservation procedure that does not use slots in the usual way. In fact, the slots themselves may not be used; the reservation procedure may use a separate cable, a separate frequency (in a broadband system), or a part of the frame that falls outside the slots.

Slot allocation may be either centralized or distributed. In a centralized system, stations wishing to establish calls must inform the central controller of their needs. Once it has received the request, the controller will allocate one or more slots to the call if free slots are available. In a distributed system the stations contend for the use of free slots, but will generally be allowed to use corresponding slots in successive frames without further overhead.

Call allocation systems have not attracted much attention, though one, the data loop exchange (DLX), was developed within RCA in the early 1970s (White and Maxemchuk, 1974). DLX was used within RCA to a limited extent and was offered as a commercial product by Electrosound Systems in 1981.

The service provided by DLX and similar systems is essentially a switched data circuit. The rigidity of the slot allocation system implies that such systems are not LANs in the sense used in this book. The hybrid systems discussed below include call allocation and do qualify as LANs.

DYNAMIC ALLOCATION

In dynamic allocation, the slots are allocated and released during a time that is much less than the duration of a call. Access to the bus generally starts with the execution of a 'gain access' protocol, which may be one of those discussed in previous chapters. This may confer the right to use only the next slot, or the right may be extended to corresponding slots in subsequent frames.

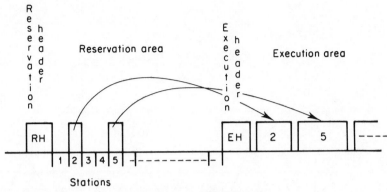

Figure 12.1 RACORN cycle.

A variety of means have been proposed to gain the use of a slot. Toshiba, for instance, has developed two LANs based on stars of optic fibres (Kunikyo and Ozeki, 1982): ACORN and RACORN.

In the Administrator Contention Optical Radial Network (ACORN) the administrator station signals the start of a cycle and each station is permanently assigned one slot. Each station transmits in its own slot if it has data. If a station has no data the administrator detects silence and indicates the end of the slot by transmitting a special signal.

In the Reservation ACORN (RACORN) the cycle is divided into reservation and execution areas. Each reservation area slot is permanently assigned to one station and a transmission in a slot reserves one, variable-length, slot in the execution area. This is shown in Figure 12.1.

The IEEE Reservation Method

An interesting algorithm is under development by the Reservation Subcommittee of the IEEE LAN Standards Committee (Project 802). This algorithm may be seen as deriving from polling, token-passing, or contention systems, depending on one's point of view (Capetanakis, 1979a, 1979b; Mori and Norigoe, 1976).

The algorithm starts with the transmission of an 'all stations' poll. The poll will be issued by a polling unit, though for resilience all stations may have the ability to act as polling units at need.

If no station transmits, then the poll is reissued and this may be repeated indefinitely. To establish that no station has transmitted the polling unit must wait for the slot-time of the system, i.e. the round-trip propagation delay plus the station response time:

1. If one station transmits then that transmission is successful and the poll will be reissued after it is complete.
2. If more than one station transmits then their transmissions collide and will be aborted.

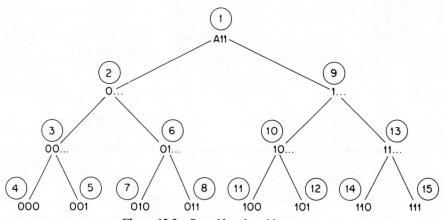

Figure 12.2 Searching the address tree.

So far the algorithm is indistinguishable from slotted CSMA (see Chapter 11).

At this stage the polling unit issues a selective poll inviting stations in the lower half of the address range to respond. If a collision again occurs the polling unit again halves the address range and re-polls. When it finds zero or one response, the polling unit will cease to explore the address space and will poll the upper halves of the address ranges. Figure 12.2 shows the order in which the address space is explored if a collision is explored at every level except the lowest. Since this method reserves transmission capacity by searching the address tree it seems reasonable to call it Dynamic Reservation by Address Tree Search (DRATS).

Figure 12.3 shows the sequence of events when stations 2, 3, and 7 are

All stations poll
Stations 2, 3 and 7 collide
Poll: 0—3
Stations 2 and 3 collide
Poll: 0—1
(Silence)
Poll: 2—3
Stations 2 and 3 collide
Poll 2
Transmission (2)
Poll 3
Transmission (3)
Poll 4—7
Transmission (7)

All stations poll
⋮

Figure 12.3 Collision resolution in a tree search LAN.

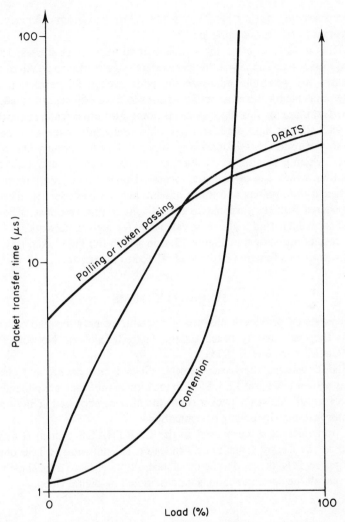

Figure 12.4   Performance of polling, contention, and DRATS
networks under varying load.

simultaneously ready to transmit. There are assumed to be eight stations with
addresses 0–7.

In this case, the process completes with less polls than would be required in roll-
call polling (seven rather than eight). As the proportion of stations that have data
to transmit rises, however, DRATS begins to require more polls than roll-call.

To compensate for this the polling unit may recognize when the load is high
and then switch to roll-call polling. DRATS may also use a hybrid scheme in

which tree searching starts several levels down. For maximum efficiency, the level may be varied to reflect changing load.

DRATS is unusual in attaching significance to network addresses. The allocation of addresses to stations will therefore affect system efficiency. An even spread of addresses will generally minimize the polls needed for resolution and it is especially desirable for the most active stations to have well-separated addresses.

The performance of this algorithm has some attractive features (Arthurs and Stuck, 1982). Under light load, stations will usually gain access to the channel within one slot-time. This is markedly superior to both polling and token bus techniques, which both require $n/_2$ slot-times on the average, but not quite as good as contention, which can offer instant access. Under heavy load pure tree search is less efficient than polling and token passing but more efficient than contention. DRATS shares with the former two the advantage that response is bounded; it can never exceed a period that can be calculated for a given network.

These results are shown in Figure 12.4, in which the time taken to transmit a packet is shown as a function of the load offered to the network.

HYBRID SYSTEMS

Hybrid systems provide a mixture of dynamic reservation and call allocated capacity. They are mainly based on the Slotted Envelope Network (SENET) concept (Coviello and Vena, 1975).

In SENET systems the basic frame is divided into packet and circuit subframes, as shown in Figure 12.5. Slots in the circuit subframe are allocated for the duration of a call, whilst the packet subframe may be allocated in any convenient manner; for instance, by polling or contention.

These principles have been used in the CARTHAGE system (Favre, 1982) developed at the Centre Commun d'Etudes de Télédiffusion et Télécommunications in France. It is intended to be developed ultimately into a local network that will integrate all the communications modes, including digital video.

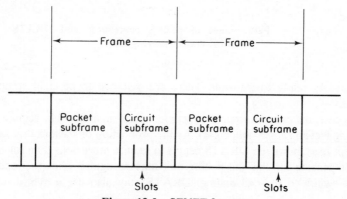

Figure 12.5   SENET frames.

CARTHAGE is implemented as a ring, each segment of which is a bundle of optic fibres. One fibre is used for voice, data, and network control, whilst the others provide video circuits. The video circuits are switched by video switches, under the control of specialized CARTHAGE stations, but are not otherwise integrated into the system.

The data fibre carries signals at 8M bit/s and traffic is divided into a succession of 'multiframes'. Each multiframe consists of 20 frames of 128 slots each. One slot lasts 1 μs and contains 8 bits. Each frame is divided into a packet subframe of 32, 64, or 96 bytes and a circuit subframe containing the remaining 96, 64, or 32 slots respectively. This is shown in Figure 12.6.

The packet subframe provides stations with a burst data rate of 2, 4, or 6M bit/s and use of these subframes is controlled by a token-passing discipline. Broadcast, datagram, and packet virtual circuit modes are all supported in a conventional manner. The packet format is shown in Figure 12.7.

Circuits are established by making a connection request which specifies the called station, required throughput, and the nature of the intended transmission. Requests may be met in a variety of ways:

1. Video circuits are provided by a separate switching unit and the video fibres.
2. Voice circuits are provided by allocating one slot per frame to the circuit.
3. Data circuits may be provided by allocating a few slots per multiframe or by establishing a virtual circuit in the packet subframes.

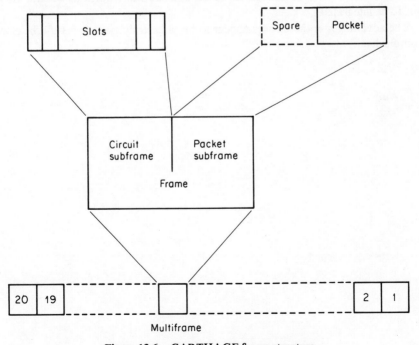

Figure 12.6   CARTHAGE frame structure.

Figure 12.7   CARTHAGE packet format.

Hybrid systems such as CARTHAGE provide a means of managing and integrating the disparate needs of video, voice, and data communications. This advantage is, of course, purchased at the price of extra complexity in the capacity-sharing algorithm. In the case of CARTHAGE, for instance, the network station supports the multiframe/frame/slot structure, together with four distinct means of allocating capacity with a frame.

A number of hybrid reservation systems have been reported including those of Hanson, Chou, and Nilson (1981), Capel *et al* (1981) and Nilsson, Chou, and Graff, (1980). Amongst commercial products the Amdax Cablenet[tm] system (Kong and Lindsey, 1982) makes sophisticated use of reservation techniques to support up to 12,000 terminals on a site up to 25 miles in radius.

CONCLUSION

Reservation methods offer attractive performance for certain kinds of traffic. Their most distinctive advantage, however, appears when traffic of several kinds has to be integrated.

The advantages in these cases appear to be sufficiently great to justify the extra complexity.

13. SLOTTED RINGS

The general principle of a slotted ring is that the data transmitted on the ring are divided rigidly into a number of slots. The slotted structure rotates rapidly, passing the slots from station to station. Stations may place data in empty slots, causing the data to be sent on to other stations.

The method was originally developed at Bell Labs. for public networking (Pierce, Coker, and Kropfl, 1971), but interest later focused on local area networks.

The best known slotted ring is that developed at the Cambridge University Computer Laboratory in the 1970s, and known as the Cambridge Ring. (The developers received the 1981 technical award of the British Computer Society for their work and several suppliers have developed products based on it.) Rings have been installed in a number of universities and other academic institutions in the UK, and sales to commercial organizations started in 1981.

THE CAMBRIDGE RING

The description that follows refers to the system developed and installed by the Computing Laboratory at the University of Cambridge (Wilkes and Wheeler, 1979), unless otherwise specified. 'Cambridge Rings' developed elsewhere differ in various ways from this system.

Data are transmitted between stations in bit-serial form as 5 V pulses. The standard wiring is two unshielded twisted pairs, each providing one channel. Each channel is fully balanced and, in each bit-time, transitions on both channels indicate a 1, whilst a transition on only one channel indicates a 0. This signalling system has been proven over distances of 200 metres, but it is usual to place stations no more than 100 metres apart to ensure continued operation in the event of a station failure. Channels are coupled to the station logic by transformers, and the electronics is so arranged that if the station fails the repeater acts as a purely passive coupler.

Stations are powered from the ring, the power being carried as 50 V d.c. either on the signal wires or on separate wires provided for the purpose. Optical fibres may also be used to carry the signal, though they cannot, of course, carry electrical power for the stations.

The general configuration of a ring is shown in Figure 13.1. Stations are identical except for the monitor and logging stations. The monitor station initializes the ring and maintains the integrity of the slot structure. The logging station records errors for the benefit of maintenance staff.

Data on the ring are divided into a number of slots known as minipackets, each of which is 38 bits long. The number of slots may be wired into the electronics, or it may be determined by the monitor station during initialization. In a ring with stations at 20 metre intervals and an operating speed of 10M bit/s, each minipacket occupies about 300 metres, so that a ring restricted to a single building will not have room for very many minipackets. In fact, the ring is very unlikely to be the exact size for an integral number of minipackets and it must therefore be artificially extended by a shift register in the Monitor Station.

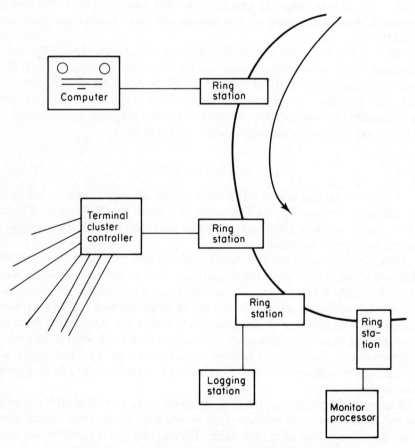

Figure 13.1   General configuration of a Cambridge Ring.

After an upgrade or an extension, it may be necessary to redetermine the effective size of the ring. This will also be necessary if, as discussed in Chapter 8, the ring can recover from failures by using alternative routes.

The ability to do this automatically, and thus to set the number of slots and the size of the monitor station shift register, eases the task of network management and is especially valuable during error recovery. It was not part of the original design but has been implemented by Racal in its Planet network.

Maintaining Ring Integrity

Several methods of monitoring the integrity of the ring are built into the design at the physical level (OSI level 1). Each slot is terminated by a parity bit (Figure 13.2) which is checked by each station that sees the slot. If the parity is incorrect, the parity bit is reset for transmission and the station unit sends a reporting packet to the logging station indicating the fault (Wheeler and Hopper, 1979). Reporting packets are deleted by the monitor station.

The monitor station also writes random numbers into empty packets and, since empty packets are subject to parity checks, this means that basic check of integrity operates continuously even if no useful data are flowing.

Packets are sent with the monitor bit unset, and normally reach the monitor station in this condition. The monitor sets the monitor bit of every full packet. If the sender fails to empty the packet on its return the monitor station will find the monitor bit already set on the second cycle and will empty the packet, thus making it available to others.

The failure of a repeater will normally cause it to become a passive component in the ring and the failure of a station unit will normally cause it to cease functioning. Neither condition causes any problems to other ring users.

The full–empty bit indicates whether the slot contains a real minipacket, rather than random data. This bit is used by the medium access control (at the data link level).

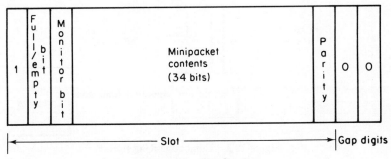

Figure 13.2   Slot format.

Transferring Data

Computers are normally connected to the ring through an access box, station unit, and repeater, the whole forming the station (as shown in Figure 13.3). The repeater manages the flow of bits on the ring, the station unit implements the minipacket protocol, whilst the access box provides conversion between the network specific functions of the station unit and the attached computer. The interface between the computer and access box is usually provided on the computer's own internal bus.

The format of the minipackets is shown in Figure 13.4. Only 16 of the 38 bits are useful data, the remainder being taken up with addresses and response bits. A total of 254 addresses are available for user stations, addresses 0 and 255 being reserved for system use.

A station with data to transmit may only use a slot if it is marked 'empty'. It will then set the full–empty bit to 'full' and transmit a minipacket in the space provided. The response bits are set by the destination statioon for the benefit of the source, to which the minipacket returns.

As it passes round the ring the minipacket is regenerated by each repeater, causing a delay of about 150 ns (1.5 bit-times) at each. As each packet passes through a repeater it is copied into a shift register as well as being output to the next station.

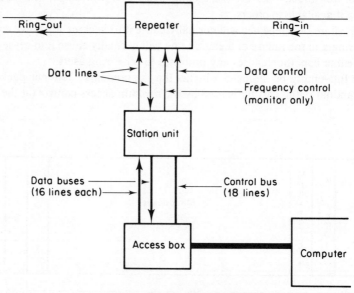

Figure 13.3   Cambridge Ring station.

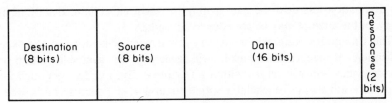

Figure 13.4   Cambridge minipacket.

At any given time each station will be in one of three modes:

1. Receptive to packets from all sources.
2. Receptive to packets from one source only.
3. Deaf.

When a station receives a minipacket addressed to itself from a station to which it is not deaf, it captures the packet from the shift register and sets '01' ('accepted') into the response bits of the outgoing packet.

The minipacket now returns to the sending station, which sets the full–empty flag to empty, making it available to other stations. To prevent one station from hogging all the available transmission capacity, the sending station is not allowed to reuse the packet itself. The sending station may recognize its own packet either by counting the packets on the ring or by reading the source address. The former was used in the original system at the University of Cambridge, but requires that either the number of packets on the ring is fixed or that all stations must always know the actual number.

The above account is rather simplified. Though each station will normally be able to accept packets from any source, this will not be true for a short time after it has accepted a packet. During this period the shift register will contain the received packet and so cannot be overwritten by a new packet. If a packet for the same station is detected, it will be rejected with the response bits set to '00'. The station may also adopt a restricted mode of operation in which it will accept packets from just one sender. In this case packets will be rejected with response bits '10'.

Because of these various possibilities, the sending station may get its minipacket back with any one of four values in the response bits, viz:

11   Destination absent
01   Packet accepted
10   Destination deaf
00   Destination busy

This information will be passed to a higher level protocol for appropriate action. If the destination was busy, the packet may be sent again immediately. If the destination was deaf the packet may be resent either immediately or after a delay, or the attempt may be abandoned altogether.

The Cambridge Ring exhibits a very low latency. Operating at the usual low utilization an empty minipacket will generally be available within a few microseconds and will return within a few more. Even under very high load an empty slot will always be available within about $4(n + 1)$ microseconds, where n is the number of stations on the ring.

The price paid for these advantages is that the ring is very inefficient in its use of transmission capacity—60 per cent. of the total bandwidth is taken up by the control bits, thus restricting the total available capacity of a ring to 4M bit/s. Each station, however, may only have one minipacket on the ring at any one time and is also not allowed to reuse its own returned minipackets. The capacity available to a single station thus depends on the number of packets on the ring and is given, approximately (Wilkes and Wheeler, 1979), by

$$\text{Capacity} = \frac{4}{n + 2} \text{ M bit/s}$$

where n is the number of minipackets. Thus 1.3M bit/s is the largest capacity that can ever be available, and this would be reduced to 0.5M bit/s if there were six packets on the ring. Despite the fact that all packets are processed by all stations the standard ring does not have a broadcast mode (Wilbur, 1980). However, at least one commercial system, Logica's Polynet, does have this facility.

Protocols

The basic service provided by the ring is an addressed minipacket (with a broadcast option in some systems). A bit error rate of about 10^{-11} is found in practice (Binns, Dallas, and Spratt, 1982).

This service may be used to carry data directly in suitable cases (see, for instance, Leslie, Banerjee, and Love, 1981) but it has a number of limitations:

1. There is no addressing within the station, so that each pair of stations can conduct only a single conversation.
2. There is no error detection between stations. (The slot parity bit only protects individual segments.)

To surmount these limitations, Cambridge University have defined the Basic Block Protocol (BB). BBP is a simple datagram protocol using the format shown in Figure 13.5.

For terminal support and similar purposes, a virtual call protocol known as the Byte Stream Protocol has been implemented on top of BBP (Johnson, 1980). As originally defined, this fell somewhat short of the requirements that have since been identified for a Transport (OSI level 4) Protocol. An enhanced form, known

Header 1001	Length	Port number	Data	Checksum
4 bits	12 bits	12 bits	Up to 1,024 minipackets	16 bits

Figure 13.5   Basic block format.

as Transport Service Byte Stream Protocol, has been defined by Dallas (1980) and is currently being implemented (Dallas, 1981) (see Figure 13.6).

An alternative, and rather simpler approach, has been developed at University College, London (Rubinstein, Kennington, and Knight, 1981). The University College team were interested in providing a population of terminals with access to various computers, including several running Unix. They calculated that a substantial proportion of the work of the terminal interface unit they intended to build would be occupied in running BBP, whilst many of the ring messages would be single characters.

They therefore defined a format for the two data bytes in each minipacket, shown in Figure 13.7. The format supports a protocol, known as the Single Character Protocol (SCP), which establishes a virtual circuit between a terminal multiplexor and a computer interface unit in the form of two simplex channels. To avoid ambiguity, the channel numbers are allocated by the receiving end of each

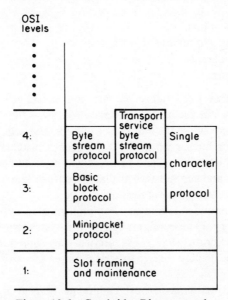

Figure 13.6   Cambridge Ring protocols.

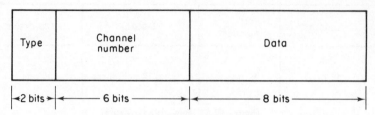

Figure 13.7   The University College single character format.

simplex channel. These channel numbers are then used in transmission minipackets. Flow control is implemented within SCP but, in view of the high basic reliability of the ring, there is no provision for error detection and control. SCP has a reset function which is used 'to escape from awkward situations'.

PRACTICAL EXPERIENCE

Cambridge Rings have been used extensively on academic sites in the United Kingdom both for research and to support populations of terminal users. Their use on commercial sites began in 1981.

One of the best documented installations is that at the University of Kent at Canterbury, now called Signet. Interest in LANs started in the mid-1970s (Spratt, 1976). A LAN was required to provide:

1. A flexible means of connecting equipment so that changes could be accepted gracefully.
2. Peer communications.
3. Remote job entry to remote mainframes.
4. Sharing of peripherals.
5. Centralized filing.

Initial developments were rather *ad hoc* and excessively dependent on the particular mainframes in use at the University (Spratt, 1981). In 1978 the Computing Laboratory considered a number of options and selected the Cambridge Ring as the basis for further work. An X.25 packet switch was rejected on the grounds of cost and inflexibility, and Ethernet was rejected because of the lack of information. Advice and support was available from the University of Cambridge and this was an important factor in the final decision.

By 1980 the Computing Laboratory had implemented two rings, both wholly within the Laboratory. (The configuration in 1981 is shown in Figure 13.8; see Binns, Dallas, and Spratt, 1982.) The service ring supported the University's 1,300 computer users whilst the engineering ring was used for tests and as a source of spares.

The ring provides terminal to host communications using the Byte Stream Protocol, and supports a file transfer mechanism between the hosts. In addition,

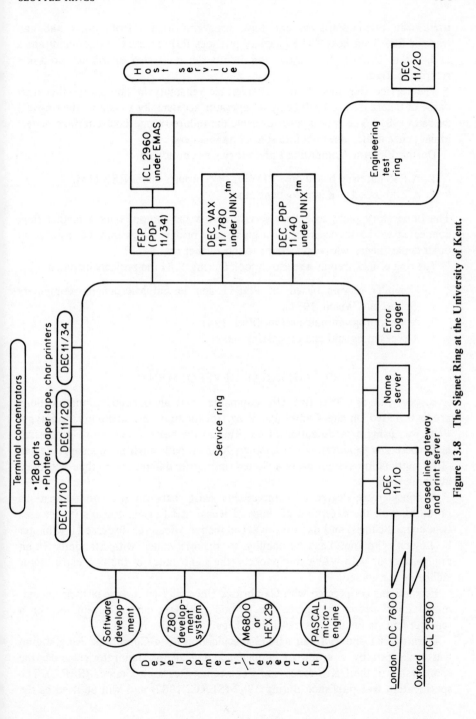

Figure 13.8   The Signet Ring at the University of Kent.

users with microcomputers can have programs loaded from hosts and can transfer files from hosts. The gateway provides RJE access to large mainframes at London, Oxford, Newcastle, and Edinburgh, and also distributes or prints returned output.

The service ring has shown considerable reliability in operation—the main cause of failure during 1980 being an operator accidentally switching the ring off! (Spratt, 1981.) The ring is also resilient; the failure of one host interface or terminal concentrator does not interfere with the others.

During 1982 the Computing Laboratory was developing:

1. A PSS gateway based on a PDP11/34 computer under RSX11M.
2. A Z80-based terminal concentrator.

The Laboratory plans to extend service across the campus over a further ring, connected to the service ring by a high-speed bridge. Rings may be installed in other departments, with connections to this further ring.

The ring is also used as a research tool. During 1981 the projects included:

1. Compiler servers based on PDP11 and Pascal Microengine computers (Schutt and Welch, 1981).
2. A microprogrammable server (Bird, 1981).
3. A typesetting and text processing server.

COMMERCIAL DEVELOPMENTS

By the end of 1981, five UK companies had announced communications products based on the Cambridge Ring. In addition, one company, Linotype-Paul, was using a modification of the Ring as the basis of new word processing and typesetting products, whilst another, Xionics, had constructed a sophisticated office automation system using a slotted ring rather different from that developed at Cambridge.

A considerable degree of compatibility exists between the communications products, with the exception of those of Racal and Logica. Racal's Planet uses twin coaxial cables, and has the advanced recovery features discussed in Chapter 8. Logica's Polynet has the facility to operate either with standard 38-bit minipackets or with 40-bit minipackets (the significance of the two extra bits is still being considered).

Ferranti has cooperated with Cambridge University on the use of their uncommitted logic arrays to replace the 80-odd packages currently required for a repeater and station unit. Ferranti chips became available in 1982.

During 1981 and 1982 an agreed specification for a Cambridge Ring station was developed by a group of suppliers and academic laboratories under the sponsorship of the UK Science and Engineering Research Council (SERC). The specification was published during 1982 (SERC, 1982) and will be used as the basis of network procurements for the academic community in the United Kingdom.

Most vendors started by providing a mixture of asynchronous V.24 and microcomputer bus access channels. 1982 has seen an increasing variety of such interfaces, together with the appearance of a variety of data processing and office

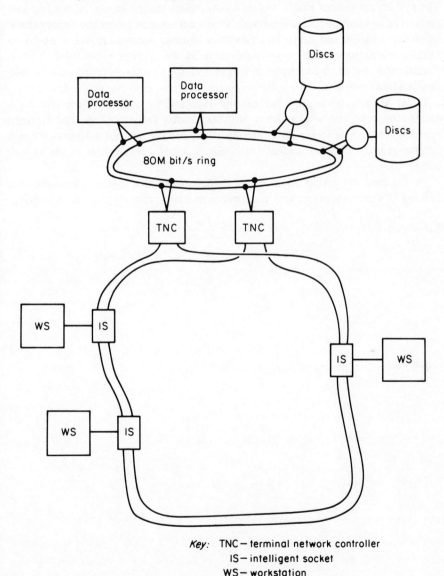

Key: TNC — terminal network controller
IS — intelligent socket
WS — workstation

Figure 13.9   The XiBus office automation system.

automation devices including workstations, file servers, name servers, logging stations and gateways. The experience of the Science and Engineering Research Council's Project Universe (Kirstein *et al*, 1982) will doubtless result in new and better bridges and gateways becoming commercially available during 1982 and 1983.

The system consists of multifunction workstations placed around a building and connected to the XiNet LAN through 'intelligent sockets', a central facility (itself based on a high-speed ring), and gateways to other sytems. XiNet is based on parallel transmission over multi-wire cable at an aggregate rate of 8M bit/s. Packets may be up to 256 bytes in length and are structured in accordance with IBM's SDLC protocol.

Initial XiBus systems provided text and data facilities under which processing is divided between the workstations and the shared facility. Store and forward speech ('voicegrams') were added during 1982, and the internal protocols are said to give priority to voice packets in order to avoid irregularities in the speech output.

At the time of writing Xionics had demonstrated the ability to connect to a number of word processors and mainframes and was promising further interfaces.

14. REGISTER INSERTION RINGS

Register insertion rings were first devised for use in speech and voice–data integrated systems. They have also found application in distributed processing systems.

Implementations vary considerably, but the logical principle is shown in Figure 14.1. The ring station includes a register or buffer placed in parallel with the ring.

In normal operation the register is switched out of the ring (state a). The attached device may place a new packet in the register whenever it is free, after which the station will wait for an inter-packet gap on the ring. As the gap passes, the register is switched into the ring (state b) and its contents transmitted.

To ensure that data received from the ring are not lost during transmission the station must either buffer incoming packets or transmit only when it detects an empty incoming packet.

Each station reads packets from the ring and determines those intended for itself. These packets are passed to the attached device and are either removed from the ring or marked 'empty' so that they will be removed by a central monitor station.

Figure 14.1b also shows the ring station removing a packet addressed to itself. Since the destination of a packet cannot be known until the address has been read, the ring must, in practice, include a buffer at least as long as the address.

When the incoming packet is not addressed to this station it is retransmitted on the ring as shown in Figure 14.1c. Some of the options for register insertion rings have been discussed by Hafner, Nenadal, and Tschanz (1975).

All register insertion rings share the characteristic that the length of the ring varies over time and, in particular, increases as the offered load increases. To maintain low delay packets must therefore be kept short. These rings also have the characteristic that, since packets are removed or emptied by the receiving station, the same 'slot' on the ring may be used more than once per cycle. This allows such rings to transfer data at a rate in exess of the raw speed of the ring.

THE SYSTEM FOR INTEGRATED LOCAL COMMUNICATIONS (SILK)

SILK was developed at Hasler's laboratories specifically to provide both voice

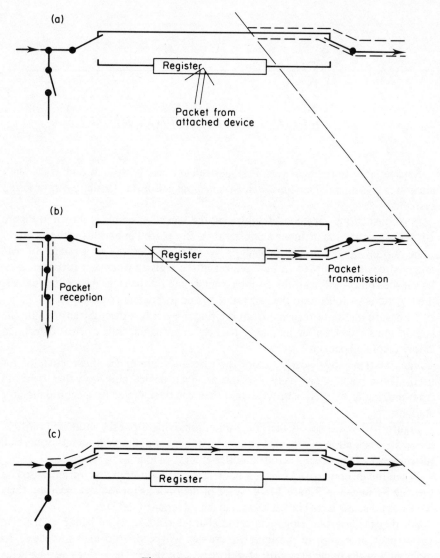

(a)

Register

Packet from
attached device

(b)

Register

Packet
transmission

Packet
reception

(c)

Register

Figure 14.1   Register insertion.

and data transmission on a single site. The system was first described in 1973 (Hafner, Nenadal, and Tschanz) and first offered commercially in 1981.

The signals on the ring take the form of minipackets of up to 16 bytes, separated by idle bytes. The format of a minipacket is shown in Figure 14.2.

The acceptance of a minipacket by a ring station involves the replacement of the received minipacket on the ring by an idle minipacket. Each idle minipacket comprises an address but includes no data. Idle minipackets waste space on the

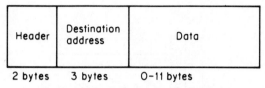

Header	Destination address	Data
2 bytes	3 bytes	0–11 bytes

Figure 14.2   SILK minipacket format.

ring and are suppressed by a monitor station termed the main block. The main block maintains the integrity of the ring by:

1. Maintaining bit synchronisation.
2. Removing minipackets that have circled the loop completely.
3. Transmitting test minipackets to check the integrity of the ring and the continued functioning of the ring stations (which are known as local blocks).

The main block also accepts error reporting packets from local blocks and supports local alarm and diagnostic equipment.

The key features of the local block are shown in Figure 14.3. There are three high-speed registers interconnected by switches and supervised by control logic which, for speed, is hardwired rather than programmed. Each local block supports up to seven devices, each attached through an appropriate data communications equipment (DCE) or, in the case of Hasler's own digital telephones, directly. To transmit via the ring, the DCE places a correctly formatted minipacket in the output register.

As soon as the control logic detects either idle bytes or the end of a packet at the output switch (S2) it connects the output register to line and transmits its contents. During this time a transient packet may be being built up in the shift register. When the output register is empty S2 will connect the shift register to the ring output so that this minipacket can be sent on. (Exceptionally, transmissions from the output register will be blocked if the shift register is in danger of overflowing.) Since minipackets are of variable length and are placed in the output register at the convenience of the DCE, transient packets are subject to varying delays. Under especially adverse conditions the shift register may overflow, causing data to be lost, though simulation studies have shown this to be very unusual (Schultze, 1979).

Incoming packets are placed into the shift and receiving registers one byte at a time. The address is read as packets enter the shift register and is compared with the addresses of the attached devices. If the address matches, the minipacket is allowed to build up in the receiving register for transfer to the attached device through switch S3. Switch S1 disconnects the ring from the shift register and idle bytes are fed to the shift register, though are not stored by it. Thus the incoming minipacket is truncated into an idle packet, and is transmitted in that form.

When the shift register is empty and there are no data in the output register, the system transmits idle bytes on the ring.

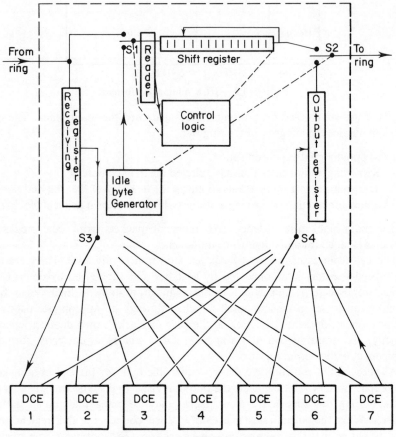

Figure 14.3   A SILK local block.

The SILK Product

The loop is constructed using either coax or optic fibre cables, or a mixture of the two, and carries data at 16.896M bit/s. For resilience, each local block is connected to both the next and the next-but-one block in both directions, and further redundancy is also possible (the question of ring topology was discussed in Chapter 8).

For telephony, the SILK digitizes data at 64,000 bit/s according to the usual pulse code modulation scheme (8,000 eight-bit samples per second). Samples are transmitted in groups of four per minipacket and, to save bandwidth, no packets are transmitted during silent periods.

SILK provides a limited range of call management facilities (e.g. shortcode dialling, 'follow me', 'camp on busy') to the vendor's own digital telephones. There is also an analogue line interface that is compatible with the Public Switched Telephone Network though, by 1982, the SILK had not been approved for PSTN connection by any European PTT.

For data transmission a range of DCEs is available that support:

1. CCITT X.21 (circuit switched) transmission at speeds up to 96k bit/s.
2. CCITT X.21 transmission with HDLC framing and error control.
3. Datagram operation.
4. Multiplexing of up to eight V.24 circuits on one X.21 circuit.

THE DISTRIBUTED DOUBLE-LOOP COMPUTER NETWORK (DDLCN)

The DDLCN was developed at the Ohio State University by Liu and coworkers (Wolf and Liu, 1978) as a research tool. It is an extension of an earlier network, the Distributed Loop Computer Network (Reames and Liu, 1975; Liu, 1978) which also used register insertion.

DDLCN differs from SILK in being primarily intended for inter-computer communication, and it therefore allows much larger packets. In addition, packets are removed by the destination station, and this requires the station to have two buffers. To provide a transmission path in the case of the failure of one segment of the ring, the ring is double (see Figure 14.4)—hence the name. The basic design of a ring station is shown in Figure 14.5 (Wolf and Liu, 1978).

Packets are received into the input buffers and their addresses checked by the microprocessor. Packets for this station are then removed from the ring and passed to the attached device. Other packets are transferred to the output buffer when it is free and are then transmitted to line. The output buffers may also be filled by the attached device.

To maximize the efficiency with which the loop is used, the station does not simply send a packet by the physically shortest route, since this might involve heavily congested stations. Instead, the station chooses the best route dynamically, using its measurements of traffic flow.

The DDLCN also makes extensive provision for recovery from the failure of individual stations or sections of the loop. By the use of special circuits (not shown in the previous figure) each individual ring segment can be made to carry signals in the reverse of its usual direction. In addition, each output buffer can be connected to the input buffer on the other ring, thus allowing it to transmit its contents via the other ring should its own outgoing segment fall.

The management of these facilities is a matter of some complexity. Each station contains a bit-map indicating the current status of every segment of each loop. This map is updated from status change messages that are broadcast by stations that detect a change.

By applying fairly complex algorithms to this map, the DDLCN is able to

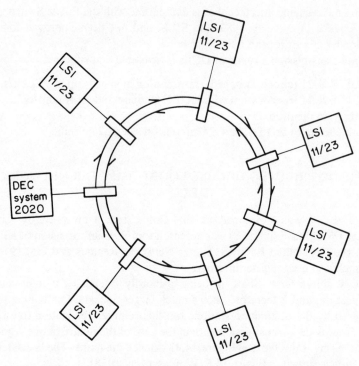

Figure 14.4   DDLCN prototype. (After Liu, Tsay, and Tian, 1982.)

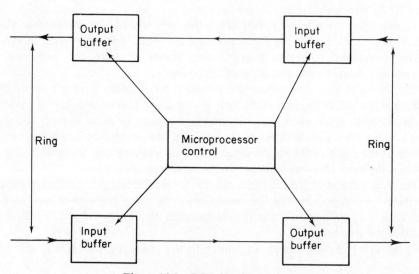

Figure 14.5   DDLCN ring station.

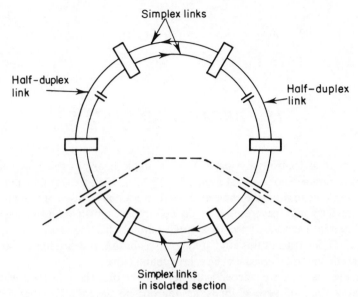

Figure 14.6   DDLCN under multiple failures.

provide degraded service even after several ring segments have failed. The network will even, by operating links in the half-duplex mode, survive the combined failure of both rings in one segment and of segments elsewhere as well. Figure 14.6 shows how the DDLCN would cope with one fairly horrific set of simultaneous failures.

The initial implementation of DDLCN (Liu, Tsay, and Lian, 1982) used twisted wire pairs to interconnect six PDP-11/23s and one DEC System-20. A distributed operating system, the Multicomputer Integrator Kernel (MIKE), has been developed to run on the network. MIKE leaves the operating systems of the attached computers largely unchanged and runs mainly in the loop station microprocessors.

MIKE provides a unified system-wide view of the resources on the network and also provides protocols for cooperation amongst the attached computers. Internally it consists of a number of autonomous processes running on the various machines and communicating solely by message passing.

One interesting feature of the system is the concept of a guardian. A guardian is a permanent process that provides other processes with controlled access to certain resources. The operating system of each of the attached computers is treated as the guardian of that computer. Guardians also exist within MIKE for control of access rights, data types, and other data structures within the system.

OTHER DEVELOPMENTS

Low-speed terminal support networks based on register insertion have been developed by two UK companies under the names Clearway and Multilink.

15. BROADBAND CABLES

The potential transmission capacity of a single coaxial cable—as calculated from information theory—is at least 1,000M bit/s. No existing electronic device is, however, able to drive the cable at more than a small fraction of that speed.

The capacity may nevertheless be divided into a number of independent channels or bands, each restricted to a small part of the frequency spectrum (see Figure 15.2). Systems of this kind are known as broadband systems or, since they are generally based on coaxial cables, broadband cables.

Since the channels are independent, they may be of several different widths and may carry data of several kinds at appropriate speeds. The signalling and capacity-sharing techniques may also vary; only the allocation of frequencies needs to be fixed for the whole cable.

The division shown in Figure 15.1 is typical of that used in Community Antenna Television (CATV) systems. In a CATV system a single antenna captures television broadcasts from a remote broadcasting tower or from a communications satellite. The various TV channels are separated in frequency at source, and the separation is maintained on the cable that is used for local distribution. The television signal is carried in analogue form by modulating—i.e. varying—the signal transmitted. The principle is, of course, the same as that used in radio broadcasting.

Television is the analogue signal most often found on broadband cables but a carrier may also be modulated with a voice signal or with the signals from an analogue facsimile machine. A standard TV channel conventionally occupies one 6 MHz channel, though more than one channel may be used if very high quality video is needed.

One of the longest established broadband cable systems is that used within the Mitre Corporation's buildings at Bedford, Massachusetts. Mitre is a non-profit research and development corporation that works mainly for the US military. Mitre now employs about 2,000 staff and makes considerable use of computers. Figure 15.2 shows the frequencies used by the internal Mitre network (Mitrenet) (Meisner, 1980).

This illustrates the way in which a broadband cable can reflect the variety of business communications.

162

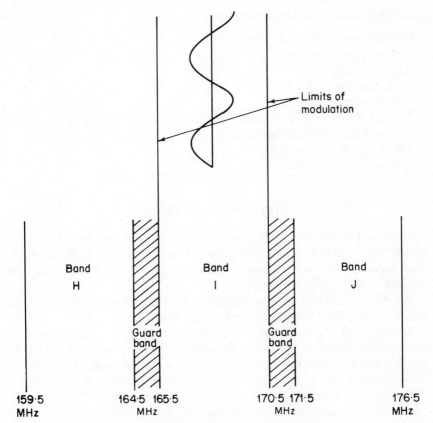

Figure 15.1   Frequency bands on a broadband cable.

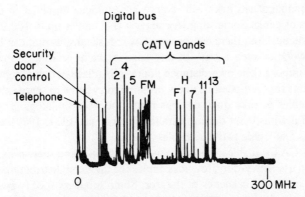

Figure 15.2   Frequency spectrum of Mitrenet. (Courtesy
of the Mitre Corporation.)

Mitrenet carries 15 services including:

Commercial broadcast television
Closed circuit television
Building access control
Mitre educational broadcast
Integrity monitor channel
Network status channel (a video channel showing the status of the network according to network management)
Mitrenet (370k bit/s service)
Mitrenet (1M bit/s service)

THE COAXIAL CABLES

Broadband cable networks have the form known as a 'rooted tree'. This may be realized by a trunk between buildings with branches to each building, or by a trunk between floors with a branch to each floor, or both (see Figure 15.3). More complex topologies are also possible.

The 'root' of the tree is, curiously, known as the 'head-end'. It is here that, in CATV systems, the TV broadcast is placed on the cable.

Because CATV systems were originally installed for one-way transmission alone, many broadband cable systems consist of two such one-way cables. The 'inward' cable carries signals from the devices to the head end, whilst the 'outward' cable carries signals to the devices. 'Receive only' devices, like televisions, need only be attached to the 'outward' cable, whilst CCTV cameras, if present, would be attached to only the 'inward' cable. Interactive devices, whether terminals or telephones, must be attached to both cables. This is shown in Figure 15.4.

Large broadband networks will require an analogue amplifier in each 500 to 1,200 metres of cable. Some suppliers suggest that cables up to 100 kilometres in length are practical, but there can be very few industrial sites that can benefit from a single network of such a size. In any case, capacity-sharing systems such as CSMA/CD impose their own distance limitations (discussed in Chapter 11). The long cable runs that are possible allow broadband systems to serve extensive sites, and allow cables to take quite devious routes between buildings. The amplifiers require careful adjustment during installation (Roman, 1977, 1979), especially in large systems and where two-way cables are used.

Standard CATV cables may be used in broadband networks, and it is customary to use heavy-duty, low-loss cables for the main distribution trunks, and cheaper cables for the branches of the tree. Some suppliers specify special cables. Wang Labs. uses a rigid extruded-shield cable in Wangnet, whilst Figure 15.5. shows the trunk cable used in the Videodata system.

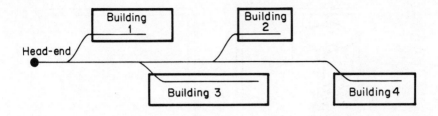

(a) Branches to buildings

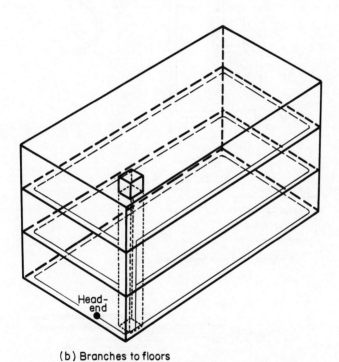

(b) Branches to floors

Figure 15.3   Topologies for broadband cable.

The special trunk cable has two advantages:

1. The thick shielding and insulation provide protection against mechanical damage (most Videodata systems are in industrial and semi-industrial environments).
2. The cable is semi-rigid and can therefore be installed without cable trays—a useful saving and a considerable convenience.

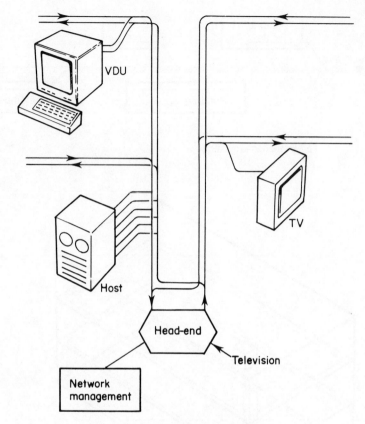

Figure 15.4   A broadband cable tree.

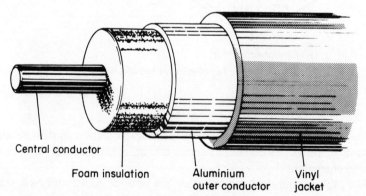

Figure 15.5   Cross-section of a Videodata cable. (Illustration by courtesy of IS/3M.)

Most broadband cable networks have separate inward and outward channels. In a two-cable system, this is achieved by physical separation, but in a one-cable system it is usually achieved by a separation in frequency. Signals travelling inward to the head-end are at lower frequencies than those travelling outward.

The frequency spectrum on a single cable is usually divided in either the mid-split or subsplit manner as shown in Figure 15.6.

Midsplit provides for 111 MHz in both inward and outward directions, enough bandwidth for 18 TV channels, but requires, if broadcast TV channels are to be carried, that they be shifted to frequencies in the outward range and that the receivers be modified accordingly. Subsplit allows broadcast television to be carried at its normal broadcast frequencies, and is therefore the system usually chosen when upgrading a TV cable system for interactive use, or where broadcast television must coexist with other services. A subsplit cable provides only 25 MHz each way for interactive services, but this is likely to be adequate for most purposes.

The head end may be little more than a convenient point to insert broadcast tv signals and to place the network management equipment. but if interactive services are to be provided on a single cable then it must include a frequency shifter to re-broadcast in the outward band the signals received on the inward band. The Mitrenet head-end equipment is shown in Figure 15.7.

Frequency shifters are found in some two-cable systems, because the frequency shift reduces the problem of cross-talk in the modems serving interactive devices, though it adds to the cost of the network. If frequency shifting is not required, a two-cable system may have a completely passive head-end. In Wangnet the inward cable is simply bent round to form the outward cable.

Whilst two-cable systems are commonest, some manufacturers produce systems based on a single cable (Videodata is one example). Single-cable systems have the advantage of requiring less cable than two-cable systems. Though they provide less bandwidth, a single cable provides so much bandwidth that this will very rarely be a problem. It is, in practice, hard to find broadband systems in

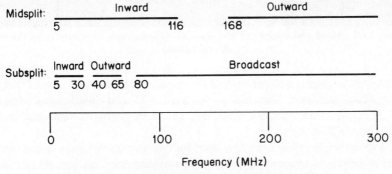

Figure 15.6   Frequency division on broadband cables.

Figure 15.7   Head-end equipment on Mitrenet. (Photograph by courtesy of the Mitre
Corporation.)

which even as much as 50 per cent. of the capacity is used—and most of that will
be broadcast television. Since many non-data CATV and closed-circuit television
(CCTV) systems use only one cable, they can more readily be upgraded to one-
cable systems than to two.

CATV technology has been developed for one-way transmission and may thus
be used directly in two-cable systems. One-way amplifiers are simpler and better
proven than two-way amplifiers. The one-way cables that are found in two-cable

systems are easier to install than two-way cables. They may also be operated at higher efficiencies, since no conflict arises between requirements for transmission in the two directions (Roman, 1977).

Modern CATV amplifiers are able to report their own performance to the network management centre, which can thus obtain early warning of problems. In Mitrenet this philosophy is taken a stage further. Special taps provide a path between the inward and outward cables at a selected monitoring frequency. These taps are distributed throughout the cable network and are usually switched off. Every few seconds each is switched on (by remote control from the head-end), and the electrical characteristics of the resulting circuit are determined by listening on the inward cable for a transmission on the outward cable. The results are compared with those obtained during installation, and deviations are notified for preventive maintenance.

Network management can also measure and track the performance of controllers and modems—e.g. the number of erroneous packets sent by the former and the drift in output frequency of the latter.

By the use of methods such as these, of which there is now substantial practical experience, a broadband network can provide very reliable service to users.

DATA ON BROADBAND

Digital data may be carried in a radio frequency channel by modulating the carrier with a bit stream, in much the same way that an audio modem modulates an audio-frequency carrier for transmission over telephone lines. The various data channels may be operated at different transmission rates, under different protocols and for different purposes.

To provide LAN service on a broadband cable one needs a cable tap, a filter, a suitable modem, and the necessary controller (see Figure 15.8). Taps are available at low cost from CATV suppliers, and the controller is no different from that which would be used on a baseband system (Hopkins, 1977). The filter and modem, however, are more difficult.

Filters and high-speed radio-frequency modems are difficult to build and are expensive. Though their prices have fallen significantly in recent years, and will continue to fall, they remain up to 10 times as expensive as baseband transceivers of the same speed. (The Mitrenet modems are discussed by Wagner (1978).)

Because of the high cost of radio frequency modems, digital services on broadband cables have usually been operated at speeds below 100k bit/s. Appropriate cable interface units have been commercially available for most of the last decade but have been marked by a low level of functionality—V.24 circuits without protocol conversion—and simple internal architectures.

During 1981 a number of suppliers announced or released products that are significantly more sophisticated. In particular, Sytek, an entrepreneurial company based in California's Silicon Valley, began to ship its LocalNet System 20.

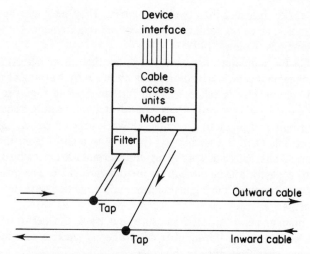

Figure 15.8   Digital access to a two-cable system.

LocalNet (Biba, 1981a, 1981b) is a midsplit two-cable system using the 70–106 MHz band for inward signals and the 226–262 MHz band for outward distribution. Each band is divided into 120 300 kHz channels, each of which is operated at 128k bit/s. The capacity of each channel is shared by CSMA/CD techniques to provide support to 200 or more terminals.

Collision detection presents difficulties in broadband systems. Baseband systems can detect a collision through the large direct current applied by the transceivers, but broadband systems do not carry direct current signals (though DC is often used to power the amplifiers). LocalNet controllers detect collisions by listening for their own packets and checking their FCSs. Any error is then taken to be evidence of a collision.

One or two terminals may access the cable through V.24 ports on each 'Tbox' and up to eight terminals may share each Tmux. Initially LocalNet provided only a transparent switched virtual call facility, but Sytek intend to provide services at all levels of the OSI reference model, as shown in Table 15.1. Sytek claims a residual bit error rate of 1 in 10^{13}.

The most ingenious feature of LocalNet is, however, the frequency management. The Tboxes and Tmuxes use frequency-agile modems—modems that can rapidly and reliably be switched from one frequency to another.

Each can be tuned so as to access up to 20 of the System 20 channels. Modems change frequency on instructions from the user. If more than 20 channels are needed then they may be connected through a central gateway known as a Tbridge. If interworking between all 120 channels were needed, some 41 Tbridges would be necessary—though this would imply a network of well over 20,000 simultaneously active terminals!

Table 15.1 Proposed LocalNet services and features.

OSI level	Service
6	Encryption Virtual terminal support
5	Name server (maps user-friendly name to network address) Access control
4	Virtual call Message service
3	Datagram service Routing between channels
2	CSMA/CD
1	Broadband cable

Network addresses thus consist of two parts, the number of the channel, and an address within that channel. A device that changes channel also changes its address, so that network addresses may have to be hidden from users by a high-level user-friendly addressing system.

This innovative mixture of frequency division and contention access has enabled Sytek to use slow, and thus cheap, modems. In this way Sytek has avoided the high costs typical of broadband systems, though at the price of a low peak transmission speed. This speed is fully adequate for terminal support, but is not sufficient for inter-computer communications. For the latter purpose Sytek offers System 40—a 2M bit/s contention system for use by minicomputers. System 40 controllers are based on faster, 16-bit, microprocessors, and can accept data from attached computers at up to 1M bit/s over a parallel interface such as Unibus.

They use the same addressing conventions and packet formats as System 20, allowing interworking through a relatively simple gateway. This interworking is limited to the maximum range of System 40 (7 kilometres) rather than to that of System 20 (20 kilometres).

Wang Labs. has chosen a different means of controlling costs. The Wangnet Interconnection Service occupies 48 MHz and includes three services:

9.6k bit/s point-to-point
9.6k bit/s switched
64k bit/s point-to-point

The point-to-point services use fixed frequency modems, with a separate frequency being reserved for each virtual circuit provided. A pool of 256 frequencies is available for the switched service. Call establishment is the responsibility of a central Dataswitch, which selects an unused frequency and sets the appropriate frequency-agile modems to it. The Dataswitch is also involved in disconnecting calls, but takes no part in transmission during a call, which occurs directly between the modems. It is interesting to note that this division of responsibilities exactly mirrors that in a computerized telephone exchange:

Wangnet Interconnection Service	Computerized telephone exchange
Dataswitch (a dedicated minicomputer)	Common control (a dedicated minicomputer)
Modem	Telephone
Destination address (typed on terminal)	Telephone number (dialled or keyed)
Multiple frequencies on cable	Multiple-switching point in matrix or multiple time slots on internal bus

Staff at Wang even refer to the technique as 'circuit switching'. The Interconnection Service occupies only a small part of the bandwidth of a Wangnet system. The complete frequency allocation is shown in Table 15.2 (Stahlman, 1982). The utility band is intended for use by television systems. The Wang band provides communications between Wang data and word processing systems, and is therefore the key to Wangnet.

The Wang band is a LAN service in which the capacity of the 12M bit/s channel is shared by a CSMA/CD discipline. Wang OIS, VS, and 2200 systems can be connected via cable interface units (CIUs) that implement protocols at the

Table 15.2 **Wangnet frequency allocation.**

Frequency range (MHz)	'Band'	Channels	Maximum speed (bit/s)	Notes
10−12	Interconnect	32	9.6k	Dedicated
12−22	Interconnect	16	64k	Dedicated
22−48	(Reserved)			
48−82	Interconnect	256	9.6k	Switched
82−174	(Reserved)			
174−216	Utility	7	n/a	Standard CATV frequencies
217−251	Wang band	1	12M	CSMA/CD
251−350	(Reserved)			

bottom five layers (physical to session) of the OSI model. The protocols themselves are proprietary.

Wang Labs. has, at present, announced no plans for the use of Wangnet for telephony. However, the choice of 64k bit/s (the PTT standard for digital voice) as the speed of one unswitched service suggests that Wang will announce a switched telephone service based on 64k bit/s circuits.

RELIABILITY

The analogue components of broadband systems are drawn from the CATV industry. Since CATV amplifiers must operate in adverse conditions—hanging from telegraph poles in a snowstorm, for instance—they have to be and are very reliable. In fact, experience suggests that in the relatively benign environment of an office, factory, or hospital, they exceed their design lifetimes by substantial amounts.

Cables, connectors, and splitters are mainly passive and are only likely to fail under physical assault. For ultra-high reliability the cables can be duplicated, although, since it will often be necessary to use the same ducts, this does not provide a fully independent system. One manufacturer will install systems in the form of a 'broken' loop. Any inadvertent break in the loop will cause the initial break to be closed, thus maintaining service to all points. This system can not, of course, work with one-way cables.

The reliability of a cable system depends crucially on the reliability of the frequency shifter at the head-end. Although these are also very reliable, large systems are likely to find it worth while having a spare unit available or even wired in parallel.

PRACTICAL EXPERIENCE

The first broadband cable systems were installed in the early 1970s by large and sophisticated organizations—mainly motor manufacturers. These systems were installed initially for low-speed data communications (they provided a robust alternative to a large mass of wires and cables), but with their possible use for television, telephony, and environmental monitoring also in mind.

One of the early users was the Assembly Division of General Motors (Smith, 1979) which operates 20 assembly plants throughout the United States. In 1974, the corporation foresaw that the years following would see the installation of a large number of terminals and computers on and around its assembly lines. After reviewing the technologies available, the corporation decided to standardize on broadband coaxial cable 'whenever possible'.

The first system was installed in 1975 and was one of what the corporation now calls its 'first generation'. Like all GM cables it was a midsplit single-cable system based on CATV components. Unlike later generations, it only provided for communications to a minicomputer at the head-end from remote locations on site. In short, the first-generation designs were overspecialized and also suffered from the inexperience of those concerned. The lessons learnt included the need to standardize components and cables and the fact that 'implementing a broadband coaxial cable network was more than running cable throughout the plant'.

The second-generation networks were installed in support of energy management systems. They included a frequency shifter at the head-end to support communications between remote locations.

The third-generation comprised networks installed in eight plants. They were designed together and in accordance with corporate standards, based in turn on the experience of the two earlier generations. Signal levels were set so as to support data, speech, or video at all points, several main cables spread out from the head-end, and the initial configuration included a substantial number of spare taps to allow for future expansion. In the interests of reliability the head-end included a spare frequency shifter that was automatically started if the main shifter failed.

Most of General Motors' systems that use the cables involved electronic 'data gathering centres' (DGCs) scattered around the site to pass data to central computers. In general the non-programmable DGCs transmit fairly complete data on a 48k bit/s channel, whilst the microprocessor-based DGCs transmit only changes in data on a 19.2k bit/s channel. Channel capacity is shared by time division multiplexing and non-standard proprietary protocols are used in all cases. The main applications are facilities management and energy management.

The General Motors cables also support a number of point-to-point and multipoint circuits, audio links and surveillance television cameras. The use of television is inhibited by the lack of standard ways of controlling the cameras from the security office. In 1982 General Motors implemented a system for monitoring and controlling plant equipment.

Though the ability to carry data, speech and video on a single cable is one of the key advantages claimed for broadband, it is rare to find this being fully exploited. One such case in an operational system is the security system on Mitrenet. Because much of its work is military, or at least of a highly confidential nature, the Mitre Corporation must maintain strict security on its site, a site that includes a number of separate buildings. Though main extrances are staffed, access through minor entrances is controlled from a central security office.

Each minor entrance has two doors in the form of an 'airlock'. Anyone may pass the outer door but they must then identify themselves to the security office. Cameras within the airlock view the person seeking entry and his security pass (which includes a photograph), and the two pictures are combined on a split screen display at the centre. Security staff can talk to people seeking entry and can lock and unlock the door. In this application audio, video, and digital data (commands to doors and door status) are used cooperatively, though it is important to note that they are carried by separate channels on the cable.

The literature includes accounts of further developments on Mitrenet (Hopkins, 1979; 1980; Meisner, 1980) and of other installations, including those of Ford (Biba and Yeh, 1979) and Brown University (Pliner and Hunter, 1982).

COMMERCIAL DEVELOPMENTS

Broadband LANs are offered to the industrial market in conjunction with energy management and process control systems. During 1980, however, it became clear that suppliers' attention had moved away from the industrial market towards the market for 'office systems'.

This has led to the development of more sophisticated products, such as Wangnet, that are able to support a distributed processing environment. There has also been a move towards greater resilience through duplication of key components, notably the cable and the frequency shifter.

Broadband networks have also begun to appear in the wider community as upgrades to CATV systems. The use of frequency division allows digital transmission services to share an existing cable with broadcast television. So far this has been limited to a few pilot trials in the United States, but during 1981 Manhattan Cable was able to transmit data more cheaply than the Bell System within the area covered by the cable.

The interactive nature of broadband systems allows households access to a number of novel services, including:

Fire and burglar alarm monitoring
Remote meter reading
Teleshopping
Instant opinion polls

These services were pioneered in Columbus, Ohio, by the Qube system. Opened in 1977, Qube had 34,000 subscribers by 1982 (*Communications News*, 1982).

By 1981 CATV systems served 22 per cent. of all US television subscribers and, as shown in Table 15.3, substantial proportions in some European countries. Few CATV systems are as sophisticated and rich in features as Qube, but the trend is clearly in that direction, especially in the United States (Gates and Tjaden, 1982).

Current telephone lines are generally limited to 2.4k or 4.8k bit/s, rates that are not really adequate for new business data communications needs. From the mid-1980s, the European PTTs will be able to offer speeds of up to 128k bit/s through their new Integrated Services Digital Networks (ISDNs), and speeds up to 2Mbit/s with special engineering. Citywide broadband networks—we might call them Community Data and Television (CDTV) networks—have the potential to

Table 15.3   Cable television penetration.

Country	Penetration into TV households (%)
Austria	2.5
Belgium	64
Denmark	50
Finland	3
France	37
Norway	23
United Kingdom	14
United States	22

(Source: *Shaw Intermedia*, 1981)

offer services that are at least equivalent to ISDN, but which could be available sooner.

As in telecommunications generally, the first tests of this facility will be in the United States. The second testbed, and one with relevance to all Europe, seems likely to be the United Kingdom. Since the general election of 1979, the British government has moved to encourage competition in the field of telecommunications. In February 1982 the government received a report from its own Information Technology Advisory Panel (ITAP, 1982). The report drew attention to the restrictive licenses under which CATV operates, the decline in CATV connections, and the new opportunities presented by broadband technology. It recommended an immediate liberalization of the rules governing CATV systems, in the belief that CATV companies would then be able to raise the large sums needed for the 'rewiring of Britain'. The British government has accepted these recommendations and will offer new cable franchises during 1983.

The very high bandwidth of a broadband cable, sufficient for up to 100,000 simultaneously active terminals on some schemes, implies considerable economies of scale. Such economies would also be available for controllers and modems if the market were large enough. These considerations suggest that a possible operator for a CDTV cable would be that organization which already has a high penetration into the community—the PTT or telephone company itself. Other factors also favour PTT participation—the possession of wayleaves and underground ducts and of rights to dig up public roads.

PTT plans for the ISDNs are still fluid to some degree, and several PTTs are known to be actively considering broadband and other LANs for their future systems. In the long run the relationship between ISDNs and CDTVs could be much closer than now appears likely.

A further consequence of the development of CDTV systems will be a need for the very large production volumes characteristic of the TV industry. This will both require and permit unit costs low enough for domestic sales. These cheap but, necessarily, reliable components will bring down the costs of broadband cables for office use.

PART III

Protocols and Internetting

Before the high-speed services of the data link layer can be used in applications and end-user services, a relationship must be established between the LAN and these applications. This relationship is provided by the upper sublayer—logical link control—of the data link layer, and by the network and transport layers.

This part discusses the protocols at these levels and shows how they are involved in the interconnection of networks.

16.   DATA LINK SERVICES

Conventional data link protocols such as SDLC and HDLC were designed for use on noisy, low-speed trunk networks. They are unsuitable for use in LANs because:

1. They do not provide for the notification of source addresses, the need for which was noted in chapter 6 (Horton and Miller, 1980).
2. They contain complex procedures for error and flow control.
3. They are unable to use the broadcast capability of the LAN.

The high speeds and low error rates of LANs allow simpler protocols to be used. This is partly because errors are less frequent and partly because there is no need to use processing power to conserve bandwidth—LAN bandwidth is cheap and plentiful. For similar reasons, wide area networks use abbreviated addresses wherever possible whilst in LANs they are often given rather fully.

At present the data link layers of the various LANs offer different services to the network layers that use them. Ethernet, for instance, provides three services—addressed packet, broadcast packet, and multicast packet—which may, in fact, be seen as variants of a single service. This service is sometimes known as the 'unreliable datagram'.

The actual reliability of a single Ethernet is, in fact, very high but the word 'unreliable' indicates that the network may, very occasionally, lose packets, and that the data link level provides neither positive nor negative acknowledgements.

The term 'datagram' indicates that the data link layer processes packets individually and without regard to the fate of other packets either from the same source or to the same destination.

In some broadcast systems (see, for instance, Tokoro and Tamaru, 1977) and in sequential systems such as the Cambridge Ring (dealt with in Chapter 13) every packet addressed to an individual station is acknowledged immediately, thus greatly increasing the confidence in correct delivery. Such a service may be known as a reliable datagram.

In ISO and IEEE documents the datagram services are known as 'connectionless' and 'acknowledged connectionless' services. The main alternative is known as 'connection-orientated' service, and in this case the data link layer keeps track of the flow of packets between various pairs of stations. It can therefore exercise some measure of control over the flow of packets.

THE IEEE DATA LINK SERVICES

The 802 draft standard (IEEE, 1982) defines two classes of data link module and a third class is under study. Class I modules support connectionless operation only, class II modules support connectionless and connection-orientated operation, while class III would support connectionless and acknowledged connectionless operation. Modules of all types can communicate in connectionless mode, since this is common to them all. The IEEE standard specifies both the services that the data link layer provides to the network layer and the format and flow of frames between stations within the data link layer. (The explanations that follow are greatly abbreviated and, hence, somewhat simplified.)

Frame formats and addressing conventions are common to all modes of operation and the LLC frame is shown in Figure 16.1. Station addresses are dealt with in the medium access control (MAC) sublayer. LLC addresses relate to 'service access points' within the LLC sublayer. This facility is intended to enable multiple independent LLCs to exist on a single data link.

Service access point (SAP) addresses are seven bits long. Individual addresses are preceded by a 0 bit, and multicast addresses start with a 1 bit. The special value '1111111' always means the set of all LLC entities at the station. Source SAP addresses are always individual or null and the preceeding bit distinguishes between commands and responses in the LLC protocols.

The null address, '0000000', may be used where a station has only one LLC entity.

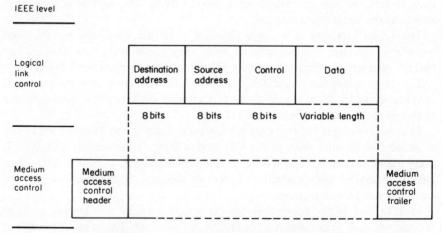

Notes: The MAC trailer includes the frame check sequence which is used to confirm the correct reception of frames.

Figure 16.1   Format of the IEEE LLC frame.

Connectionless Operation

In this case the data link layer offers three services to the network layer:

1. To send a frame to another station.
2. To broadcast a frame to all the stations on the data link.
3. To multicast a frame to a group of stations.

In each case SAP addresses (or the null address) must be given to indicate the LLC entities concerned. The actual transmission of frames is the responsibility of the MAC sublayer.

When a logical link control sublayer receives a data frame from its associated medium access control sublayer it will pass it to the network layer after removing the LLC header.

In addition to data transfer the standard specifies two exchanges that may occur within the data link layer and without reference to higher levels of the protocol. These are the exchange identification (XID) and test functions. The formats of the corresponding data link frames are described in Table 16.1.

Any station may transmit an XID command at any time. Stations receiving the XID command should then return XID responses to the station that issued the command. Command and response both carry the class of the station in their data fields, coded as shown in Figure 16.2.

Table 16.1 Formats of packets in IEEE connectionless operation.

Packet function	IEEE acronym	Command/ response bit (first bit of source SAP address field)	Control field	Data fields
Data transfer	MUI	0	1 1 0 0 0 0 1 1	Data
Exchange identification command	XID	0	1 1 1 1 u 1 0 1	Class of station
Exchange identification response	XID	1	1 1 1 1 * 1 0 1	Class of response
Test command	TEST	0	1 1 0 0 u 1 1 1	Optional
Test response	TEST	1	1 1 0 0 * 1 1 1	Copied from test command

Notes: u—undefined
  *—copied from corresponding field of command

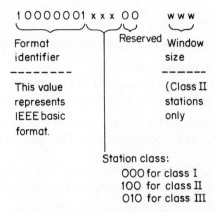

Figure 16.2   Format of the XID field.

The XID exchange may be used for a number of distinct purposes including:

1. To test the continuing operation of the responding station.
2. To determine which stations comprise a multicast group, i.e. which will respond to commands using the multicast address.
3. To determine which stations are currently attached and functioning. The broadcast function is used for this purpose.
4. To determine whether a station can operate in connection-orientated mode.
5. For a newly connected station to announce its presence to other stations.
6. To check for duplicate addresses. (A procedure is given as an appendix to the IEEE standard.)

TEST commands may also be given at any time. A station that receives a TEST command should return a TEST response to the station that issued the command. The data field should normally be no larger than the maximum specified for the particular network. If, however, some stations are known to be able to handle larger sizes, the TEST procedure may be used to locate them. If a station receives a command with an overlength data field, it should proceed as follows:

1. If it can accept and return the larger field it will do so.
2. If it can compute the frame check sequence (FCS) but cannot accept the whole field it may issue a response with a truncated data field.
3. If it cannot compute the FCS it will make no response.

Both XIDs and TESTs can be used extensively for network management.

Acknowledged Connectionless Operation

This mode of operation is very similar to the preceding one. It differs in requiring every frame to be acknowledged explicitly and immediately by the receiving

Table 16.2   Formats of frames in acknowledged connectionless operation.

Frame function	IEEE acronym	Command/ response bit	Control field	Data
Send data	CAI	0	1 1 x x 1 x x x	Yes
Acknowledge data	CAI	1	1 1 x x 1 x x x	No

station. The sender must not send a frame to any LLC entity until that entity has acknowledged the previous frame. Formats are shown in Table 16.2.

Connection-Orientated Operation

This mode has been modelled closely upon the asynchronous balanced mode of ISO's High Level Data Link Control (HDLC) (ISO, 1979). Asynchronous balanced mode is used in CCITT's Recommendation X.25, which at once keeps the IEEE proposal reasonably close to the mainstream of OSI development, and eases the interconnection of IEEE LANs and wide area networks with X.25 interfaces.

In this operating mode the logical link control establishes connections with other stations, transfers frames over these connections whilst maintaining their sequence, and closes the connections. During the life of the connection the LLC is responsible for controlling the flow of frames between the stations and for arranging the retransmission of frames that were not correctly received.

For the purpose of flow control, all data frames are numbered, separate sequences being used for the two directions of the connection. The sequence numbers are in the range 0–7 and are placed in the control field as shown in Figure 16.3.

The services that LLC provides to the network layer are shown in Table 16.3. This also shows the unsolicited indications that are given to the network layer to indicate an event in the data link, usually the receipt of a command from the other station on the connection. (The table only shows services that are involved in the maintenance and use of connections. There are other services, concerned with the management of the layer and of SAPs, as well.)

To initiate a connection the LLC transmits a 'request connection' command to the station specified by the network layer. The format of this command is shown in Table 16.4. If the remote station is able to establish the connection it will reply with a 'confirm connection' response. If it is unable to establish the connection, due perhaps to a shortage of buffer space, it will reject the connection attempt. In either case the remote station will notify its network layer by an appropriate indication (see Table 16.2) whilst the initiating station will make a suitable response to its network layer.

Like the class I commands and responses these commands and responses are unnumbered. To maintain integrity LLC starts a timer each time it transmits a

Bit 1	Value 0
Bit 2)	
)	
Bit 3)	Sequence number of this frame; set by transmitter
)	
Bit 4)	
Bit 5	(commands) Poll bit—1 indicates that the destination should respond immediately
	—0 otherwise
	(responses) Final bit—1 if replying to a poll
	—0 otherwise
Bit 6)	
)	
Bit 7)	Sequence number expected for the next data frame that the transmitter will receive
)	
Bit 8)	

Figure 16.3   Format of the control field in IEEE data frames.

command, and retransmits the command if no response has been received before the timer expires. After some number of attempts LLC will conclude that the station cannot be reached and will abandon its attempts. It should inform the network management function, if possible, if this occurs.

The sequenced transmission procedure can now be used for the exchange of data frames over the connection. LLC accepts packets from the network layer and transmits corresponding numbered data frames. If the frame is correct when its FCS is checked by the remote LLC it will be passed to the destination network layer and the LLC will acknowledge it by either:

Including its number in an outgoing data frame of its own or
Transmitting a 'frame-acknowledgement' frame containing the number

If the data link layer receives a frame with an incorrect FCS or which is otherwise invalid, it will ignore the frame. If this was a numbered frame, then the omission will be detected when the next numbered frame is received.

If the data link layer receives a frame with an unexpected sequence number it will ignore the frame but transmit a reject frame giving the expected sequence number. The transmitting LLC, which should still have a copy of the unacknowledged frames in its buffers, will then retransmit all frames from the one indicated.

Under certain circumstances, the network layer of the LLC of either station may decide that the link should be reset. This usually occurs because of serious errors in the system and allows the exchange of frames to restart from a well-

Table 16.3   IEEE connection-orientated LLC services.

Service		
Name	Meaning	Action by LLC
Requests from network layer		
CONNECT	Requests the establishment of a connection	Attempts to make the the connection
DATA	Requests the transfer of a data packet	Frame is added to queue for transmission
RESET	Requests a reset	
CONNECTION FLOWCONTROL	Limits the amount of data that can be passed to the network layer from one connection	Sets local parameters
SAP FLOWCONTROL	Limits the total amount of data that can be passed to the network layer	Sets local parameters
DISCONNECT	Requests disconnection	The connection is closed and any unacknowledged frames are lost
Indications to the remote network layer		
CONNECT	Indicates that a connection has been established from another station or that the attempt has failed	
DATA	Indicates the arrival of a packet	
RESET	Indicates that the connection has been reset by the remote station	
CONNECTION FLOWCONTROL	Requests the network layer to adjust the rate at which it sends packets	
SAP FLOWCONTROL		
DISCONNECT	Indicates closure of a connection	

Table 16.4   Formats of supervisory commands and responses in IEEE connection-oriented operation.

Function	IEEE acronym	Command/ response bit	Control field
Connection request command	SABM	0	1 1 1 1 p 1 0 0
Confirm response	UA	1	1 1 0 0 * 1 1 0
Reject connection response	DM	1	1 1 1 1 * 0 0 0
Frame acknowledgement	RR	u	1 0 0 0 $\frac{p}{f}$ r r r
Reject	REJ	u	1 0 0 1 $\frac{p}{f}$ r r r
Reset request	FRMR	1	1 1 1 0 f 0 0 1
Receive not ready	RNR	u	1 0 1 0 $\frac{p}{f}$ r r r
Disconnect request	DISC	0	1 1 1 1 p 1 0 1

Notes: rrr—received sequence number
p—poll bit
f—final bit
p/f—poll or final bit depending on context
u—undefined
*—copied from corresponding command

defined state. When instructed by the network layer, or by the remote LLC, an LLC will reset the link by transmitting a connection request command. This is treated in the same way as for the establishment of a connection.

A transmitting LLC need not wait until one frame is acknowledged before sending the next, but it may not continue to send frames indefinitely without receiving acknowledgements. The number of frames whose acknowledgements may be outstanding at any time is known as the window size. The window size may not exceed seven, since ambiguities in retransmission requests might otherwise occur. To limit their need for buffers, some stations may not be able to work with windows as large as seven. Such a station may indicate this using the window size field of an XID (whose format was shown in Figure 16.2).

When a station has the maximum number of acknowledgements outstanding, it must cease transmitting until it receives an acknowledgement.

To close a connection an LLC will transmit a 'disconnect request' frame. On receiving this frame the remote LLC will reply with a confirmation frame and will inform its network layer that the connection is no longer usable. When it receives the confirmation the local LLC will inform its network layer of the disconnection. The stations are now out of contact and are no longer able to exchange information over the connection, though they can still use connectionless operation.

THE SERVICES COMPARED

It is clear from the descriptions of the two IEEE services that the connection-orientated service is more complex than the connectionless service, and will therefore be more expensive to implement. In many cases the extra features that it provides—error control, guaranteed delivery, preservation of sequence—are essential to the application and will have to be added at higher levels if not provided by the data link layer. The further development and use of LSI will allow LLC to be provided, at a reducing cost, in hardware whilst this will take longer to achieve for higher levels of protocol. The provision of these services at data link level is also consistent with the developing standards for wide area networking.

In other cases, though, these features are either unnecessary, or uneconomic, or, as in the case of error recovery in digital speech systems, actively undesirable. In these cases, the extra complexity is simply wasted effort.

The IEEE goes some way towards reconciling these conflicting interests by specifying ways in which both cheap, datagram only, implementations and more expensive, dual-mode, implementations can be accommodated within the standard. This is clearly a sound approach.

It is also appropriate to use HDLC conventions, complex as they are, for the formats and message types associated with connection-orientated operation. HDLC is familiar to communications specialists so that this choice avoids the need for them to assimilate new material. But the definition of service access points (SAPs) appears to be a mistake. The equivalent addresses in HDLC refer to stations on the data link and are clearly essential. IEEE SAPs are either:

1. Higher level objects, such as network stations or communicating processes, or
2. Independent, and possibly incompatible, LLCs which might form part of proprietary network architectures.

The former use is clearly in breach of the OSI model—levels 3 and 4 are intended to deal with these questions. The latter may be useful but could more systematically be met by allowing several network layers to coexist.

In fact this facility violates the spirit of the OSI model in two ways:

1. If several LLC implementations exist for a single data link, then no one of them has control of that link; nor is any one able to record traffic flows. By breaking the 1:1 association between data link and data link layer the ability of the latter to control the former is reduced.
2. It requires the MAC sublayer to select the correct SAP by inspecting the destination address given in each frame. This requires all LLC protocols to have destination addresses in the same format and position in the frame, which is a restriction on them; and also requires MAC to be aware of LLC formats, which is a breach of the intended independence of the sublayers.

By way of contrast, the Ethernet packet type field is an example of clean design. The field is defined at data link level as a means of selecting among various possible network layers. (There is no separate LLC sublayer in the Xerox architecture.) A large range of values ($2^{16} = 64k$) allows considerable flexibility in the allocation of particular values.

Breaches of good design principles may be acceptable where there are pressing needs. No such needs exist in this case, and it is regrettable that the IEEE has defined the LLC layer in this way.

17. NETWORK AND TRANSPORT PROTOCOLS

The data link layer of a local area network is concerned with a single 'data link'; i.e. a single cable or a set of cables, etc., that are operated together. Wherever a LAN must be connected to another network—local or wide area—some network level functions will be needed. Transport level functions will be needed to enable attached computers to communicate. This chapter discusses some of the issues that arise at these levels and presents some solutions.

LANs AND LAYERS

In most wide area systems the typical data link is either a point-to-point circuit or a multi-drop line with a comparatively small number of attached devices. In a LAN, by contrast, the data link may be much more complex and may carry hundreds, or even thousands, of attached machines. In LANs, in fact, it has not been usual to distinguish between the data link and the complete network.

In the case of Ethernet, the data link is the set of repeaters and cable segments over which collision detection operates. In the case of a ring, it is the ring segments and repeaters, while in case of a broadband cable, it is limited to the frequencies used in the service being considered.

The network layer is concerned with communications between machines which may be attached to different data links—even machines connected only indirectly through a number of intermediate links. The network layer is therefore concerned with the routing of traffic between data links.

The network layer relies on one or more data link layers to carry data across the links. For this purpose each data link layer provides it with one or more 'data link services' (to use OSI terms). In the IEEE LAN reference model (described in Chapter 7), these services are defined in the logical link sublayer. Figure 17.1 shows the layers and sublayers together with an indication of the way they might be implemented in a typical attached computer.

If the computer is attached to several data links it will have several data link modules. Ideally, these will all present the same interface to the network router, which will chose between them according to the destination of the traffic presented to it.

It is the intention of the OSI model that each computer should have only one

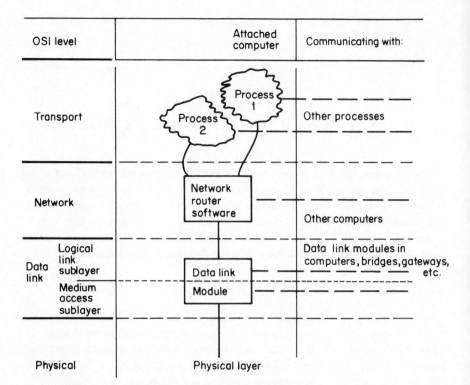

Figure 17.1   Layers of protocol.

network router—that for OSI. In practice computers must sometimes support several incompatible network architectures, and they will need several routers to achieve this.

At the network level each attached machine is treated as a single entity. Transport level protocols admit the possibility of there being several communicating processes in each machine, and provide for communication between these processes.

The transport layer has two main functions:

1. To provide inter-process communication, including communication between local processes. To do this, the layer uses a mixture of local switching and network services.
2. Where necessary, to upgrade the quality of the network service (with regard, for instance, to residual error rates) in order to make the transport level service acceptable to the processes calling it.

A number of disagreements currently exist as to the proper location of such functions as flow and error control and the assurance of packet sequencing. These disagreements make it impossible to specify the proper role of the transport layer less ambiguously.

THE NETWORK LAYER

Network layer protocols are found in most proprietary network architectures, that in SNA, for instance, being known as Virtual and Explicit Route Control (Meijer and Peters, 1982). The first set of related protocols to be used on interconnected LANs were those developed within the Xerox Corporation and based on the Parc Universal Packet (PUP) (Boggs *et al*, 1980). During 1981 Xerox began to publish the revised versions of these protocols that are used in their Network Systems 8000 range (Xerox, 1981a,b). These protocols are known as the Xerox Systems Integration Standards (XSIS) and Xerox is publishing them to encourage other vendors to implement them, and hence to increase the size of the Ethernet market.

The best-known network protocol, and the one likely to have most impact on the ultimate standards for Open Systems Interconnection, is CCITT Recommendation X.25. This is discussed below.

The Xerox Internetwork Datagram Protocol

The Internetwork Datagram Protocol is intended principally for use in an environment consisting of Ethernets interconnected by leased lines and X.25 public data networks, though other local and wide area networks could also be used. Packets are relayed between networks by 'internetwork routers'.

The protocol lies very largely at the network level (level 3) of the OSI reference model, but in a few respects, such as the reference to the socket numbers of host computers, it includes material more properly assigned to the transport level (Postel, 1980). The more complex aspects of the protocol are largely due to the need to operate in large, possibly global, networks in which the routes between some hosts may involve many intermediate links. The protocols limit the number of intermediate links between the two most widely separated networks to 14.

Within the protocol, all data and control information is carried in Internetwork Datagrams (IDs), whose format is shown in Figure 17.2. On an Ethernet, IDs are indicated by the packet type $(3000)_8$.

Network numbers are 32-bit numbers that refer either to Ethernets or to other networks to which hosts are connected. Network elements to which hosts cannot be connected, such as leased lines between networks, do not need numbers.

In destination addresses, three kinds of network number may be used:

1. 'All 0s' indicates the local network on which the packet is transmitted.
2. 'All 1s' means all the connected networks.
3. Specific addresses indicate specific networks.

Host numbers are 48-bit numbers and are unique amongst all network systems ever built. In fact, the host number of a machine is identical to its Ethernet address. In destination addresses three kinds of host number are supported:

1. Broadcast address. The value 'all 1s' indicates that the packet should be accepted by all the hosts on the specified network(s).

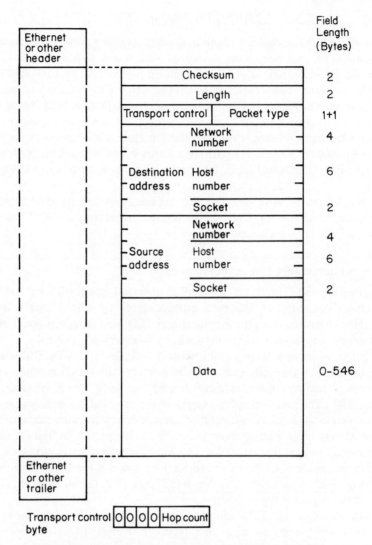

Figure 17.2   Format of the Xerox Internetwork Datagram.

2. Physical. The first bit is 0 and exactly one machine is indicated.
3. Multicast. The first bit is 1 and the address indicates a group of hosts, which may or may not be connected to the same network.

Host numbers and network numbers may be taken in any reasonable combination, including a broadcast to all hosts on all connected networks. Xerox intends to allocate blocks of host and network numbers itself to preserve global uniqueness.

In source addresses host and network numbers must specify individual host

Table 17.1 Well-known socket numbers.

Number (octal)	Function
1	Routing information
2	Echo
3	Router error
5	Receipt of remote procedure calls (Courier protocol)
⋮	⋮
40–77	Experimental

and networks. Though many hosts may receive a given packet, it always has a single source.

Socket numbers are 16 bit numbers that identify services or programs within a host. The range 1–3000 is reserved for use as 'well-known' socket numbers that should be used consistently in all hosts. Table 17.1 shows the initial well-known socket numbers. Sockets may serve as both sources and destinations of datagrams.

The checksum is described as the 'one's complement add-and-left cycle of all the 16-bit words of the datagram'. It is intended for end-to-end checking and its use is optional. The length is given in bytes, and must be an even number.

The hop count is used to prevent packets circulating forever in large networks and it is incremented each time the packet is relayed between networks. When it reaches the sixteenth internetwork router it will be discarded. The router may report this fact using a higher level protocol.

The packet-type field is used to select the higher level protocol that should process the packet. Table 17.2 lists some 'well-known' internet packet types.

Table 17.2 Well-known Internet packet types.

Number (octal)	Protocol
1	Routing information
2	Echo
3	Error
4	Packet exchange
5	Sequenced packet
⋮	⋮
20–37	Experimental

Like Ethernet itself, the Internet Datagram Protocol yields an unreliable datagram service. Where high reliability is essential, it must be obtained through the action of higher level protocols, such as Xerox's own Sequenced Packet Protocol.

CCITT Recommendation X.25

The first version of X.25 was published in 1976 as a proposed interface between computers and public data networks (Scantlebury, 1982). By 1982, 15 countries had public networks that complied with X.25, and compatible packet switches were available from a number of vendors for use in private networks. CCITT developed X.25 during this period by removing ambiguities, permitting a revised data link protocol (which would be compatible with a revised HDLC) and adding some new packet types. CCITT has also added datagram and fast select services, and extra diagnostics. The revised version was published in 1981.

Though X.25 only specifies an external interface, the nature of that interface places severe constraints on the internal structure of the network. In practice, therefore, X.25 specifies the network as well as its user interface.

The main X.25 service is the virtual call. The attached device (known in CCITT terminology as a Data Terminal Equipment or DTE) may attempt to establish a circuit at any time. The network relays this request to the indicated station which may accept or reject the call. If the call is accepted, HDLC connections are set up across the intervening data links, and a unique logical channel number is allocated to the virtual circuit so constructed. Data packets are then transported over this circuit.

Network addresses are specified in CCITT Recommendation X.121, as shown in Figure 17.3. Country codes are allocated by CCITT, and local addresses by the network operators (who may also be the PTTs). This is thus an example of an hierarchical addressing structure.

X.25 provides for a process of negotiation between stations before the virtual circuit is established. The calling DTE may specify special facilities from a CCITT list of 17 options (Scantlebury, 1982). These include one-way circuits, abbreviated addresses, and extended packet sequence numbers.

Packets are transferred over a virtual circuit in accordance with a sequencing and error control discipline similar to that described in connection with the IEEE

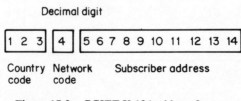

Figure 17.3   CCITT X.121 address format.

connection-orientated service in the last chapter (both are derived from the parallel facilities in HDLC). A three-bit number is generally used for sequencing, but seven-bit numbers are an option which may be selected by the DTE on networks that support this facility. The format of a data packet with extended numbering is shown in Figure 17.4.

In fast-select operation, the call request packet is allowed to contain application data. After accepting this packet the receiving DTE may clear the call, having received the data, or it may establish a normal virtual circuit.

In datagram operation, one or more virtual circuits are reserved for datagrams, though in effect these circuits terminate within the network, rather than at the called DTE. Datagrams may be transmitted without any preliminary, and their integrity and order of delivery are not guaranteed by the network. The datagram format is shown in Figure 17.5.

X.25 can be used in a local area network. Netskil, for example, combines Ethernet (at the physical and data link levels), Ungermann-Bass hardware, and ICL programs to provide X.25 service. But it suffers from disadvantages in the areas of complexity, error control, and addressing.

The emphasis on virtual circuits adds to the logical complexity of the network layer, and to the requirement for buffer space. Though a datagram service is now

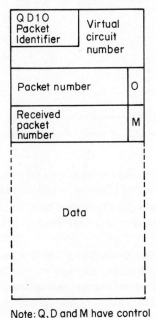

Note: Q, D and M have control functions

Figure 17.4 Format of an X.25 packet with extended numbering.

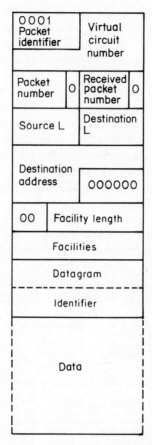

Figure 17.5   Format of an X.25 datagram.

included, this is in addition to the virtual circuit service, and includes a variety of options which will only rarely be required in local networking. The call establishment and clearing procedures are also rather complex, involving the exchange of an excessive number of request and confirmation packets (Meisner and West, 1980).

The X.25 error control was designed for use in a public network environment over noisy analogue lines. It is less appropriate for the high-speed digital lines found in LANs, with their very much lower errors rates.

The X.121 addressing convention is not suitable for the interconnection of private and public networks, since a single X.25 connection implies the existence of only one X.121 address. A large private network may require a number of distinct addresses—perhaps one for every computer. Though ways exist of circumventing this problem, they are either rather messy or capable of only small-scale application. In addition, X.25 has neither broadcast nor multicast facilities—facilities that have been found useful in LANs.

The OSI Network Layer

The OSI network layer will not be identical to X.25, though it will have many points of similarity (Tucker, 1982). The initial versions are likely to specify virtual circuit operation only (together with diagnostics and network management), but later versions will probably include datagrams as well. ISO envisage that their network layer will consist of two sublayers in respect of every actual network over which the service is to be provided:

1. The lower sublayer will consist of a suitable subset of existing network facilities chosen as the basis of the services to be provided. This sublayer will exist in attached computers as well as in network elements (such as packet switching exchanges).
2. The upper sublayer will consist of any additional protocols and procedures needed to supply services not present in the lower layer, and to enhance the quality of service to that required by transport layer protocols. This will be implemented wholly within attached computers.

To support interworking between dissimilar public networks and between public and private networks will require either an extension of X.121 (to cater for a potentially large number of private networks) or an extra level of addressing within the upper sublayer of the network layer. Figure 17.6 shows what a suitably expanded X.121 might look like.

Within the IEEE LAN Standards Committee (IEEE, 1982) there seems to be a

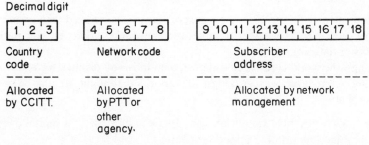

Figure 17.6   Expanded form of X.121.

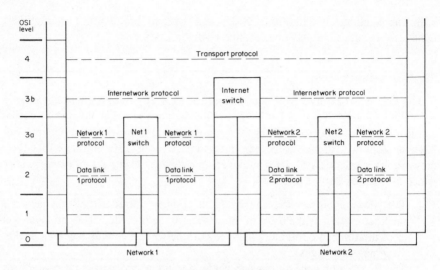

Figure 17.7   Internet protocol. (After Danthine, 1982.)

preference for a separate level of addressing in a new, 'internetwork', sublayer. (These topics have also been discussed by Danthine, 1982, and Saltzer, 1982.)

Figure 17.7 shows the concept of a separate internetting sublayer according to Danthine. The protocol is implemented by attached computers and internetwork gateways only. Within any single network, no matter how extensive, the protocol is carried transparently and is, therefore, dispensable (though it is good practice to use it so as to facilitate any subsequent use of other networks).

THE TRANSPORT LAYER

As indicated in Figure 17.1, the transport layer is concerned with communications between processes rather than between network stations or over particular networks or data links.

A single network layer may support a number of distinct transport layers providing different services. Amongst the services that might usefully be provided on a LAN are:

1. A low-latency byte stream service. This could be used for digital telephony or for the support of graphics terminals.
2. A datagram and response service. This is cheap to implement and can be used for certain kinds of file access.
3. A sequenced packet service. This can be used for file transfer, electronic mail, file access, etc.

The Xerox System Integration Standards (**XSIS**) include several protocols that lie approximately at transport level (Fishburn, 1982). These include:

Echo
Packet Exchange
Sequenced Packet
Error
Routing Information

I will present three of these, all of which are based on the Internetwork Datagram: the Echo, Packet Exchange and Sequenced Packet Protocols.

The Xerox Echo Protocol

This is an extremely simple protocol and is intended for use in testing the integrity of the network and the continued operation of attached computers. Echo packets have a packet type of 2. Socket 2 should be able to execute the protocol and others may also do so. Echo packets have the format shown in Figure 17.8.

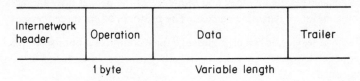

Notes: Operation 1 is 'request'
         Operation 2 is 'reply'

Figure 17.8   Format of Echo packet.

On receiving an echo request the host sends an echo reply. If the received packet was defective this will be reported using the error protocol.

If the echo request packet becomes corrupt during transmission, the host receiving it may not even be able to recognize it as an echo request. This protocol contains no provisions for reporting errors, though reports may be made using the error protocol.

The Xerox Packet Exchange Protocol

This is another very simple protocol. It is intended for functions such as status enquiries and time of day queries, and for applications in which simplicity of implementation is more important than reliability, or in which higher layers of protocol will make themselves responsible for the integrity of the interaction.

Exchange packets are denoted by a packet type of 4 and have the format shown in Figure 17.9. ID identifies the current exchange, and client type indicates the nature of the request (which may also be implicit in the nature of the socket to which the packet has been sent).

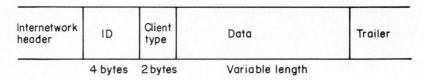

Figure 17.9   Format of exchanged packet.

Once a request has been sent, the sender will expect a reply. If no reply has been received after a suitable time, the packet will be sent again. Replies are identified by their IDs, and their client types may then be used to confirm their appropriateness.

The Xerox Sequenced Packet Protocol

This is a virtual call protocol operating between communicating processes. The protocol guarantees the integrity and sequence of the packet flow and arranges for the retransmission of defective packets. The protocol offers three services:

1. Message service, in which a message may comprise a number of packets.
2. Sequenced packet service, in which message boundaries are not distinguished.
3. Reliable packet mode, in which packets are presented in order of arrival but without duplicates; retransmitted packets may arrive late. This service gives a lower average delay which may be valuable in some applications.

All data are carried in internet datagrams which have a packet type of 5. The format is shown in Figure 17.10.

Connection IDs serve to identify the call unambiguously so that call establishment is, in essence, the process of agreeing their values. To establish a virtual call a station will allocate a connection ID (the source connection ID) to the call, and will then send a packet to the intended destination socket with a destination connection ID of 'unknown'.

If the recipient is willing to accept the call, it will allocate its own connection ID which will be notified to the caller in its first reply packet. The responding station may acknowledge the existence of the call by transmitting a system packet (with the system packet bit set), but the protocol does not require this.

Data are then transferred in numbered data packets which are acknowledged via the 'acknowledge number' in packets travelling in the reverse direction. Acknowledgements may be sent for individual packets or for groups of successive packets at the discretion of the respondent, except for packets with the 'send acknowledgement' bit set which must be acknowledged immediately. The allocation number is used for flow control; it specifies the highest number that the station receiving it may use in a transmitted packet. It will usually be increased each time packets are acknowledged.

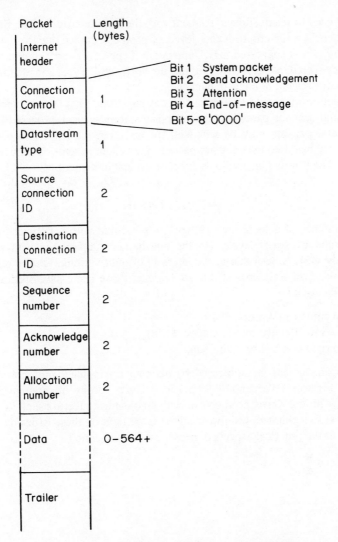

Figure 17.10   Format of the Xerox sequenced packet.

The end-of-message bit may be used to mark the end of a message (as defined by the client process). It is ignored by the Sequenced Packet Protocol. In a file transfer, for instance, messages might be logical records, disc blocks, or restartable sequences, according to the convenience of the processes managing the transfer.

The datastream type field is used to select a session or higher level protocol. It is not examined by this protocol.

Responsibility for terminating calls lies with the client process, which will typically need to reach some agreement with the remote process first. Such agreements are held to belong to higher levels of protocol, rather than to the transport level, though it is suggested that Datastream Type 254 ('end') should be used to flush undelivered packets through the network, and Type 255 ('end-reply') to acknowledge receipt of an 'end' packet.

Any station may send system packets at any time. They can be used for flow control and are not passed to the recipient station's client process. To convey urgent data, packets may be sent with the attention bit set. These packets can contain only one data byte and are passed to the client process as soon as they are received. They should be used only for time-critical information.

CONCLUSION

The designer of a local area network is presented with a difficult problem at network and transport levels. On the one hand, compatibility with standards, specifically OSI, is desirable in the interests of interworking. On the other hand, there are no firm standards at this level, whilst those being developed are, for an LAN, likely to be:

1. Too complex (Warner, 1980).
2. Too slow (Bennett and Hinchley, 1978)
3. Too rigid in network addressing.

This problem may be addressed by defining a simplified protocol with near-standard services (Warner, 1979) to client layers, or by maintaining full compatability with the Xerox protocols or with an older architecture such as SNA.

The next two chapters will throw a little more light on these issues by considering some of the practical aspects of network interconnection.

18. EXTENDING THE LOCAL NETWORK

Chapters 9 to 15 indicated the restrictions on the sizes of networks using the various technologies. In every case except that of broadband cable, the LAN is limited to a few kilometres in length, and can serve only a few hundred attached devices over a few square kilometres. Various repeaters, amplifiers, and power supplies will have to be included in the systems to achieve these maximum ranges.

A larger area can be served by installing two or more interconnected LANs of the same kind (as in Figure 18.1). The installation of several LANs on one site can

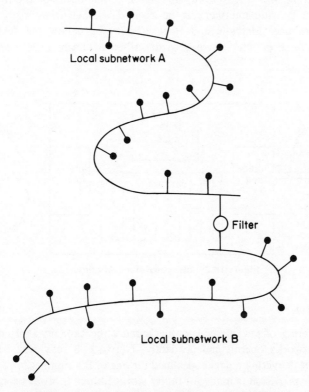

Figure 18.1 Interconnected LANs serving one site.

have additional advantages:

1. Traffic load may be effectively reduced by restricting some traffic to a single network (Gardner, 1982).
2. Slower or less reliable networks may be used in some areas to save money.
3. The consequences of the failure of one network are restricted to the area it serves.

The disadvantages of this arrangement are increased cost and complexity, and the possibility that some network functions, notably the low-level acknowledgements of some rings, cannot operate across all the networks.

In some cases it is desirable to interconnect networks of different kinds on one site. Since this can raise a great many further complexities, it will be discussed separately in the next chapter.

In most systems the only functions that the connector must perform are the selection of packets received from one LAN for retransmission on the other, and necessary buffering (see Figure 18.2).

These 'connectors' are sometimes referred to as gateways, but I prefer to follow Clark, Pogran, and Reed (1978) in reserving that term for the more complex devices that provide interworking between dissimilar networks. I shall follow Ethernet practice (Metcalfe and Boggs, 1976) by calling the device a 'filter'. Implementations of filters have been described by Leslie (1982) and Bux *et al* (1982).

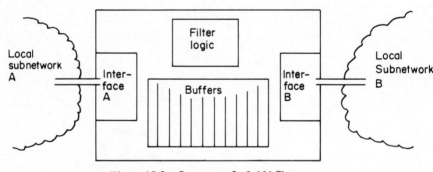

Figure 18.2   Structure of a LAN filter.

Flow Control

The buffering of packets is essential because the capacity-sharing systems on the two networks operate independently. Network B may well be busy while network A is delivering a packet destined for one of B's stations.

Whatever provision is made for buffer storage, there is always some possibility of its overflowing. A 10M bit/s LAN, for instance, can fill 64k bytes of buffers in less than a tenth of a second if all the traffic is for another LAN that is temporarily busy. Such overflows arise without notice, raising the question of what the filter should do in such a case.

If the filter has only the functions shown in Figure 18.2 then it must discard some packets. This is the view taken in Ethernet and one consistent with the philosophy of providing a 'best efforts' service, rather than 'guaranteed delivery'.

Packets may be discarded at random or according to priorities associated with the type of packet and/or its source and destination. Priority schemes may be viable in disciplined environments, such as those characteristic of military systems, but in most environments a policy of 'favouritism' is unlikely to be acceptable.

The filter may be able to report the loss of packets to their sources. This may help the source to recover quickly, but it provides little guidance on future policy, because loading changes very quickly on LANs (Shoch and Hupp, 1980a). It also has a number of disadvantages:

1. It adds to the network load precisely when that load is greatest.
2. It adds to the complexity of the filter.
3. It requires the source to accept reporting packets and, preferably, to adjust its own behaviour appropriately, probably by reducing its rate of packet transmission.

The decision as to whether filters and, by extension, other devices that are used to interconnect networks should report discarded packets is therefore one that must be made by network designers in the light of their objectives and the resources of their systems.

Routing

In order to recognize the 'A' packets that should be selected for transmission on the 'B' network, and vice versa, the filter must be able to interpret their addresses. Four main approaches may be used:

1. The source indicates that the packet should be filtered.
2. The filter knows the locations of individual stations and passes packets accordingly.
3. The filter recognises one part of the data link address as identifying the destination link.
4. The filter implements Network (OSI level 3) routing functions.

All these approaches may be used in small networks, but the choice becomes increasingly important in large networks and where the functions of the filter are extended to include switching among several subnetworks.

In source routing (Farber and Vittal, 1973) the complete route is specified by the original source. The route takes the form of a sequence of addresses of successive filters, followed by the address of the destination on the final subnetwork. Filters that implement source routing are extremely simple; indeed, this is the principal attraction of the method. The filters need neither look-up tables nor routing algorithms and, in consequence, may be cheap, fast and robust.

In source routing, the source must assume the responsibility for deciding the total route through the network. This is often an onerous burden, and the network operator will typically provide a 'route enquiry service' from which standard routes to named devices may be obtained. The use of standard routes excludes the standard dynamic routing techniques for bypassing defective elements, but the high reliability to be expected of LANs implies that this is of little importance (except in such special cases as a system for a warship or space craft). Similarly, the high speeds available on LANs make poor choices of route relatively unimportant.

Saltzer, Reed, and Clark (1981) have argued that source routing is the optimum strategy in a 'campus' environment; i.e. an environment in which a large population of diverse users is subject to only limited central discipline. Universities and research labs are the obvious examples of such environments, but the proliferation of office systems may create such environments in business organizations as well.

Apart from simplicity, Saltzer claims the following advantages for source routing:

1. The elimination of the instability, looping, and oscillation problems that can otherwise occur in large packet networks.
2. The ability to select a route with some known set of properties, for instance low delay.
3. The ability to accommodate unofficial filters between subnetworks.

Source routing is used by Network Systems Corporation in their HYPERbus network.

Where the subnetworks are small, it is possible for the filter to know the locations of all the network's stations, and it may then pass packets through in appropriate cases. This approach requires that, as in Ethernet, station addresses are unique across the whole set of linked networks, thus increasing the size of the address fields. The method has the advantage of being completely transparent to the source, but it requires the filter to maintain tables of station addresses. Some system will be needed whereby newly attached stations may announce their presence and have this information passed round the network. (The IEEE XID command, discussed in the preceding chapter, may be used for the former function, but the latter will require a further, inter-filter, protocol.) In networks that are large or which change rapidly, the overheads of this system become insupportable.

In the IMB token ring (Bux et al, 1982) the data link address comprises two parts. The first two bytes specify a ring, whilst the second two specify a station on that ring. Rings are connected by filters, known in this case as 'block switches'. The IBM filter needs to know the route to any ring that is not directly connected. If all the individual rings are directly connected, then the scheme degenerates to source routing, and no routing tables are necessary.

Like source routing, this scheme is simple to implement but it violates the integrity of the data link layer by including the addresses of data links in the layer itself. Selection of data links is more properly a Network function.

In implementing the network protocol, a LAN filter has the functions shown in Figure 18.3. In this case a clear division is made between the data link functions, which operate on a single data link, and the network functions which provide routing between data links.

When the Xerox Internetwork Datagram Protocol is used on Ethernet, packets have the address of the filter at level 2 but the address of the ultimate destination at level 3. The filter will override the level 2 addresses with those proper to the next Ethernet, but will leave level 3 addresses unchanged.

Though a normal packet will not have a filter as its final destination, the filter may receive and send network management packets (Xerox, 1981a). These may announce the connection or disconnection of a station, and report traffic volumes and patterns to a central network management facility. These reports should certainly include data on the numbers of packets that have been discarded.

This approach has the merit of clarity, but will typically require some routing algorithms and/or tables, and will therefore be slower and more complex than some of the alternatives.

Whilst implementation of the protocol's addressing functions is essential, it may not be necessary to implement other functions. Flow control is a case of particular significance. Protocols designed for use in wide area networks usually devote considerable attention to flow control, whereas those developed for LANs often completely exclude flow control from the network layer. Examples of these cases include CCITT X.25 and Xerox Internetwork Datagram, both discussed in the last chapter.

If the filter implements flow control, then this may be used to prevent the loss of packets. This adds significantly to the complexity of the filter, whilst operational

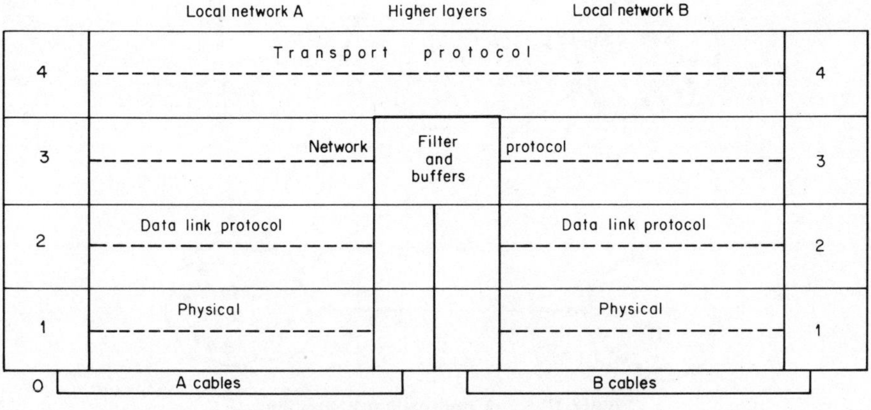

Figure 18.3 Functions of a LAN filter.

experience with Ethernet shows that very few packets are discarded in practice. It is therefore probably best to restrict the functions of the filter to selection and buffering.

COMMUNICATIONS BETWEEN SITES

Many organizations employ staff at a number of sites, possibly separated by large distances, and may have terminals and computers at all these sites. As the analysis of business communications needs in Chapter 3 showed, the communications are predominantly limited to a single site and can therefore be satisfied by a local area network at each. However, some communication may occur between people at different sites, whilst people at one site may need to use data or other facilities at another. Furthermore, the organization may wish, for policy reasons, to provide all its staff with the same facilities.

Consider, for instance, the British engineering company depicted in Figure 18.4. In 1981 the company operated a large time-shared mainframe at site A, and minicomputers of several kinds were distributed amongst the sites. The main information flows were between sites B, C, D, and E and site A, and between sites D and E (since these were managed jointly).

The company had an immediate requirement for online and RJE access to the time-sharing system, and was developing some TP systems. Though there was little exchange of data between the minicomputers, the company suspected that

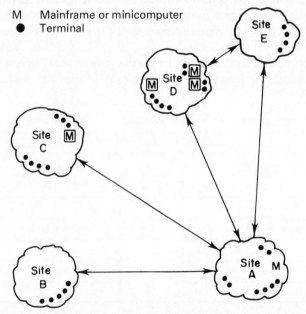

Figure 18.4   A multi-site organization.

this would change and that electronic mail might also be introduced in the future. Various sorts of distributed processing also seemed possible.

One reasonable solution to the company's problems was therefore to install a LAN-based terminal support network at each site, with appropriate communications between sites. The LAN would have had enough capacity to accommodate the likely requirements of future systems.

Since LANs use packet switching techniques, and are intended to provide a service with low transit time, the call establishment times associated with the PSTN, or even a public data network, make it impractical to establish a new connection for each transmission. Instead, the effect of a direct connection between sites is needed. In the circumstances the main options were:

1. One or more leased lines.
2. A permanent virtual circuit on the British national Packet Switching System (PSS) (an X.25 network).

The choice between these depends principally on the relative costs, bandwidths, reliabilities, and the expected traffic pattern. In other places, dedicated microwave links, satellite circuits, circuit switched data networks, and existing corporate data networks might also demand consideration. In this case, leased lines were chosen since the volume of batch data made PSS too expensive.

The Inter-Site Connection

The equipment used to interconnect LANs in this way has often been termed a gateway. Again, however, it seems desirable to distinguish between the limited facilities required here and those of full gateways. I shall make this distinction by using the term 'bridge' to indicate a connection between physically separated LANs over some trunk facility but, distinctively, without giving LAN users access to the wider capabilities of the trunk facility. This may also be seen as avoiding the complexities of the trunk network, as indicated by Figure 18.5.

Specifically, an X.25 network might be used to carry traffic from site A to site B, but a bridge would not allow the user to establish calls on that network to other locations (see Figure 18.6). A gateway, by contrast, would allow LAN users to establish and use X.25 connections to any subscriber on the X.25 network.

The routing options here are essentially the same as those given above in connection with filters, but the balance of advantage and disadvantage is rather different:

1. Source routing is less suitable, since the optimum use of trunk facilities is now more important and configuration changes at remote locations are less likely to be known locally.
2. Explicit knowledge of the locations of stations becomes completely impractical in a geographically distributed network.

Figure 18.5   A bridge.

3. If the sites are connected by a public packet network, then the bridge end-points will have to be concerned with the network level protocols of that network.

The user of a separate network layer is clearly indicated where bridges are used. Where traffic is heavy, the 'end-points' of the bridge are likely to be connected by dedicated circuits. These may be leased as digital facilities or they may be

OSI level

4							

OSI level							
4							
3		LAN level 3	X.25	LAN Level 3 protocol / X.25	X.25	LAN level 3	
2		LAN level 2	HDLC		HDLC	LAN level 2	
1		LAN level 1	V.24		V.24	LAN level 1	
0	LAN cables		PSS			LAN cables	

Figure 18.6   LAN-to-LAN bridge via PSS.

analogue lines with user-supplied modems.

Where leased lines or a wide area data network are used, the data link protocol used on the trunk element will be different from that on the LAN. These differences arise from the delays and high error rates characteristic of long distance transmission:

Data link	Bit error rate	Transit time (μs)
Ethernet	10^{-9}	5
Cambridge Ring	10^{-11}	5
Leased line (100 kilometres)	5×10^{-6}	800
Packet switching service	Very low	10,000
PSTN	$10^{-3} - 5 \times 10^{-6}$	50,000

The high error rate implies both the use of short packets (128 bytes maximum in the case of PSS) and the use of error detection and packet acknowledgement disciplines such as HDLC and SDLC in the data link layer. (This is shown in Figure 18.6.)

For high reliability, the bridge may consist of several physical circuits, possibly independently routed or using different technologies, and the bridge hardware must monitor the status of these routes. If one circuit becomes inoperable, the bridge should retransmit lost data over another circuit, as well as informing network management of the failure condition.

Where traffic is light the bridge may be implemented over a virtual circuit on a data network (Ansart *et al*, 1982). Wide area networks such as Transpac, Tymnet, or private networks under SNA usually have their own error control and network management facilities, so it may not be necessary for the end-point to implement these itself. (However, this cannot be assumed and may be true only for network interfaces that are themselves expensive to implement.)

These characteristics and others define the work that must be done by a bridge. An interesting example, in which several Ethernets were linked by radio, has been reported by Shoch and Stewart (1979).

The Xerox Ethernet–Radionet Bridge

Radionet is a digital radio system operating in the San Francisco Bay area of Northern California and based on contention principles (Kahn *et al*, 1978). The bridge end-points (known here as gateways) may receive internetwork packets of up to 564 bytes, and must fragment these into Radionet packets of not more than 254 bytes.

The fragmentation of a 290 byte packet is shown in Figure 18.7. The Radionet packet starts with a Radionet header (RH) of 22 bytes, and is followed by 4 bytes of encapsulation. The encapsulation is used by the receiving gateway to reassemble the original packet correctly (Shoch, 1979).

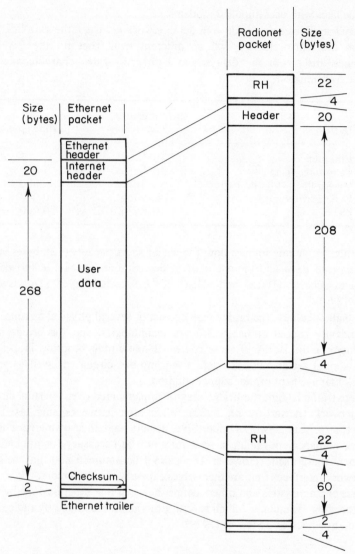

Figure 18.7   Packet fragmentation for a Radionet bridge.

Radionet packets are transmitted separately and, if the full complement of fragments of one packet has not been received within a period known as the *reassembly timeout*, then all packets are discarded by the gateway. (In the experiment, about 0.1 per cent. of packets were lost in this way.)

Though radio is a broadcast medium, Radionet does not provide either broadcast or multicast service to users. The gateway therefore simulates this by

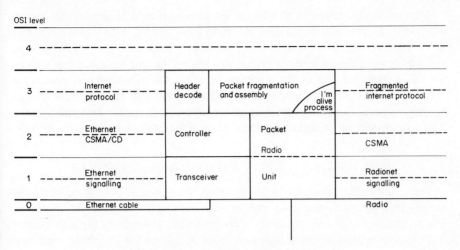

Figure 18.8   An Ethernet–Radionet gateway.

broadcasting multiple copies where necessary (Dalal, 1977). In addition to carrying packets for users, each gateway also transmits an 'I'm alive' packet to every other Radionet gateway (only five in practice) every 10 seconds. This enables each gateway to know which other gateways are functioning and serves to avoid the problems that some higher level protocols encounter when a circuit becomes operative in one direction only.

SERVICES ACROSS BRIDGES

We have assumed so far that the object of the bridge is to make all of site A's services available at site B, and vice versa. This is obviously both practical and desirable for a virtual call service operating at moderate speeds, but there may be limitations in other cases. Operating at 10M bit/s, the LAN will be able to load a 64k program in a twentieth of a second, whereas if a 9.6k bit/s bridge intervenes this process will take nearly a minute. Similarly, it would take over two hours to transfer a 10M byte file across this bridge, even if no other trunk traffic was flowing. At the transport level, then, the bridge should at least give warning of its low speed. There will also be a need for some flow control so as to prevent the bridge from constantly discarding packets.

There may also be difficulties in providing a minipacket service across the bridge. Heavy use of the service would lead to inefficient use of the bridge unless an alternative form of encapsulation were used for minipackets. More significant, perhaps, than this complexity is the delay. A minipacket can circle a typical Cambridge Ring in about 10 µs, but would take at least 4,500 µs to cross a 100 kilometre 10k bit/s bridge. A low-delay service is clearly impossible under these circumstances.

A question also arises as to whether broadcasts should be propagated across the bridge. In practice, broadcasts are most often used to locate resources, and while such resources as time-sharing hosts and electronic mail systems may reasonably be accessed across a bridge, this will not be true for a disc that is to be used as a paging device or for a printer on which the user wishes to produce a copy for his own use. A layered approach allows broadcasts to be easily restricted to one network. Suitable addressing conventions, such as are embedded in the Xerox Internetwork Datagram Protocol, allow a multicast to a group of LANs.

THE IMPLICATIONS FOR WIDE AREA NETWORKS

These difficulties stem in large measure from the mismatch between the LAN—high-speed, simple data link control protocols—and the WAN—low-speed, complex data link protocols. This mismatch arises from the high cost of fast trunk communications, a high cost based in part on the telephone engineers' assumption that connections require constant transmission rates and can tolerate (relatively) long setup times. Bridge traffic will, however, reflect the statistics of local traffic. Can we find any wide area technology that can exploit these statistics in the same way that the LAN does locally?

The public packet switching networks can do this to some extent. X.25 connections can operate at speeds up to 48k bit/s, and connections at up to 2.048M bit/s will be available within a few years in some countries. Although the rental for these connections is substantial, users only pay call charges for the traffic they actually send, making the operational costs much less than those of a dedicated link at the full speed.

The latest round of satellite data services for business (those being offered in the United States by Satellite Business Systems, and in Europe by the PTTs on Telecom-1) allocate capacity by Time Division Multiple Access (TDMA). TDMA is a dynamic reservation system similar to some of those described in Chapter 12. But because of the central control of the network and the long distances between ground and orbit, a delay of at least half a second always intervenes between asking for new capacity and obtaining it. Though much shorter than the time taken to establish a call on the PSTN, this is still a long delay by LAN standards.

As we suggested in Chapter 15, the future may see alternative public data networks based on broadband cable technology, and, if some dynamic time division technique is used, these networks will be able to exploit the statistics of packet flow.

It is noteworthy that, while the PTT's initial plans for the Integrated Services Digital Network of the 1980s and 1990s were based on fixed allocation strategies, there has recently been greater interest in dynamic allocation systems of the kind needed to complement LANs. Those advancing these ideas within the PTTs have, however, a hard task, in view of both the enormous installed base of circuit switching equipment and the inertia of the organizations themselves. It would be overoptimistic to simply assume that they will win this argument.

Addressing in Networks

It is clear from the theoretical discussion in the last chapter and from the practical considerations in this one that we may distinguish five levels of addressing at and below the network level. These are shown in Table 18.1, which also illustrates the fact that the requirements of public and private networks are rather different. A subscriber to a public network may be a single user with a single terminal. A subscriber may also be a local, national, or even international, private network.

A variety of views exist as to the correct relationships between these addressing requirements and the OSI model. The Xerox Internetwork Protocol, for instance, recognizes private networks but not site networks; each Ethernet is treated as both a network and a data link.

There is presently a danger that extra layers and sublayers will have to be introduced to compensate for the limitations of individual addressing systems. The division of the network layer into network and internetwork sublayers now seems to be certain (Danthine, 1982), whilst a division into three has been suggested by, for instance, Fishburn (1982).

I do not propose to solve this problem here, but I wish to suggest some guidelines for a solution. The guidelines concern the recognition of site networks as addressable entities and the correct relationships between public and private networks.

Table 18.1   Addressing levels.

	Scope	Entity addressed	Notes
a	World	Country	As in the X.121 country code
b	Country	Network	Public networks: as in the X.121 network code
			Private networks: requirement discussed in last chapter
c	Public network	Individual subscriber	Follows X.121
		Private network	
	Private network	Site network	Discussed in connection with bridges
d	Site network	Data link	Discussed in connection with filters
e	Data link	Station	Discussed in connection with filters

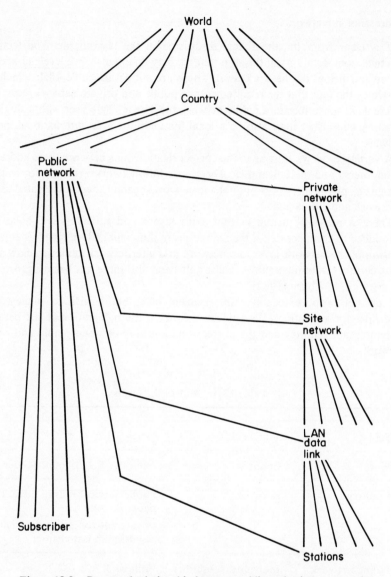

Figure 18.9   Proposed relationship between public and private networks.

A site network is a collection of LAN data links on one site connected by high-speed filters. It is necessary to recognize the site network as an addressable entity in order to:

1. Allow addressing from public and larger private networks.
2. Restrict the use of those LAN services that require high speeds to the area that can support those speeds.

3. Allow broadband networks to be addressed as single entities comprised of multiple services.
4. Allow local autonomy in the allocation of data link and station addresses.

Any comprehensive addressing scheme should treat public and private local networks with, at least, formal equality, just as PABX extensions may use the PSTN and may, in some cases, be dialled directly from the public network.

It follows that site networks and individual LAN data links should be able to attach to the public network, and that wider private networks should also be allowed appropriate attachment. (Some private networks are international in scope, being operated by multinational companies, common carriers, and affinity groups such as SITA and SWIFT. In an ideal world these would be treated as extra-territorial to any PTT. This, however, is clearly a counsel of perfection and will suggest a dangerous radicalism to many CCITT people. It therefore seems best not to insist upon it.) Figure 18.9 shows the resulting relationship between public and private networks.

It follows from this account that the site network *is* the local area network, so far as analysis and protocols are concerned, and that a lower sublayer of the network layer is necessary to define a LAN. A single upper sublayer, which might be based on an extension to X.121, should suffice for all necessary interworking between networks.

19. COMMUNICATIONS GATEWAYS

The previous chapter discussed how fairly similar local networks could be interconnected. The required connector only needs to implement the physical and data link layers of the two networks together, when they are not adjacent, with some control of the trunk facility being used.

This simple approach is excellent when the networks to be connected use the same network layer protocol. But it breaks down when this is not the case, and a more complex connector will then be necessary. This connector may be called a gateway.

THE NEED FOR MULTIPLE LOCAL NETWORKS

The need to interconnect dissimilar local networks may arise in several ways. There may be technical reasons for installing LANs with different facilities. For example, the need for television distribution in a hospital or college might indicate a broadband network, whilst the need for low-latency delivery might mandate a minipacket ring in a technical area of the same organization. Then again, particular computers and word processors may be compatible with only certain, proprietary, LANs, and may require those LANs for efficient operation.

On a large site there are advantages in interconnecting the LANs that serve a single building or department via a backbone network with different characteristics (Danthine, 1982).

Even when no adequate technical reason exists, there may still be insufficient central control to insist on the adoption of compatible networks by independent departments or operating companies. Though little need for intercommunication may be apparent at the time of installation, such needs have a habit of developing over time as the scope of systems, and the ambitions of their developers, increases.

Finally there is the question of cost. Though an organization may be willing and able to standardize on Ethernet (or the Cambridge Ring, or on a proprietary product), it may be unable to afford the costs of connecting all its existing machines. It may then choose to connect micros to the network via a micronet and terminals via multiplexors, as shown in Figure 19.1. Within a few years the costs of connection will have fallen substantially, and the organization will then be able to connect all its machines directly and expand their ability to interwork

220

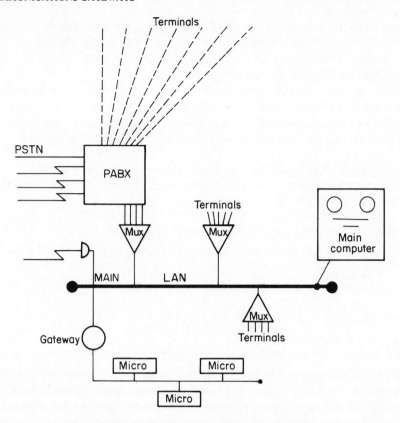

Figure 19.1 An example of multiple local networks.

across it (Flint, 1981). Several Micronet suppliers are developing gateways to other LANs for this purpose.

Other common cases include the need for terminals to gain access to networked resources across a PABX and the need for office workstations to gain access to data and programs on existing TP, time-sharing, and CAD systems. Office systems research by Butler, Cox and Partners (Flint, 1982b) has shown that the benefits of a sophisticated office system may be greatly increased if it can link with other systems and networks.

INTER-SITE COMMUNICATION

Site networks may be connected by bridges over leased lines or other networks. Each bridge end-point implements an inter-site, as well as the local area, protocol, and must therefore provide some conversion between dissimilar protocols. But the end-point uses the inter-site element in a very limited way, since its only concern is to pass complete packets to the distant end-point. LAN protocols at OSI transport level and above pass unchanged and uninterpreted across the inter-site link. The facilities of the intervening network are largely irrelevant to the user of a bridge, because they are not available to that user.

There are many circumstances, however, in which the user of a local network would like access to the facilities of another network.

Table 19.1 lists some of the kinds of network that might be of interest. This is very far from being a complete list but it illustrates the scope of the problem.

Table 19.1   Networks with which interworking might be useful.

PSTN—analogue interfaces (via modems)
     —(in future) high-speed digital interfaces as defined for ISDN

Private circuit switching networks supporting X.21 interfaces

Public and private packet switching networks supporting X.25, X.28, and X.75 interfaces

Private data networks constructed according to proprietary architectures such as SNA

Affinity group networks such as SWIFT and SITA

Public and private videotex networks

Access to public networks may be useful in order to access external databanks and computer bureaux, to send and receive electronic mail of various kinds, and to interrogate computers operated by suppliers to determine the state of orders. In the future, public network links may serve for electronic funds transfer and to receive orders from members of the public.

Access to private networks may be useful in order to gain access to large computers or to files on data processing computers. Office systems, in particular, will often find such links essential.

Figure 19.2 illustrates, graphically, the concept of a gateway from one network into another.

THE CONNECTION PROBLEM

The most basic problem in interworking between networks ('internetting') is to establish some reliable connection between processes in machines on the connected networks. Where the required access is intended for use by terminals, as it often will be, this is in fact the largest part of the total task.

The gateway usually takes responsibility for establishing and closing a virtual circuit between the networks and for transferring data over that circuit, but it takes no responsibility for control of the screen, remote login procedures, etc. In

Figure 19.2   Crossing network environment boundaries.

other words, its functions are restricted to the network, transport, and (perhaps) session layers of the OSI model.

This approach itself poses some problems since older networks have not been designed on the basis of a layered model and since, even where this has been done, differences of intention and interpretation may still exist. The attempt to connect networks at different levels is likely to cause problems (see, for instance, Piney, Parkman and Fluckiger, 1980) but cannot always be avoided.

The gateway shown in Figure 19.3 implements protocols up to the transport level for both networks. The physical and data link layers pose no problems, since they relate to single networks, and thus no information needs to be passed between the corresponding layers of the networks. The main functions of the network layer are addressing, error control, and flow control, and here some interaction is necessary.

The principles of internetting have been discussed by Pouzin (1977), Gien and Zimmermann (1979), Higginson and Kirstein (1981), Elden (1981) and Sunshine (1977).

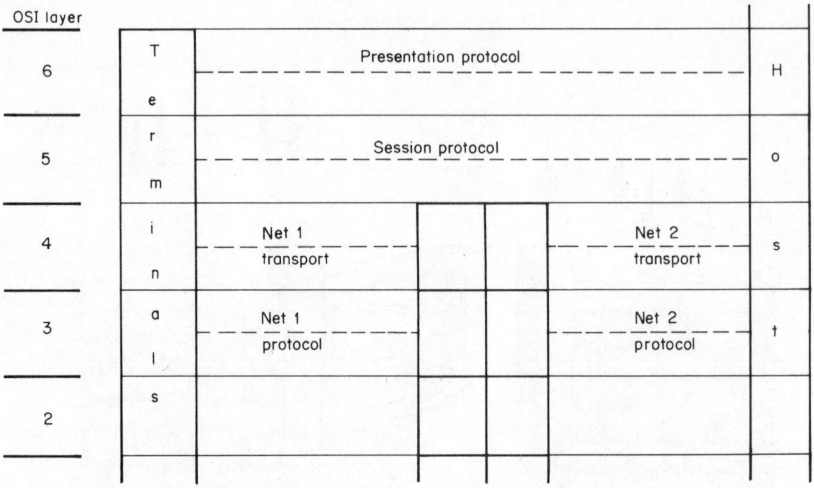

OSI layer							
6	T e	Presentation protocol					H
5	r m	Session protocol					o
4	i n	Net 1 transport				Net 2 transport	s
3	a l	Net 1 protocol				Net 2 protocol	t
2	s						

Figure 19.3   Protocols at a simple terminal gateway.

Addressing

Where the networks use different network protocols three main methods exist for addressing through gateways:

1. An explicit call extension function in the gateway.
2. An implicit call extension function, with a table for converting between net 1 and net 2 addresses.
3. The introduction of a global internetwork sublayer as discussed in Chapter 17.

The first method is usually quite convenient and is completely general. The net 1 user can construct a call to any net 2 host whose address he knows. He will, of course, need to be a recognized user of that host before his call will be accepted. If the networks are operated by different organizations, or even by different departments of the same organization, the gateway may need to limit the use of net 2's facilities to selected users. It need not be concerned with the remote host, since that has recognized the user and will presumably do its own accounting (Dallas, 1982).

The second method improves on the first by relieving the user of any need to know net 2's addressing scheme, but at the cost of a mechanism for keeping the address conversion tables sufficiently current (Sherman, Gable, and Chung, 1982). (This is similar to the problem of keeping internetwork routers consistent in a single extended network, one solution to which has been published as the XSIS Routing Information Protocol; see Xerox, 1981a.)

The gateway's knowledge of remote hosts may now be used as the basis of further services to users. These include:

1. Automatic execution of the login protocol to the host, either in the user's name or in the name of net 1 itself. In the latter case the gateway may need exercise access controls and to perform accounting functions in respect of the user's use of remote host facilities. (In practice the limitations of the host's billing system may make this last function impractical.)
2. Automatic selection of an alternative host, if the one normally accessed is unavailable.
3. Automatic invocation of protocols at and above transport level, with necessary protocol conversions.

The third method is the most powerful and general but it requires cooperation from the hosts on net 2. Where net 2 is an existing network, such as a corporate TP network or a public data network, this will usually be impractical.

The first method is the most generally applicable, though the second and the third (which is a kind of generalization of the second) will become increasingly attractive as the connectivity of networks increases.

Access controls are likely to be an important part of the functions of gateways in the future. Controls may be used both to restrict access to information and (expensive) services and, by analogy with call barring on PABXs, to prevent users making expensive calls (Dallas, 1982).

Error and Flow Control

Error control is generally based on the return of positive and negative acknowledgements to the source. Positive acknowledgements are returned for correctly received packets and negative acknowledgements for packets that are corrupt, out of sequence, or otherwise in error.

Real computers are able to accept data only up to a certain maximum rate. To avoid exceeding this rate, therefore, computers use the flow control features of networks to restrict the flow of data to them. Chapters 16 and 17 presented the flow control mechanisms used in various connection-orientated (virtual circuit) protocols.

Where both networks provide virtual call services, the gateways will use these services for terminal support. The relationship between flow control in the two networks is complicated by the facts that they may use different mechanisms, that they may allow different numbers of unacknowledged packets to be outstanding, and that packets from one network may have to be fragmented to be carried by the other. (This point was discussed in connection with a Radionet bridge in the last chapter.)

Though logically distinct, error and flow control are closely related and are often implemented by a single network mechanism. This mechanism may be called 'circuit control'.

Networks differ not only in the particular mechanisms they use for circuit control (consider the various protocols presented in Chapter 17) but also in the significance they attach to them. Even for X.25 there is a divergence of practice between PTTs. In some public data networks the circuit control functions operate end to end, whilst in others they operate only between a host and the local network equipment. (Scantlebury, 1982). These interpretations are compared in Figure 19.4.

Where both networks attach only local significance to circuit control, the gateways may follow this practice without causing any problem. Where both attach end-to-end significance, the gateway may retain this level of service by delaying its acknowledgement until it receives the necessary acknowledgements from the further party (Gien and Zimmermann, 1979). This technique obviously increases the time taken for the host to obtain a reply, and, where the host is directly connected to a high-speed LAN, this may lead to a protocol timeout being exceeded, and consequent confusion. In some cases, this problem has made it impossible to interconnect networks. (Sherman, Gable, and Chung, 1982, have implemented a system that avoids this problem by measuring the round-trip delay to other hosts.)

Where one network is based on end-to-end significance and the other on local significance the problem is rather more subtle. Direct connection of the services will produce a composite service that does not have end-to-end significance, causing a reduction in the quality of services to hosts attached to the former network, and an increased response time to hosts on the latter. The second problem may be avoided by implementing host-to-gateway significance on the first network and local significance only in the second. This, in essence, is the

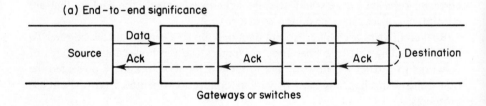

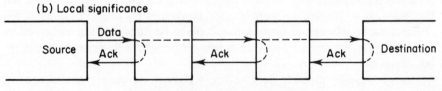

Figure 19.4   Significance in protocols.

route taken in CCITT's Recommendation X.75 for the interconnection of public data networks.

The quality of service problem, however, can only be solved by introducing a new layer of protocol on the network that has local significance. If this is an existing network, and access to all its hosts and services is desired, then any resulting problem must simply be left to the care of the higher level protocols.

Datagram Networks

In datagram networks all packets are processed independently of one another and there is, therefore, neither error nor flow control at network level. (The XSIS Internetwork Datagram Protocol presented in Chapter 17 operates in a datagram network). A gateway between two datagram networks is therefore fairly simple since its only functions are address translation and, sometimes, the fragmentation of large packets.

The concept of a connection, a continuing association between two communicating partners, will often reappear at the transport level. In such cases the networks must generally be matched at that level as well as at the network level.

The connection of datagram networks and virtual call networks is more difficult. The lack of error and flow control functions in the former is particularly troublesome. Since the network has no concept of a call the gateway must, if the initiative comes from that side, establish calls across the virtual circuit network at its own discretion. The gateway must also take a decision as to when the circuit should be closed, since it will receive no 'call clear' instruction. This is usually done when the circuit has been idle for an extended period, possibly 10 minutes.

Where a call is started in the virtual call network and must be extended across the datagram network the problem is less severe. Most datagram networks have, in fact, some transport level connection for virtual circuits and these may be mapped to the transport level of the virtual call network.

CONNECTIONLESS SERVICES

Some datagram networks provide broadcast and multicast services.

To pass a broadcast into a virtual call network the gateway will have to establish circuits to every host. This is rarely sensible, since the hosts will not be able to interpret the message.

Multicasts may, however, usefully be simulated by a virtual call network. If a public data network were used to link a number of local networks then a multicast to that group of networks might easily prove useful. (Though this is rather like a bridge, it could be used in circumstances where a permanent bridge would be inappropriate.)

THE COMPREHENSION PROBLEM

So far this chapter has dealt with the work needed to establish connections between processes in computers on different networks. There is, however, no guarantee that such processes will be able to communicate. As when two people without a common language share a telephone line, connection alone does not establish communication.

Most internetwork communication falls into one of four categories:

1. Terminal support.
2. File transfer.
3. File access.
4. Electronic mail.

In each case the gateway may provide some assistance to the user if the desired compatibility between networks is lacking.

Terminal Support

This is both the most useful and, probably, the easiest of the tasks. Terminals operate in quite a limited variety of ways and, indeed, the same terminals may be acceptable to both networks (though through different mechanisms). The conversion of terminal support protocols has been discussed by Gien and Zimmermann (1979) and by Zimmermann and Naffah (1978). Ball *et al* (1976) have reported on Rochester's Intelligent Gateway, a machine that converts terminal and host protocols through a common internal format.

File Transfer

Most networks have one or more protocols for file transfer. Each protocol allows the source and receiving files to be identified and then establishes one or more connections over which the contents are moved. Error control is essential but may be regarded as part of the transport layer. There is usually, also, some provision for marking places in the file in order to assist restarts following a failure (Day, 1981; Finnington, 1982). Though the elements are common, most proprietary protocols are intimately related to the structures used for data storage on the vendor's own computers. They are therefore rather difficult to relate to one another.

File Access

LANs typically have a protocol for file access; indeed, access to shared disc files is often an important part of their value. In Micronets this has often reflected the storage system used by preexisting micros, and is therefore rather difficult to relate to other systems. In more powerful systems, such as Xerox Network Systems and the Apollo Domain, less machine-dependent protocols are used, making conversion work easier.

Wide area networks often do not have file access protocols *per se* since all access is expected to be by a TP terminal addressing a telecommunications package on the host computer. It may therefore be necessary to make the conversion via terminal emulation in the gateway. This is unlikely to be satisfactory.

Bucciarelli and Errico (1982) have described their experience in moving a distributed filing system from a wide area network to a LAN.

Electronic Mail

Electronic mail is increasingly often found in networks of all kinds. Electronic mail systems (EMSs) vary considerably from those that merely transfer a file of text on demand to highly sophisticated systems (such as Comet and OnTyme) that allow the interactive preparation of messages, circulation lists, and multiple levels of urgency.

Clearly, messages cannot be transferred from sophisticated to simple systems without some loss of function. It appears, however, that local and wide area electronic mail requirements are rather different. In the local area the EMS is best seen as a part of an office automation system, with requirements for electronic filing and retrieval, word processing, and linkage with other electronic systems. In the wide area the key requirements are support for a variety of customer devices, ranging from intelligent typewriters to LAN-based office systems, very wide connectivity, and prompt delivery of urgent mail.

During the 1980s the PTTs will introduce EM services based on the Teletext standards (Dewis, 1982) which will be a reasonable match to the wide area requirements. The main gateways required will, therefore, be between sophisticated local EMSs on LANs, and Teletext provided over PSS or the PSTN. Such gateways have been discussed by Naffah (1981) and by Higginson and Kirstein (1981), and an EM–Teletext gateway has been reported by Hanna and Wakeman (1981).

CONCLUSION

The proliferation of incompatible networks, locally, nationally, and internationally, makes it essential to be able to interwork between these networks. Gateways have, therefore, an assured place in future networks.

Most networks installed to date have been designed to support terminal-to-host communications. Such communications form a *de facto* standard in internetworking. Gateway developments will therefore focus on virtual circuit support, with some conversion of terminal protocols. This will serve three purposes:

1. Terminal users may access hosts on other networks.
2. Hosts can allow access from terminals on other networks.
3. Computers, most notably intelligent workstations, can emulate terminals and thereby gain access to hosts on other networks.

In most cases the user is likely to be aware that he is using a gateway, since such gateways are easiest to develop and avoid the need to maintain address translation tables. In the longer term, workstations and gateways will assist the user in accessing these facilities.

Another development in gateways will be the appearance of transparent gateways into alien networks. Such gateways will enable the user of an office workstation to access files on other systems and networks as if they were local, and to prepare and despatch electronic mail in the same way for correspondents on many networks.

20. LAN STANDARDS

Standards are useful to users. They provide a degree of confidence that devices which conform to the standards will in fact work, and they reduce the price of equipment by facilitating economies of scale in manufacture. In the case of complex systems of hardware or software, they make it easier for staff to assimilate new systems. Thus, a programmer who has once mastered one application of X.25 or IBM's DL/1 data management system will be able to master another more rapidly than he will an equivalent system using, say, Internetwork Datagram or IDMS.

Standards also change the marketplace in which users and suppliers must both operate. Successful standards allow users to buy similar machines from a variety of sources. Thus the QWERTY keyboard allows any typist to operate almost any typewriter, whilst the V.24 interface (EIA RS232 in the United States) provides data processing managers with a wide choice of terminal suppliers.

For this reason, standards are favoured by small suppliers, who wish to gain a share of the 'plug compatible' market. They are often resisted by large and established suppliers, who see the non-standard nature of their equipment as making it difficult for existing users to shop elsewhere. In data processing, standards have been largely set by market acceptance rather than by formal standardization activities. IBM is, therefore, the largest source of DP standards.

Telecommunications standards are rather different. Standards are essential to communications, and especially to the public networks operated by the PTTs and by other common carriers. Telecommunications standards have therefore often been fixed by official standards bodies, most notably the International Standards Organisation (ISO) and the Comité Consultatif International Télégraphique et Téléphonique (CCITT).

LANs share the natures of both fields. Though clearly communications systems, they are restricted to single sites. At the transport level and above, the issues of protocol design are very similar to those found in public and private wide area network. Below that level the special nature of the LAN is increasingly relevant, but, at least at network and transport levels, alignment with standards is desirable to facilitate interworking with other networks.

At the data link, physical and medium levels, standardization provides the benefits of economy and familiarity. It will also allow users to buy specialized devices, such as database machines, from a variety of sources, rather than being restricted to a single supplier.

Standardization work has proceeded largely independently for each of the four kinds of LAN:

Mainframe LANs
Office LANs (covering micronets, minicomputer LANs, and integrated office
    networks)
Process control networks
Home Bus standards

Standards work on mainframe LANs has been conducted by Committee X3T9.5 of the American National Standards Institute (ANSI). This led, during 1982, to the definition of a 50M bit/s standard consisting of hardware based on CDC's Loosely Coupled Network and protocols derived from work by the US National Bureau of Standards (NBS). X3T9.5 expected to present its results to ISO committee SC13 during 1983.

Committee 65A working group WG6 of the IEC is developing a local network for process control (IEC, 1980). The standard will be known as PROWAY and is intended for use in heavy industrial environments. The Committee expects to complete its work by 1985.

During 1980 an organization called the Home Bus Standards Association was formed under the auspices of SRI International (Shaffer, 1980). The association aimed to develop standards that would allow a wide variety of domestic machines—toasters, ovens, central heating systems—to communicate. The Association expected to produce a draft standard for low-speed communication over power cables towards the end of 1982.

The leading role in LAN standards, however, has been taken by the US Institute of Electrical and Electronic Engineers (IEEE).

The work began at the Spring Compcon of 1980 (Sze, 1982) when a number of engineers and other professionals in the computer industry decided that a standard would be valuable in the fields of office automation and distributed processing. The group was subsequently recognized by the IEEE and constituted as 'Project 802—Local Network Standards'.

At its formation, a significant proportion of the project group wished the IEEE to adopt Ethernet essentially unchanged as its own standard. By the end of 1980 a majority of the group had rejected this position. They disliked the statistical nature of Ethernet's response and preferred to define a standard that was not based on contention.

The 802 Committee dealing with the data link layer therefore divided, more or less amicably, into two parts. One part was to work on contention whilst the other began to develop token passing. This work resulted in draft B of the standard (IEEE, 1981) which was circulated for voting in November 1981. This draft was rather poorly received by the IEEE membership (*Data Communications*, March 1982) whose criticisms included the following:

1. The contention proposal was not compatible with Ethernet.

2. There were too many options that could be independently selected. One member of the 802 project calculated that there were over 10,000 conforming, but mutually incompatible, sets of options.
3. The token-passing section was complex and confusing, because it attempted to cover both rings and buses.

During the months that followed, project 802 expanded and restructured its draft standard and brought the contention section much closer to Ethernet. Draft C (IEEE, 1982) was circulated for voting in May 1982.

The work of project 802 has been notable for the very considerable efforts that have been put into it. The project group has over 500 members, of whom about 100 attend meetings. A major contribution has also been made by corporations such as DEC, Xerox, IBM, AT&T, and Hewlett-Packard.

During 1982, the European Computer Manufacturers' Association (ECMA, 1982) intervened in the standards debate by publishing a contention standard closely based on Ethernet and differing from the IEEE draft. ECMA thus gave Ethernet its first endorsement by a semi-official body. ECMA has also contributed to the definition of standards at higher levels of the OSI model. During autumn 1982 the IEEE aligned its contention standard with Ethernet and the ECMA position, whilst progress on token-passing standards began to suffer from disputes over patent rights and licensing.

THE DRAFT IEEE LOCAL NETWORK STANDARD

Figure 20.1 shows the options in the standard according to draft C (IEEE, 1982). The division of the data link layer into two sublayers was discussed in Chapter 7.

The logical link control (LLC) sublayer was described in Chapter 16 where the various options were also described. Connectionless service is common to all classes of station, so that all 802-compliant stations will be able to interwork using that mode of operation. This uniformity also isolates the technicalities of the LAN from higher level protocols (except where they concern network management). Provided that it only uses connectionless operation, any network layer that runs on one 802 LAN can be moved to any other. Of course, it will run more slowly if the new LAN is itself slower, but it will run correctly.

Protocols that use connection-orientated or acknowledged connectionless service will, of course, only operate on stations in classes II and III respectively.

The medium access control (MAC) sublayer provides two options for the address format and three options for the capacity-sharing algorithm. (A fourth, very similar to that described in Chapter 12 as Dynamic Reservation by Address Tree Search (DRATS), is under development.)

The address formats are shown in Figure 20.2. The first (I/G) bit distinguishes between individual and group (multicast) addresses. In 48-bit addresses the second bit (L/UPC) is reserved to distinguish between those allocated as part of a

OSI layer	IEEE sublayer	Option
2 Data link	Logical link control (LLC)	**Station classes:** I —connectionless operation only II —connectionless and connection-orientated operation III* —connectionless and acknowledged connectionless operation **Service access points:** One (null address is used) Several Duplicate MAC service access point address detection procedure*
	Medium access control (MAC)	**Addresses:** 16 bit 48 bit—locally administered —universal product code

Capacity sharing algorithm:

	CSMA/CD		Token bus		Token ring	
OSI layer	Speed (bit/s)		Speed (bit/s)		Speed (bit/s)	
1 Physical	10M					40M
			20M			20M
	10M	10M	10M		4M	4M
	5M*		5M			
	1M*		1M	1M	1M	

Medium (OSI layer 0):

	CSMA/CD		Token bus		Token ring	
Cable:	Coax	Optical fibre	Coax		Shielded pair	Coax
Topology: Tree	Rooted tree	?	Bus with stubs	Bus with drops / Rooted tree	Ring	Ring
Encoding: Manchester	Miller	?	Differential Manchester		Differential Manchester	
Signalling: Baseband	Vestigial sideband / Broad band	?	Frequency shift keying / Phase continuous	Phase coherent / Phase shift keying / Broad band	Baseband	

Figure 20.1 Options in the IEEE draft standard.

Key:
*At draft C (IEEE, 1982) of May 1982 these items were provisional.

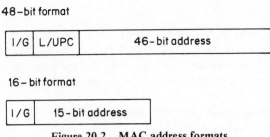

Figure 20.2   MAC address formats.

Universal Product Code (UPC), i.e. as proposed for Ethernet, and those allocated in some other way ('locally'). In both cases the value 'all 1s' indicates a broadcast to all stations.

The contention (CSMA/CD) option is extremely close to the relevant parts of the Ethernet specification. Unlike Ethernet, however, the IEEE intends to permit operation at 1M, 5M, 10M, and 20M bit/s and over a variety of physical media. Many of these combinations are not fully specified.

The baseband coax medium and its physical layer are only specified for operation at 10M bit/s and are substantially identical with the Ethernet specification (DIX, 1980).

The broadband coax option is defined for a single-cable midsplit system with a frequency shifter at the head-end (Chapter 15 explains the significance of these choices), though two-cable systems are also permitted. Each station detects collisions with its own packets by making a bit-by-bit comparison between the transmitted and received versions of the packet.

The token-bus algorithm was described in Chapter 10. Three distinct cable configurations are described with associated signalling conventions. All are based on CATV components but only one is broadband, the others being baseband systems designed for low-cost implementation.

The token ring system is similar to the IBM token ring described in Chapter 10. Shielded twisted pairs can be used at speeds up to 4M bit/s, whilst coax cable is defined for use at speeds up to 40M bit/s.

THE PROGRESS OF STANDARDISATION

Journalists like to ask questions such as 'When will there be a LAN standard?'. In the sense of a single, generally accepted, standard the answer is clearly 'never!'. There is no universal standard for terminal interfaces or for wide area networks, and LANs will be no different.

As with these other fields, however, a small number of field leaders will certainly emerge. These will, by sheer sales value, become tomorrow's *de facto* standards. There will also, of course, be *de jure* standards resulting from the work of the IEEE and others. These two processes will come together on at least two specifications:

1. The token ring. If, as seems likely, **IBM** announces office automation products based on the IEEE 4M bit/s ring, it will establish this technology very firmly in the market. The token ring has the potential for telephony as well as for data communications, so the possible market size is very considerable.

2. Ethernet. Xerox, Intel, and DEC already have a number of other companies interested in developments based on Ethernet. These companies include ICL, Siemens, Nixdorf, Ungermann-Bass, and Olivetti (Metcalfe, 1982). As the use of VLSI reduces the costs, many other companies are likely to produce Ethernet products.

It is also possible to identify a number of proprietary systems that may become *de facto* standards without the help of the standards community. In mainframe LANs, HYPERchannel is already the dominant product in its class and the range of interfaces now available will make it hard for a competitor to overtake it. The announcements by Tandem and SBS of HYPERchannel interfaces are important pointers here.

In the minicomputer networks field the main contender is Datapoint's ARCNet, which was the first such product to obtain a substantial user base. It was not until 1981 that Datapoint realized that ARCNet was a powerful selling point in itself, and its advertising campaign that year exploited this systematically for the first time. The announcement, in 1982, of a facsimile interface and of a deal with Tandy under which their micros can use ARCNet confirmed Datapoint's intention to develop their LAN further.

In the field of micronets, Zilog's Z-Net and Corvus's Omninet are possible contenders. Each is backed by a major participant in the micro market. Z-Net will become available on micros from other suppliers through licensing deals, whilst Corvus has a great deal of expertise already in interfacing its disc controllers to a wide variety of micros. It is, however, certainly too soon to predict the winners of this race and I shall not attempt to do so.

At higher levels of protocol we may identify five sources of standards:

1. The Xerox Systems Integration Standards. The success of these standards probably depends critically on the success of Xerox's own network systems, to which frequent reference has been made in this book.

2. The US Department of Defence. DoD's protocols have been developed through work on ARPANET and have influenced Xerox's protocols. They have also been packaged for Unix machines by 3Com as the Unet[tm] communications package.

3. ISO.

4. Digital Research. If CP/Net and MP/Net are as successful as CP/M has been then this will define a set of *de facto* standards.

5. IBM. Anything that IBM does is likely to be widely emulated.

At the time of writing one can only say—Watch this Space!

PART IV

Consequences and Implications

In November 1979, Technical Committee 6 of the International Federation for Information Processing (IFIP TC6) held a conference on Integrated Office Systems at Versailles. During that conference the workshop on Local Area Networks concluded that:

'Local networks are a means, not an end. They have no intrinsic value'. This was a rather surprising conclusion for a group of technical experts to reach, but it is basically correct. A local network has no intrinsic value—it cannot produce accounts or calculate stresses—but it adds value to computers that do have such value.

This part discusses the value that a LAN may contribute both in directly practical ways (Chapter 21) and in facilitating new architectures (Chapters 22 and 23).

21. THE PRACTICAL VALUE OF A LAN

The attempt to assess the real value of a LAN presents certain difficulties. There are certainly many people claiming to know the value of LANs but, when we have excluded the self-interested claims of suppliers, most of them are relying on general and theoretical arguments of the sort given in the first part of this book.

It is obviously desirable to base an assessment of LANs on the solid ground of user experience. Unfortunately, experience of local area networks is rather limited. Several thousand LANs had, by 1981, been installed throughout the world. Most fell into one of three categories:

1. Bundled LANs, installed as part of a distributed data or word processing system.
2. Home-built LANs, designed and built by the user organization, usually in order to learn more about LAN technology.
3. Pilot LANs, purchased from a commercial vendor but installed as part of a learning and evaluation exercise.

Bundled LANs are installed because the purchaser sees value in the complete application system. Until 1982 the Datapoint ARCNet was the biggest selling LAN, but the purchasers saw themselves as buying distributed processing systems, which happen to include a rather novel communications facility, rather than 'local area networks'. In other cases the system has been installed for word processing or office automation rather than data processing. In all these cases the LAN element has not usually been separately evaluated, or even costed, making the success of the LAN difficult to determine.

Home-built LANs have usually been intended to serve the needs of a population of real users (rather than network designers). They have typically been developed on an *ad hoc* basis and with the use of large amounts of expensive manpower. (See, for example, Christman, 1973.)

Pilot LAN installations have also usually involved highly skilled staff and have often been made without the usual cost-benefit exercises. Their small size, atypical users and, often, the near-experimental nature of the hardware, makes them unsuitable as a basis for general conclusions.

In interpreting the experience of existing LANs, then, there is a considerable lack of:

1. Accurate costings.
2. Experience of use and maintenance in commercial rather than research environments.
3. Comparisons with other technologies for local networking.

In consequence, this chapter will use a mixture of theoretical arguments and appeals to experience.

One or more of four reasons are usually given to justify the installation of a LAN. The same reasons are given by the suppliers of bundled systems to justify their choice of a LAN for their systems, so these two cases may be treated together. The reasons are:

1. To provide interworking between compatible machines.
2. To provide interworking between incompatible machines.
3. To provide resource sharing.
4. To provide the basis of a communications or systems architecture.

A LAN provides a suitable basis for the interconnection of machines that produce very bursty traffic, though it may also be used for other devices. In its most basic form the LAN provides for the transparent carriage of packets between the machines. LANs have been employed in this way so as to reduce the wiring costs or to simplify the network interfaces.

A LAN may go beyond transparent connection by providing conversions between the protocols native to the various attached devices. This increases the value of all the devices by easing the exchange of information between them.

It is often convenient to provide some group of users with only a single printer or other piece of hardware or a single instance of a file or database. The high speed of the LAN allows devices to access it as if it were local to them.

The final reason is sufficiently important to be dealt with separately in the next two chapters.

Chapter 7 indicated that LANs could be divided into five groups according to the most powerful data device that each kind of LAN can support effectively. The five kinds are:

1. Terminal support networks (TSNs).
2. Micronets—which support microcomputers.
3. Minicomputer networks.
4. Integrated office networks—which support mini and microcomputers, office machines and telephones.
5. Mainframe networks.

The significance of the various advantages claimed for LANs varies according to the kind of LAN in question.

TERMINAL SUPPORT NETWORKS

These networks are normally used to give a number of terminals access to one or more computers. They may also provide communication between terminals or, more usefully, between micros, word processors, or facsimile transceivers.

If all terminals need simultaneous access to the computer, then access might conventionally be provided by direct wiring. A LAN will involve much shorter cable runs than this configuration, though these will be balanced by the costs of the TSN interface units. Figure 21.1 shows the costs of supporting a population of terminals in a large open-plan office when the computer is either on the same floor or is ten floors away. The advantage of the TSN is much greater if the computer is on another floor, since all the direct cables then require line drivers.

It is clear that the TSN becomes cheaper than direct cables where the terminal penetration is high. The exact crossover point depends critically on the position of the terminals, presence of usable ducts, and on the particular TSN and terminals being compared. It also depends on the availability of a high-speed interface to the computer. Table 21.1 compares the costs of providing 30 computer access ports, with or without a high-speed multiplex interface of the kind discussed in Chapter 3. It is clear that the savings are considerable.

The LAN provides other advantages as well; it will be cheaper to extend to support extra terminals, cheaper to extend should it be necessary to move the computer, and it will support communications between terminals without involving the shared computer. In addition, it will be possible to add extra facilities, such as a telex interface and switch, without affecting the computer(s).

Where the terminals are thinly scattered round a large site, however, the LAN may easily be more expensive than direct connection by individual cables.

A number of special circumstances may change the balance between a TSN and direct cables for a particular site:

1. A need for secure circuits (usually obtained by encryption).
2. A need for non-electrical connections (usually obtained by the use of optical fibres).
3. A need for the cables to pass through electrically noisy or irradiated areas.
4. The ability to use existing cables—whether installed for telephony, CCTV, or other purposes—for the communications.

Any one of these circumstances can have a profound effect on the cost and even the feasibility of certain options. It is also necessary to be sure that the local requirements really are restricted to low-speed terminal-to-host communication. If there is a requirement for other communications then there may be advantages in using a single network for the several kinds of communications.

Where the average utilization of the terminals is expected to be fairly low there may be more terminals than computer ports. It is usually possible to restrict such terminals to speeds that are readily and cheaply available over telephone lines and

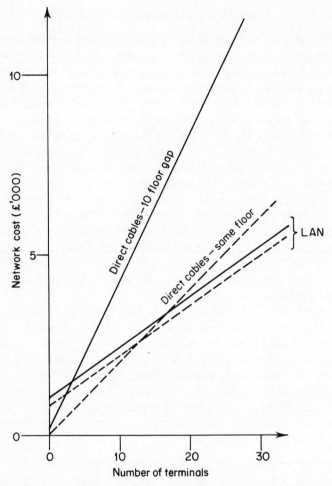

Figure 21.1   Costs of LAN and direct cable for terminal support.

Table 21.1   Cost comparison of multiplex and multiple simplex interfaces (typical cost of providing 30 logical ports in the United Kingdom, 1982).

30 Simplex connections		Multiplex connection	
30 computer ports at £250	£7,500	Computer port	£3,000
30 network ports at £150	£4,500	Network port	£2,500
1 chassis for network processor		Network processor	£1,000
with common logic	£1,000		
Total	£13,000	Total	£6,500

this may prove to be the cheapest solution for terminals that are used in this way. Where the utilization exceeds one or two hours per day, as it is likely to if the facilities offered are genuinely useful, then the cost of the switching capacity on the telephone system must be allowed for, and this will usually outweigh the costs of a separate data network.

Prior to 1981, most LAN-based terminal support networks used broadband techniques. They were significantly more expensive than has been assumed above, though their operating speeds and facilities were no better. Due to the high cost of modems and the skills needed to commission a broadband system, these TSNs were cost-effective only when a large site had to be served or when changes were especially frequent.

During 1981 a new generation of TSNs appeared that was based on minicomputer LANs. These provided a number of extra facilities, most notably switching, but were still rather expensive. LANs optimized for terminal support (notably by operating at low speeds) became available during 1982 (Willis, 1982).

In the future the TSN market is likely to become very competitive, depressing prices further. This will push the balance further towards LANs as that part of the cost due to electronics declines relative to that due to the purchase and installation of cables. Some TSNs are listed in Table 21.2.

A TSN may provide interworking between incompatible devices through the use of an attached protocol converter or by mapping all terminals to a network virtual terminal. This feature can be used, for instance, to allow ICL terminals to access IBM hosts, and vice versa. Such access can either provide convenience to the user or it can reduce the number of terminals that must be purchased. The most attractive use of protocol conversion, however, has been the substitution of (cheap) ASCII terminals for (expensive) synchronous terminals such as IBM 3270s.

Figure 21.2 shows the costs of providing access to synchronous computer ports using:

(a) The manufacturer's terminals.
(b) ASCII terminals and a protocol convertor on every synchronous port.

In a larger network where there are both ASCII and synchronous terminals and computer ports, the protocol convertor may be present as a network server. This is cost-effective where both terminals and ports are connected to incompatible devices for a significant part of the time.

A TSN may also provide conversion between word processors (which, although based on microcomputers, generally communicate by emulating terminals). These conversions are especially valuable in organizations that have installed a number of incompatible word processors. In the United Kingdom, at least, there are many such organizations. Interworking between incompatible word processors adds to operational convenience and is most cost-effective where there are a substantial number of such WPs with significant needs to exchange data. Since each individual word processor is unlikely to spend more than a few

Table 21.2   Terminal support network products.

Supplier	Network	Speed (bit/s)	Capacity-sharing algorithm	Notes
Sytek	LocalNet System 20	128k	CSMA/CD	Broadband
Real Time Developments	Clearway	56k	Register insertion ring	
Nine Tiles Information Handling	Multilink	250k	Register insertion ring	
IBM	R-Loop	20k, 38.4k	Polled ring	

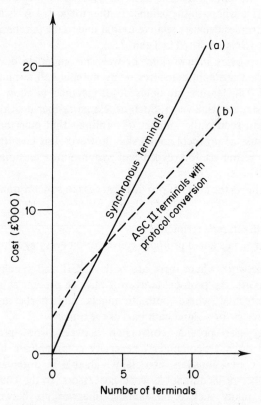

Figure 21.2   Costs of access to synchronous computer ports.

minutes in such communications each day, a single protocol convertor, shared through the TSN, can meet the needs of a large number of word processors.

Resource sharing is not generally a significant issue in TSNs, unless the computer ports are regarded as resources. Once installed to provide terminal-to-host communication, though, it can provide shared access to word processing, electronic mail, and gateways to other networks as shown in Figure 21.3. The economics of this depend on the proportion of the day during which each terminal

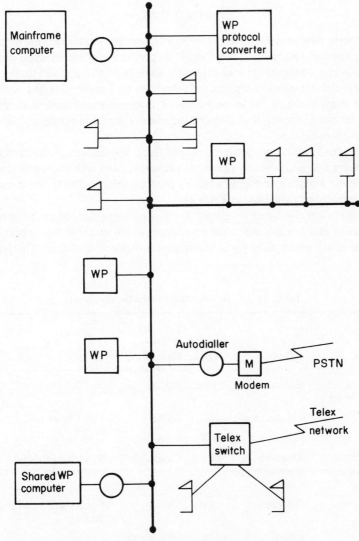

Figure 21.3 Resource sharing on a terminal LAN.

uses the shared facility; the higher the proportion, the less the advantage of sharing. In some cases the shared facility may exhibit economies of scale. In the case of a telex interface, for instance, the monthly rental can be shared amongst all the devices that use the connection.

Finally there is the question of convenience. Many users need to send a telex or type a letter occasionally. They will benefit from being able to do so from that terminal at which they more commonly interrogate databases or solve polynominals.

MICRONETS

Micronets now provide a cheap way to interconnect similar micros. By the end of 1981 the cost had fallen to less than $100 per micro for the cheapest products. Ring and bus configurations also provide savings in the costs of cable. Initial micronets did not provide support for terminals, thus preventing any economies through the sharing of cables and network management. Future networks will include terminal support, thus allowing the costs of the basic network to be shared amongst more devices.

Direct communication between micros finds application in electronic mail systems, for war and business games, and in schools and colleges, where it may be desirable for a teacher to follow a pupil's progress (Shirer, 1982). Some currently available micronets are listed in Table 21.3.

Micronets are also being developed to allow incompatible micros to interwork. This facility allows each individual user to install the machine that is best for his personal needs whilst allowing communication between machines. The practical

Table 21.3 Commercially available micronets.

Supplier	Network	Speed (bit/s)	Capacity-sharing algorithm	Notes
Digital Microsystems	Hi-Net	500k	Polling	
Nestar	Cluster One	240k	CSMA	For Apples
Acorn	Econet	210k	CSMA	
Research Machines	Research Machines Chain	800k	CSMA/CD	Z-Net and CP-Net compatible
Corvus	Omninet	1M	CSMA	For Apples and CP/M micros
Zilog	Z-Net	800k	CSMA/CD	

value of this is sharply reduced by a number of factors:

1. Micronets for a variety of machines are substantially more expensive than those for a single kind of micro.
2. Effective interworking between, for example, Apple Writer on an Apple and Wordstar on a Superbrain requires protocol conversion up to the presentation level (level 6) of the OSI Reference Model. In most practical cases the necessary conversions are not available.

The key to the development of micronets has been resource sharing, especially the sharing of fixed discs. The earliest micronets were developed as extensions to disc controllers and allowed several micro users to share the cost of the disc. The sharing of discs among a number of micros is desirable for reasons of economy, data integrity, performance, security and to avoid duplication.

Figure 21.4 shows the substantial returns to scale shown by disc storage, the cost of storing a single document on a large disc being as little as one-tenth that of using a single floppy disc. In addition, the storage on a 10M-byte fixed disc can be

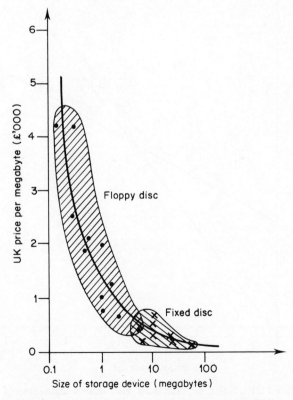

Figure 21.4   Returns to scale in data storage (1981).

more fully utilized than can that on a hundred 100k-byte floppy discs. One user's spare space may be borrowed by another user, provided that the controller can keep track of the space allocations (though this advantage is counterbalanced by the ability to hold a large library of floppies next to each micro, whilst the fixed unit must itself hold all the data that may be needed).

Figure 21.5 shows the resulting costs after these factors, and the costs of the micronet, have been allowed for.

Fixed discs also show much higher performance than floppies. The shorter seek times and higher transfer rates can, if the network has sufficient speed, enable a micro to load programs up to ten times faster. The large capacity of the fixed disc also allows a single user to work easily with files which would spread over several

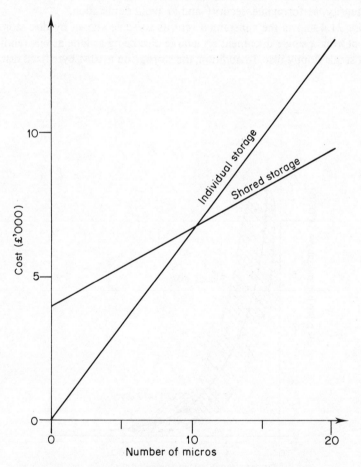

Figure 21.5   Costs of individual and shared data storage for microcomputers.

floppies, and to perform conveniently operations that would require repeated disc changes on a floppy-based machine. In the future, the power of an uprated disc controller may be available to provide associative searches of textual files, a valuable facility in emerging office systems.

The single fixed disc can be kept in its own room (which may be locked for most of the day). It can therefore be shielded from extremes of temperature and humidity, as well as from the common floppy experiences of being sat on, or drenched in coffee. Data will therefore be better preserved on the fixed unit and this advantage may be increased by taking a single archival copy of the whole unit at convenient intervals—a process that is often omitted altogether on a single-user system.

This approach also improves security. Confidential files can be restricted to selected users, with the door to the 'disc room' serving as a tangible barrier against intrusion.

Finally the use of a common filing system avoids the need to copy programs, address lists, survey data, etc., a process which takes time and often leads to there being multiple distinct copies—no one of which is completely accurate.

Other peripherals that can usefully be shared between several micros are high-speed and high-quality printers. Each is an expensive device for which a single user will have only occasional use. In the case of the high-speed printer, economies of scale apply, though to a lesser degree than for disc storage. There are also practical issues. To print a large document on a slow printer might take several hours. If a shared high-speed printer is used, the document may well be ready by the time the user has walked down the corridor to the print room. Even if it is not, the user can continue working on his own micro—it is not occupied in driving the printer.

The arguments are even stronger in the case of the letter-quality printer. Such a printer may cost as much as twice the price of an individual micro. Furthermore, it may need to print on a variety of stationery types at different times, and must be aligned precisely. These are tasks that are better done by a specialist operator than by the manager or professional who wrote the document. It will often be convenient for one person to combine the job of looking after the printer with that of typist or secretary. It is also desirable to confine the noise made by an impact printer to a room shared with other noisy machines, such as photocopiers and binders.

Similar arguments apply to the sharing of gateways to other networks. Cheap modems are becoming available for micros, but are restricted to low speeds. To use higher speeds, or to gain access to a sophisticated network such as SNA, or to a public data network, or to use a multiplex interface to a data processing computer, all require complex software that leaves little room in a micro for application programs. In any case users will typically have only intermittent needs to access such facilities so that fewer modems need be provided if they are shared.

Figure 21.6 shows, schematically, how a micronet could serve the office of a

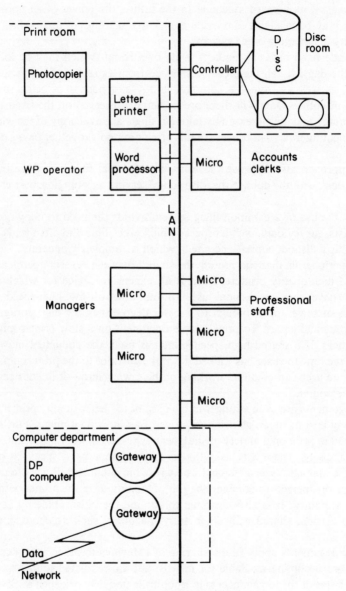

Figure 21.6   Office micronet.

company in the professional services field. A micronet forms a good basis for a distributed office automation system. If there are already a few micros, the network can readily be justified by savings achieved through resource sharing. It then provides a smooth upgrade path, with scope for almost unlimited expansion.

MINICOMPUTER NETWORKS

Minicomputer LANS provide communications between minicomputers and intelligent workstations based on powerful processors. They may also support microcomputers and terminals (usually by supporting a virtual circuit on top of the packet facility). Some minicomputer LANs are listed in Table 21.4.

Viewed as a means of interconnecting minicomputers a LAN offers only modest benefits. Though requiring less cabling than a conventional network, a LAN is only of substantial benefit if:

1. There is a significant number (more than, say, six) of computers on the site.
2. The computers are dispersed across the site.
3. The computers require high-speed communications.

Table 21.4   Commercially available minicomputer LANs.

Supplier	Network	Internal speed (bit/s)	Capacity-sharing algorithm	Notes
DEC Xerox Intel 3Com Interlan	Ethernet	10M	CSMA/CD	
Logica Toltec SEEL Racal–Milgo Acorn	Cambridge Ring	10M	Empty slot	Ring
Hasler	SILK	17M	Register insertion	Ring
Datapoint	ARCNet	2.5M	Token passing	Star
Wang	Wangnet Wang Band	12M	CSMA/CD	Broadband
Sytek	LocalNet System 40	2M	CSMA/CD	Broadband

Though not unknown, these conditions are not often met in practice. Such communications as are needed can often be provided by a mixture of magnetic tape exchange and data communication at terminal speeds.

In the future, the installation of intelligent workstations for engineers, managers, process operators, and other skilled staff will create a need for a suitable local network. Since micronets will typically be too slow, requirements for minicomputer LANs will develop.

The LAN might also be used to provide interworking between incompatible minis. The problems here reflect those of micronets. Effective interworking requires resolution of the differences in coding, filestore structure, job control language, and a number of other matters. Partial and *ad hoc* solutions have been developed in a number of research laboratories but no general solution is commercially available. In my view, no general solution is likely to become commercially available because:

1. Too few users require communications between incompatible minis. Only a large, and rather undisciplined, organization is likely to have a variety of incompatible minis on one site. These will usually have been acquired for well-defined tasks that were seen not to require interworking with incompatible machines. Used in this way, minis are less subject to the 'application sprawl' that forces mainframes into repeated upgrades. Minis are thus less likely to develop unforeseen communication requirements.
2. The task of resolving the incompatibilities is very complex, yet will rarely justify large-scale expenditure by the user since cheap *ad hoc* solutions are often possible.

A minicomputer LAN can also provide resource sharing. In the case of disc storage this is advantageous for workstations and small minis. Larger minis will usually justify their own disc units for performance reasons—access to a 30M-byte disc will usually be faster than a one-tenth share of a 300M-byte unit. Where exchangeable discs are used, the convenience of the operator will usually require the discs to be local. In principle, shared use of a large archive might be preferable to a local tape library, but most minis make too little use of tapes for this to be very advantageous.

Similar considerations apply to printers, except that an operator will certainly be needed in this case. Shared access to a communications gateway is advantageous but, with the low speed of trunk networks and the need, typically, for terminal handling logic, a LAN is not obviously the best choice. In the cases of both discs and printers, any distribution of functions is likely to be frustrated by the operating systems. Like those on mainframes, these generally assume the installation of all the system components in a small area.

These rather negative conclusions will be modified by changes in the market. As LAN interfaces become available, it will become attractive for vendors to introduce mini-LAN interfaces and minicomputer compatibility on such specialized devices as database machines, laser printers, COM units, and giant archives. Minicomputers may find some use for these machines; intelligent workstations certainly will.

INTEGRATED OFFICE NETWORKS

The Integrated Office Network (ION) is an extension of the minicomputer LAN. It has enough transmission speed, typically 10M bit/s, to support interworking between fairly powerful minis, and it can also support telephones, terminals, and microcomputers.

Viewed as a means of connecting similar machines, the ION offers no more than a minicomputer LAN, but the essence of the ION is that it connects dissimilar devices. The ION thus requires more internal complexity than other LANs and this makes it more expensive than any one of the other kinds. The complexity arises because of the different communications requirements of the various kinds of attached device. This is shown particularly clearly in Table 21.5. In addition the ION will need considerable bandwidth if it is to support any number of telephones.

By the end of 1981 three manufacturers—Hasler, Prolink, and Xionics—had announced IONs, but each was expensive for the simpler kinds of attached device. Amongst the vendors known to be actively working towards IONs were IBM, AT&T, Wang, and Olivetti.

The term ION indicates a network in which all the attached devices share a single logical LAN service; i.e. they all have access to the same shared bus. It therefore excludes broadband LANs in which devices of different kinds are connected to distinct services at different frequencies. A broadband LAN will be able

Table 21.5 Communications requirements.

Device	Peak speed (bit/s)	Typical peak/ average ratio	Tolerant of		Nature of communication
			Delay?	Error?	
ASCII terminal	1.2k	50	Yes (1 s)	No	Byte stream connection
Synchronous terminal	19.2k	100	Yes (3 s)	No	Bursty connection
Telephone	64k	$2\frac{1}{2}$	No	Yes	Connection
Microcomputer	500k	Very high	Yes (100 ms)	No	Datagram
Minicomputer	5M	Very high	Yes (100 ms)	No	Datagram

to avoid some of the complexities inherent in the ION, but it will be unable to deliver the same comprehensive support. Moreover, broadband systems will continue to be markedly more expensive than baseband systems for years to come.

A broadband LAN may be adopted as a halfway house, an interim solution that could be developed into either a full ION or a more sophisticated broadband cable. Figure 21.7 shows how this might happen over the next decade.

There seems little doubt that, at least during 1983 and 84, it will be cheaper to install a number of separate networks than to install a single ION. After that date, the cost of the complex logic needed in an ION may have fallen sufficiently to make it attractive in direct economic terms. In general, an ION will be cheaper than separate networks if:

1. There is a wide variety of devices to be supported.
2. The site is physically large, increasing the importance of cabling costs.
3. The organization needs to move people and equipment at short notice.
4. There is a large number of minicomputers and intelligent workstations.
5. The site is inadequately provided with ducts for cables.

Even before costs have fallen substantially there will be other advantages in the ION. It will support interworking between the various kinds of attached device.

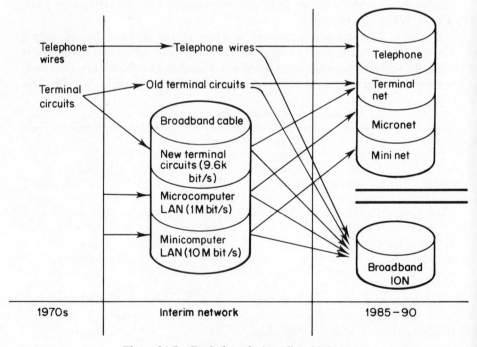

Figure 21.7   Evolution of a broadband LAN.

Though this can be achieved by the use of suitable gateways and protocol convertors, it rapidly becomes very cumbersome and is unlikely to be implemented comprehensively. An ION will encourage the development of links between systems and applications leading to improved communications within the organization. The ION will also reduce the disruption otherwise involved in moving people and equipment.

The importance of these advantages must be considered by each organization for itself but it appears that, for most European organizations, the technical problems are too great and the penetration of data processing and office automation systems too low to justify a commitment to an ION before the mid-1980s. For many organizations there will be no need even then because of the central restriction of installed machines to a few, largely compatible, types, or because of the prior installation of a satisfactory network of one of the simpler kinds.

IONs provide little extra in the area of resource sharing, but they do open opportunities for new systems architectures.

MAINFRAME LANs

Most mainframe computers have been developed to operate in isolation from other computers, except insofar as they manage subsidiary processors in order to complete their own tasks. The attitude of their designers has been compared, unkindly but truly, with the Ptolemaic view of the universe that was overturned by Copernicus.

This view provides little scope for communication between mainframes, though most manufacturers have introduced multiprocessor systems that involve high-speed communication over very short distances.

Large users have, however, developed various needs for communications between their large computers. These needs are based on more fundamental needs:

1. The need to use specialized machines.
2. The need to share work between large computers.
3. The need to preserve existing investment in software.
4. The need to run a collection of incompatible machines as a coherent computing utility.

In many cases a computer centre has started with a single large mainframe and has enhanced it progressively to meet needs for greater computing power and more online access. When the limits of the original system are reached, further needs for computer power may be met by a 'supercomputer' such as the Cray 1, an extra mainframe, or a specialized machine such as ICL's Distributed Array Processor (DAP). The need for more online access will be best met through front-end processors to manage the terminal network and to support users in operations, such as editing files, that do not need the power of a mainframe.

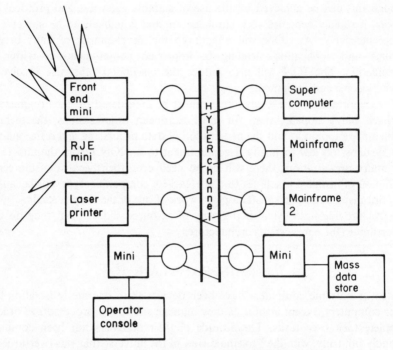

Figure 21.8   Computer centre with HYPERchannel.

The computer centre may also have specialized peripherals such as graph plotters, microfilm cameras, very large archives, and laser printers. It is not always convenient to attach these permanently to a single mainframe, if only because any failure of that machine would make the peripherals unavailable to all the machines.

Shared peripherals, and the need to adapt rapidly as individual machines fail or are removed for maintenance, complicate the operational control of the computer room considerably—even discovering the state of the several machines can become a complex task. It is therefore attractive to use a specialized machine to support and assist the computer operators.

A large computer centre can therefore easily find itself with a need for communication among half a dozen or more incompatible machines, and a suitable LAN can readily find application in such an environment. The LAN will need a high operating speed, and it will need to connect to suitable high-speed interfaces on the various machines. Since these interfaces will generally have been developed for quite different purposes, such as controlling a set of disc drives, considerable software development is likely to be needed.

A large computer user may have many millions of pounds worth of computer equipment, and an investment in data and systems that is at least an order of magnitude greater and is essential to his business. Such users are able to invest substantial sums in order to meet their needs.

By 1982 HYPERchannel was the only product that could form the basis of such computer room communication. (Though CDC's Loosely Coupled Network tackles some of these problems, it is only offered in conjunction with CDC computers.) HYPERchannel provides communications at up to 200M bit/s between a wide variety of mainframes and large minis. Figure 21.8 shows a typical HYPERchannel installation, somewhat idealized (Binney, 1981; Thornton, 1980; Wolfendale, 1980). Similar systems have been developed by a number of sophisticated users. These include the Manchester University Exchange and the Octopus network at the Lawrence Livermore Laboratory (Fletcher *et al*, 1975).

SUMMARY

It is clear that LANs can provide real practical benefits. These benefits depend on the circumstances of the site being considered.

When used to connect compatible machines, a LAN does offer a 'data ring main'. It saves on cable and installation costs and provides communications managers with operational flexibility.

The value of a LAN increases with the number of connected devices, the distance between them, and the number of logical connections to the network that each needs.

A LAN offers benefits when considered purely as a means of connecting terminals to computers. Direct financial benefits arise from savings on wiring and from the use of multiplex computer interfaces.

In the other cases, however, the costs and value of inter-computer communication will rarely be sufficient, on their own, to justify the LAN.

When a LAN is used to enable incompatible devices to interwork it provides some convenience to users and some financial savings. The savings are greatest where the pattern of accesses fluctuates most widely and unpredictably. This advantage is limited, however, by the lack of suitable protocol conversion software.

Interworking between incompatible machines requires large investments in development effort. It is therefore important for terminals, where the volumes are great, and for mainframes, where the benefits are great. It is less likely to be beneficial in other cases.

It is in resource sharing, though, that LANs have been most valuable. Resource sharing is attractive where the resource needs special operating skills, where it is very expensive, where there are economies of scale, where the resource is physically intrusive (e.g. noisy), and where the application requires there to be a single resource. One or more of these conditions is met in the case of printing and data storage in many DP and office automation systems, and resource sharing is the feature that has done most to justify LANs.

All the advantages are largely financial. They are therefore readily understood by management, and may be used to justify the purchase of a LAN without any need to raise the complexities of LAN operation or of systems architecture.

This, however, is a mixed blessing. It may lead to certain costs, the cost of cabling, for instance, being overlooked, and it may also lead to short-sighted decisions. As with computers and word processors, it may lead to the installation of a number of incompatible local networks with unfortunate, and expensive, long-term results.

CAVEATS

Several general cautions are necessary at this point.

1. I have written that a LAN 'can do' this or that. These are general statements of technical feasibility, and it does not follow that every, or in some cases, any, commercially available LAN actually does do the functions described.
2. Where a commercial product does provide the function discussed the supplier may make an extra charge, thus upsetting the apparent economics.
3. The machines and cables already installed may make it impossible to realize some of these advantages. It may be cheaper to extend an existing system than to install a completely new one.
4. Many of the products offered in the market are new. They have been developed, and will be maintained, by companies with little track record in communications technology. They may not work well, or even at all!

In short, the selection and installation of a LAN is a task requiring professionalism and care. The final part of this book shows how the general principles of requirements definition and product evaluation may be applied to the choice of a LAN. But first I will discuss the new architectures made possible by LANs.

22. NEW COMMUNICATIONS ARCHITECTURES

The power and flexibility of the LAN provide a number of opportunities for new approaches to the design of communications networks. From the architectural point of view, the key features of the LAN are:

1. It supports the sharing of expensive resources among user devices.
2. It provides universal connectivity at relatively high speed without masses of direct cables.
3. It eases the addition and removal of devices, allowing a wide variety of system configurations to be created and then varied to meet the changing needs of the users.

A variety of novel communications architectures can be based on LANs; this chapter discusses two of them. Since there is no standard terminology for discussing architectures, I have been obliged to name them informally as the Terminal Service Architecture and the Two-Bus Architecture.

Figure 22.1 shows a schematic of a conventional data network. A central mainframe supports local terminals via a local cluster controller. Communications with remote terminals are via a communications processor and trunk circuits to cluster controllers at the remote sites. Virtual circuits are multiplexed on the trunk circuits using a protocol that is common to the communications processor and the cluster controller.

This network might be implemented using components from any one of a dozen suppliers. In the case of an IBM installation, the protocol would be SDLC and the components might be:

3081 mainframe
3705 communication processor
3274 cluster controller
3278 terminal
trunk circuits from the PTT or a common carrier

The network architecture, as distinct from the topology, is shown in Figure 22.2. This figure serves to illustrate a diagram convention that will also be used later to present the new architectures.

259

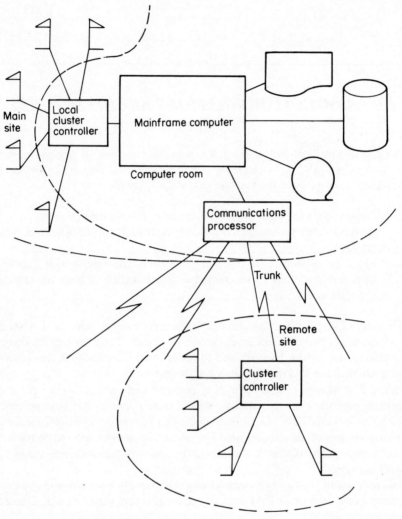

Figure 22.1   Conventional data network.

TERMINAL SERVICE ARCHITECTURE

This architecture is based on a terminal support network (TSN). Terminals of various kinds may be connected to the TSN, either through individual interface units or, where terminals are clustered together, through a multiplexor.

The TSN will offer a number of communications services, including a replacement for direct connections and circuits switched under user control. There will also be a name server from which the user can determine the nature and addresses of the facilities currently accessible via the TSN.

Computers will normally be connected to the network through a high-speed

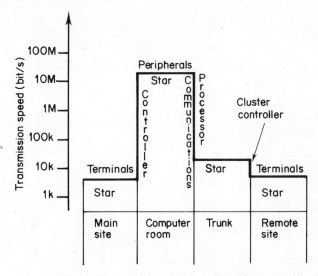

Figure 22.2   Conventional architecture.

multiplex connection, but low-speed channels will be available for computers for which no suitable network interface is available. The use of the more complex interface will allow the TSN to maintain a closer check on the status of the attached computers. This information may be made available to users via the name server or via a separate network 'noticeboard'. Attached computers will be able to post messages to this noticeboard.

The architecture allows other services to be attached, limited only by the ingenuity of the developers. Obvious examples include gateways to public data networks, electronic mail servers, telex interfaces, and interfaces to the PSTN.

Figure 22.3 shows what a typical network might look like when implemented under this architecture. The architecture itself is depicted in Figure 22.4.

Where terminals communicate in burst of tens or hundreds of bytes the traffic can be carried by any kind of LAN and layered protocols used at and above the data link level (Marathe and Hawe, 1982). Though the overhead, which is typically 50–150 per cent., is substantial, even a TSN has a sufficiently high speed to make this of little account.

A different case arises with systems in which the transmission is by single bytes. This technique is used to good effect in the Unix system to enable application programs to look at each key depression. Since different programs attach significance to keys in different ways, it is necessary to pass every byte directly to the host computer, and this is often done before displaying it on the user's screen. The host will normally echo the character to the screen ('echoplex' working) as a check, but it may decide to revise the whole screen on the basis of that one character.

In this case the use of layered protocols will impose an overhead which is

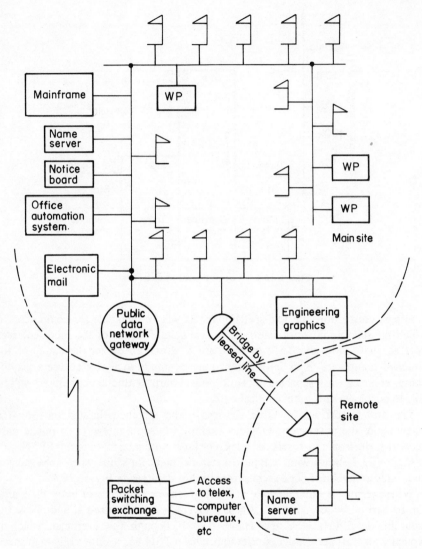

Figure 22.3   Resource sharing on a terminal support network.

unlikely to be less than 1,000 per cent. The Xerox protocols described in Chapter 17 would impose a much greater overhead than that. Those protocols, of course, were not designed to support terminals.

This overhead may overload both the TSN and its interface units, yet the inclusion of headers for high-level protocols in each packet offers little value to the terminal user. It may therefore be desirable to use a more compact and economical protocol to support these terminals. (A suitable protocol for the Cambridge Ring has been discussed by Rubinstein, Kennington, and Knight, 1981.) It is sometimes

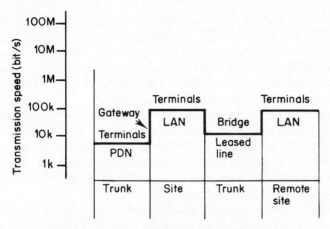

Figure 22.4   The terminal service architecture.

possible to avoid this problem by exporting the echoing of bytes to the TSN interface unit under the general control of the host computer. In many cases, however, the interface unit has too little processing power for this to be feasible.

Higher Level Protocols

The Terminal Service Architecture will need to include a number of protocols above the data link level. At the network level a routing protocol will be needed so that several data links can be installed on a single site and in order to support the use of inter-site bridges. This problem has been addressed in Sytek's LocalNet (discussed in Chapter 15) where the distinct data links are the separate frequencies used by System 20 services.

At the transport level the architecture will need a connection-orientated protocol which will operate between processes in the interface units (Davidson, 1982). Processes in terminal interface units represent the corresponding terminals whilst those in host interface units represent the virtual computer ports to which those terminals may work.

A standard protocol will be required to access the name server and notice-board. These may be implemented as either distributed (Davidson, 1982) or shared (centralized) facilities.

The architecture may stop at that level, in which case it will only provide a transparent service between terminals and hosts, a direct wire replacement. As discussed in the last chapter the general problem of device incompatibility may be relieved by providing protocol convertors (i.e. convertors of session and presentation layer protocols) on the network. Unfortunately the number of such convertors increases as the square of the number of protocols to be supported. Above a certain, modest, number a better solution is needed.

There are two main approaches to this problem: parametric control and the virtual terminal (Day, 1981). The parametric approach has been used in the CCITT '3X' protocols (CCITT Recommendations X.3, X.28, and X.29) as shown in Figure 22.5. The essence of this approach is that each terminal describes itself, using X.28, to an X.3 Packet Assembler–Disassembler (PAD). The host then obtains this desciption, the 'PAD parameters', from the PAD using X.29, and must adjust its own terminal handling accordingly.

Though simple for the network designer, the approach has several defects. The number of parameters tends to increase rapidly as the range of terminals is widened. X.29 specifies only 12, but Telenet, a US common carrier, has 50 in its corresponding protocol and a new proposal lists more than 120. Worse than this is the fact that each new parameter must be understood by every host, undermining the advantage of the standard protocol.

In the virtual terminal approach, an idealized network virtual terminal (NVT) is defined for host-to-terminal traffic within the network. The usual way of using this to date (for instance, on ARPANET) has been for hosts to drive all terminals as if they were NVTs, and for Terminal Interface Processors (TIPs) adjacent to the terminals, to convert between NVT and the properties of actual terminals.

An alternative, which might be more attractive when the terminal control functions of the host are already fixed, is for a Host Interface Processor (HIP) to convert host terminal handling to NVT. Both arrangements are shown in Figure 22.6 and the application of the principle to the support of ASCII terminals on 3270 ports is shown as a protocol diagram in Figure 22.7.

In practice, for simplicity, most NVTP systems attempt only to convert between terminals of broadly similar designs. Terminals are therefore divided into a number of classes, typically:

Scroll terminal
Page terminals
Data entry terminals

In the future further classes—graphics terminals for instance—may have to be added.

The chief advantages of this architecture are essentially those of the TSN that is its main component:

1. The network uses less cable than conventional stars.
2. Because of this, it is more attractive to run the LAN to all points at which terminals might eventually be required, thus making moves very simple.
3. The network can be independent of any particular supplier of computers or word processors.
4. New devices can be connected immediately using the transparent service, and given access to the network virtual terminal protocol at a later date.
5. Interworking between incompatible devices is supported.
6. All terminals can be given the use of a new service without changing any

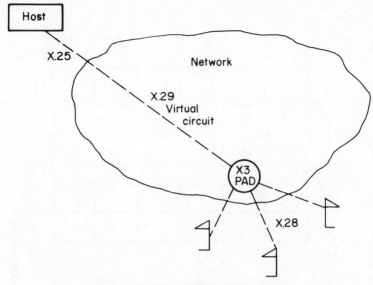

Figure 22.5   The CCITT '3X' protocols.

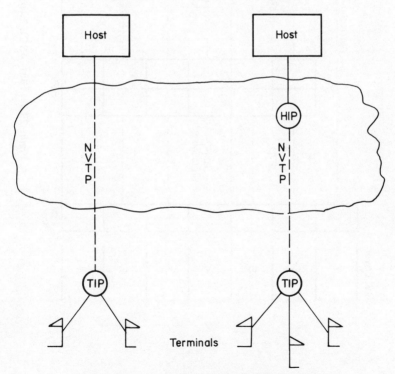

Figure 22.6   Network Virtual Terminal Protocol.

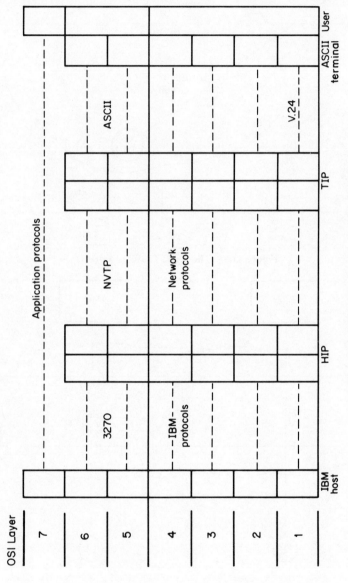

Figure 22.7   IBM–ASCII interworking via NVTP.

existing computers, and without requiring extra cables. The new service is simply attached to the network and its name declared to the name server.

7. Network operation is independent of any host and thus more reliable.

By early 1982 no vendor had announced a system based on a full terminal service architecture, though Ungermann-Bass (Net/One), Sytek (LocalNet) and

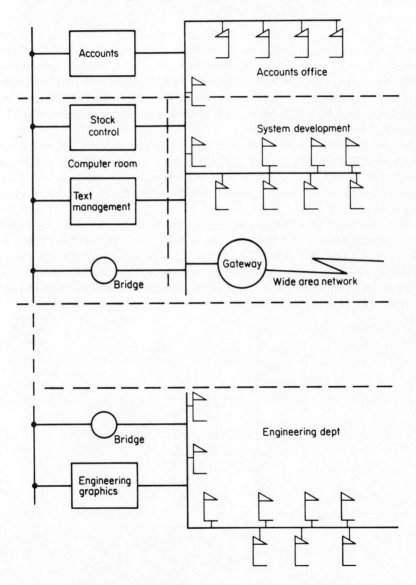

Figure 22.8 Terminal support in a two-bus architecture.

Network Systems Corporation (HYPERbus) had announced sophisticated terminal support networks. No vendor had based his system on a NVTP. Being based on high-speed buses both Net/One and HYPERbus are able to support minicomputers and intelligent workstations as well as terminals.

THE TWO-BUS ARCHITECTURE

Though cheap and flexible, the Terminal Service Architecture fails to provide high-speed data transmission services, the need for which was identified in Chapter 4. Since terminals are often much more widely dispersed around a site than are computers, there is the possibility of using one LAN for the terminals and another, faster but more expensive, for the computers (thus reflecting the division between data circuit and office wideband communications developed in Chapter 4 and shown in Figure 4.1).

Figure 22.8 shows how this architecture might be used on a site with several computers. The terminals are all attached to a terminal support network through which they are able to access both the computers and other resources. The TSN is carried to all parts of the site in order that existing and future terminals can easily be connected.

Since the range of a TSN is sometimes rather limited, it may be convenient to use the minicomputer LAN to provide a bridge between separate TSNs. For instance, on a large site each building might have its own computers and TSN but be joined by a minicomputer LAN. The figure shows this method used to link a main building, containing several departments, with an engineering department a little distance away.

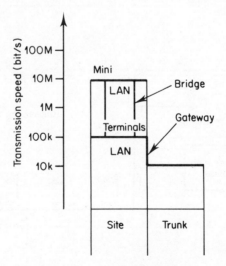

Figure 22.9   Two-bus architecture.

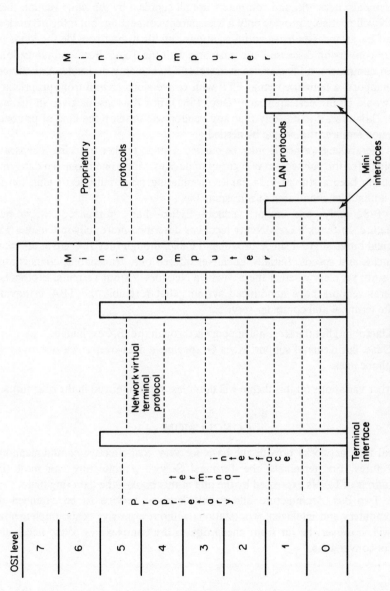

Figure 22.10 Protocols in the two-bus architectures.

Figure 22.9 shows the speeds and places covered by this architecture. Figure 22.10 shows the protocols used in the architecture.

If terminals, network, and computers are all supplied by the same vendor, then the TSN will probably provide only a transparent connection; but if the network is supplied by an independent communications vendor it may provide the kinds of protocol conversion discussed in connection with the TSA. For communications between computers, a file transfer protocol (FTP) is highly desirable. As with terminal support, a network virtual FTP with conversions to and from proprietary FTPs would be the best approach (Day, 1981). For the reasons given in the last chapter, however, it is unlikely that any vendor will develop the kind of protocol conversion features that would be needed.

This hierarchical principle may be carried a stage further by using a separate technology for the connection of a group of devices within one room. To date, this has usually been a star of V.24 cables terminating on a multiplexor unit, but in future it might be an infrared or ultrasonic bus.

By 1982 only one major vendor—Sytek—had announced a two-bus architecture. In Sytek's LocalNet (which was described more fully in Chapter 15) the logical buses share a single broadband cable, though they operate at different frequencies and speeds. Initially LocalNet offered only transparent connections, and it is not yet clear whether there will be a Network Virtual Terminal Protocol.

Several vendors have announced systems that resemble the TBA in having separate terminal and computer services:

1. Datapoint, but the terminal support is through the ISX exchange.
2. Case, but terminal support is via Grapevine, a data-over-voice system using phone lines.

Further variations on this theme will doubtless be announced in the near future.

CONCLUSION

Local area networks provide the basis for very cost-effective communications architectures. For terminals, the Terminal Service Architecture can meet the expectations of LANs expressed by the title of this book—the data ring main.

The Two-Bus Architecture allows this level of service to be extended to minicomputers and intelligent workstations without excessive costs. Implementations will, however, be far from cheap due to the complexities of the necessary protocol conversions.

23. *NEW SYSTEMS ARCHITECTURES*

LANs provide new opportunities to the designers of processing systems, as well as to those of communications networks. The features of LANs with the greatest importance to the systems architect are that:

1. Expensive resources may be shared between user devices.
2. The component parts of a system may be separated in space. Conventional systems, by contrast, often require components to be in the same room and processes to be in the same computer.

A wide variety of new architectures can be based on a LAN. This chapter discusses three of them—Workstation Network Architecture, Office Machines Architecture, Distributed Mainframe Architecture—together with the processing systems which embody them.

Each of these architectures, like each new communications architecture, is related to one or more kinds of LAN. The relationships are shown in Figure 23.1.

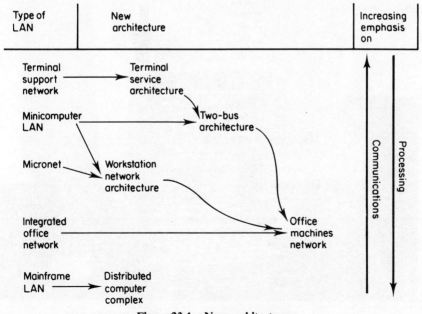

Figure 23.1   New architectures.

271

THE WORKSTATION NETWORK

A distributed processing system may be based on components of the following three kinds:

1. Workstations that provide the local processing needs of individual users.
2. Servers that support and coordinate the work of the individual workstations.
3. A LAN to link workstations and servers.

As discussed in Chapter 3, these workstations will be based on computers supplemented by the displays and other peripherals appropriate to the needs of the user. The architecture may be implemented using computers with sizes varying from an 8-bit Apple to a 32-bit supermini, depending on the users and their applications. In each case, it is likely to be the workstations which provide most of the value and which incur most of the cost—hence the name.

Workstations have been developed by a number of commercial and research organizations. Managerial workstations have been developed by Office Technology Ltd. (Davies, 1982) and professional workstations by Xerox (Fishburn, 1982) and Bolt, Beranek, and Newman (Greenfeld, 1982). Engineering and programmers' workstations have been developed by Symbolics, Three Rivers, and Apollo Computers.

Figure 23.2 shows the Buroviseur—an integrated workstation developed at

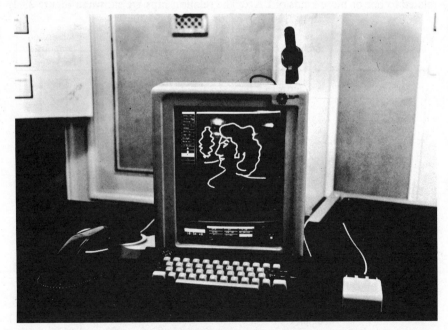

Figure 23.2   The Buroviseur workstation. (Courtesy of Kayak.)

INRIA in France (Naffah, 1981). This workstation can manipulate speech, data, text, and image and can also be used as a telephone.

Microcomputer Workstations

The use of personal microcomputers in offices has been inhibited by two factors:

1. The limited power of the individual micro.
2. The lack of any means of coordinating the work of individual micros.

The Workstation Network Architecture addresses both of these problems.

The prices of processor chips are already so low that very large amounts of processing power can be afforded—during 1981 a move towards 16-, and even 32-, bit chips was already apparent. The limitation on auxiliary storage can, of course, be remedied by sharing a large fixed disc, and file servers with capacities up to 300M bytes were expected during 1982.

The effective size of the main store may be increased by overlay techniques. The high transfer rate of fixed disc and network makes it possible to overlay or page both programs and data, where a floppy disc would simply be too slow.

The effective size may be increased in another way as well. A stand-alone micro (or other computer) must run the code for support functions as well as for applications. These functions include print formatting, printer control, disc management, and the implementation of communications protocols. In a LAN all these tasks may, as shown in Figure 23.3, be transferred to shared utilities and replaced by the LAN interface. The economy inherent in this architecture may be used to reduce the cost of the individual workstation or to increase its capabilities.

The LAN itself provides a channel for rapid communications between workstations. To use this channel to coordinate the work of the various programs and users will, of course, require suitable software. Initial versions of micronet software such as CP/Net inhibited this by failing to support peer communications. A similar problem recurs at the application software level, where the maintenance of compatibility with single machine, and monolithic, operating systems such as Apple DOS, has inhibited the necessary developments.

To realize the advantages made possible in a network of microcomputer workstations will require new thinking on the part of system developers. In the micronet market, effective exploitation of the new architectural possibilities remains a task for the future.

The economies in main storage are less significant for workstations based on 16-, rather than 8-, bit computers.

Shared Network Resources

The workstation network will include a file server to provide workstations with the use of large, high-performance files and with access to shared data (Swinehart,

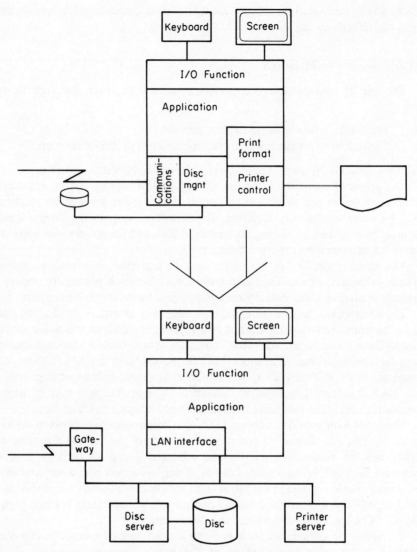

Figure 23.3   Enlarging the power of the micro.

McDaniel, and Boggs, 1979). For text systems, the file server may provide associative retrieval through the use of special hardware and software (Harding, 1982). For data processing applications, especially where several applications must share the files, the server may provide data independence and maintain a complex logical structure in the data, i.e. it will perform the functions of a Database Management System (DBMS) (Canaday *et al*, 1974; Farrel, 1976; Lowenthal, 1982).

Though some workstations may have their own printers there will usually be a print server. This will use one of the modern non-impact techniques to allow printing of both text and graphics at high speed. A powerful print server may be based on a laser-xerographic printer and can replace both office printers and duplicators, thus reducing the need for manual handling of the printed output.

Gateways to other networks and computer systems may be established as communications servers. In some cases they will be invoked automatically by the attempt to use some other facility and will be transparent to the user, who will suppose the alien system to be part of the workstation network.

The server concept need not be restricted to such universal functions as filing, printing, and communications. There may be servers for compilation and for specialized kinds of computation—array processing for instance. There may also be servers for applications that need to be accessed by several users. These might, according to circumstances, include staff time recording, expense claim processing, electronic mail, electronic publishing, the arranging of meetings, and the updating of a shared program library.

These applications share the characteristic that they require the server to exercise some privilege that could not be freely extended to all users, e.g. the right to update payroll files or to inspect users' personal diaries. The server gives the user all the legitimate benefits of that privilege and assists him in his task, but also imposes appropriate disciplines. General principles for the design of servers have been discussed by Needham (1981).

The assistance provided by the server might include guidance in staying within the rules for expense claims, which are very complex in some organizations. Disciplines might include the referral of expense claims to the correct authorizing officer before payment, or the restriction of update access to a particular program to one programmer.

Process Structure in WNA

There are several advantages in constructing a large software system as a set of communicating processes. The most important are:

1. The definition of compact individual components which are easier and faster to construct than the corresponding parts of monolithic systems.
2. Localization of errors to a single process.
3. The ability to re-use processes in similar but different systems.
4. The ability to assemble new systems dynamically as needed by users.

These advantages, however, only obtain if the interfaces between the components are designed for the purpose. They must, in particular, be specified in terms of logical service requests and responses rather than in terms of the supposed behaviour of the communicating processes.

A LAN allows designers freedom as to where they place particular processes, and the workstation network may exploit this in several ways. Figure 23.4 shows a series of processes that are supporting a user in analysing data held partly in conventional files and partly in a database.

In a stand-alone system, of course, all the processes will run on that system. If the system is a minicomputer, and more especially if it is a microcomputer, there may be insufficient resources to allow this structure to be used, and a monolithic system with less flexibility will result.

In a centralized system the division of functions is made at E–E', so that only the components in direct association with the workstation hardware are run in the workstation.

In the first resource-sharing micronets, the functions were divided at about the line denoted by A–A'. Again the processes in the workstation were simplified and consolidated due to shortage of resources, and also because the similarities between micros and other computers were seen less clearly at that time. In addition, these early systems provided only a single shared disc unit.

The Workstation Network Architecture (WNA) formalizes the protocols necessary to use the processes, and provides a standard means of invoking proceses across the network. WNA thus makes it easy to vary the way in which processes are allocated to machines.

Figure 23.4 shows several ways in which the processes might be divided between a workstation and a shared server:

1. B–B' divides the system into file, database, and data dictionary servers which provide the common functions related to data. The workstation then provides the query processing functions.
2. Line C–C' differs only in including the processing needed to support a variety of user views in the database server.
3. Line D–D' restricts the workstation to just those functions needed to support the dialogue with the user.

Each of these partitionings of the total processing has advantages in certain circumstances. Centralization will be favoured by low utilization of the workstation and requirements for very large amounts of processing. Distribution will be favoured by high workstation utilization and by the existence of great variety in the tasks that the users undertake.

It has been usual in the past to fix the division between central and distributed elements at the time the system was originally conceived. This approach has prevented many manufacturers from exploiting the opportunities provided by

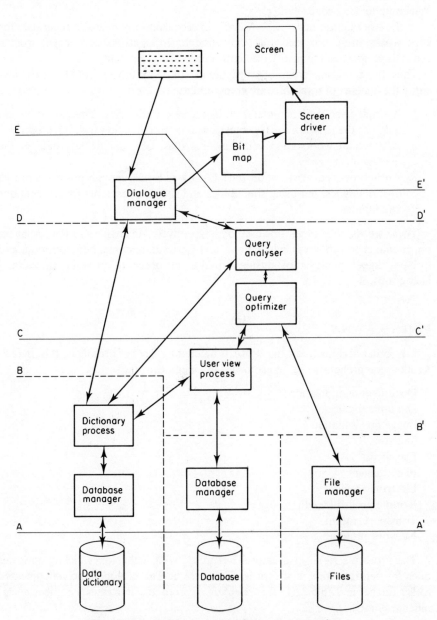

Figure 23.4   Process structure for query processing.

microcomputers, just as they were unable to exploit the advantages of minicomputers a decade earlier.

In the workstation network, however, this decision may be made separately for each workstation, provided only that enough workstations can benefit from a centralized approach to justify the central processing capability.

Thus the following types of workstation, amongst others, could coexist and enjoy the benefits of total software compatibility:

1. A single user minicomputer with its own local disc files. This station would only use the network for file transfer and communication with other users.
2. A powerful workstation with no local files, not running any data or file management processes.
3. An abbreviated workstation (line D–D') with just enough power to run its own dialogues, but using shared files and shared processors for applications and utilities.

These workstations might be used by, respectively, an engineer, a lawyer, and a line manager to run stress calculations, text retrieval, document composition, and (pre-packaged) analysis of business trends in order to produce tables and histograms.

Protocols in WNA

Like other architectures, the WNA is defined by a set of protocols. It is, in fact, a rather comprehensive set of protocols and includes:

Document manipulation
Data manipulation
Image manipulation
Statistics
File access
File transfer
Electronic mail
Remote procedure call
Transport station
Network protocol

The protocols stand in a natural hierarchy, with higher ones calling on lower ones for services; this is shown in Figure 23.5. The protocols are documented rather further in Table 23.1. This selection of protocols illustrates a number of significant points:

1. At level 5 of the OSI model, and above, processes are unable to tell (except, perhaps, by timing effects) whether they are interacting with local or remote processes. The procedure call protocol conceals this fact.

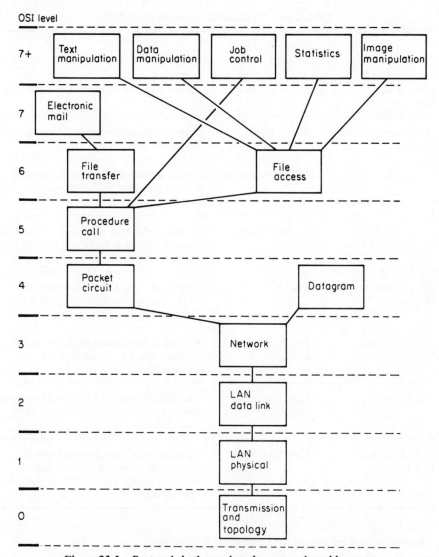

Figure 23.5   Protocols in the workstation network architecture.

2. The same protocol may be interpreted differently by different processors and on different occasions. Thus the data manipulation protocol provides direct control of stored data when directed to the file manager but not when directed to either component of the database system.

Figure 23.6 shows the protocol structure used in Xerox 8000 series network systems. It differs in many important respects from the hypothetical example

Table 23.1   Workstation network protocols.

Protocol	Process(es) by which interpreted	Other notes
Job control language	Job scheduler	Causes tasks to be loaded, given access to files, etc.
Data manipulation language	File manager	Causes file manager to act directly on stored records
	User view process	Causes actions on records in the user view maintained by the database system
	Database manager	Causes actions on records as defined in the conceptual schema maintained by the database manager
Text manipulation language	Text manager	Causes changes to text documents or to the textual parts of composite documents
Electronic mail	Electronic mail server	Recovers documents from the server or sends them to it for onward forwarding
File transfer	File transfer process	Copies files, parts of files and views, or parts of views, of databases to other files and views
Data dictionary language	Data dictionary	Notifies the dictionary manager of changes in managed storage and retrieves the characteristics of parts of that storage

discussed above but shows the same general principles:

1. The protocols are defined explicitly.
2. The protocols are arranged in a hierarchy that covers everything from signalling levels on the cable to the format and interpretation of print files.

Xerox is publishing the protocols used in their network systems in order, as with Ethernet, to create *de facto* standards. Similar standards at this level may be derived from IBM's SNA, Digital Research's CP/Net, and the US Department of Defence protocols (promoted by 3Com through their Unet package for Unix computers).

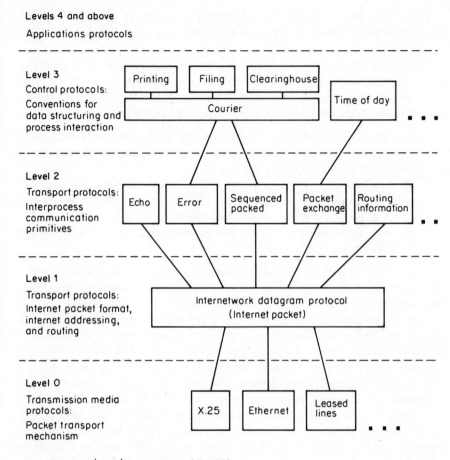

Figure 23.6 Xerox systems integration protocols. (Courtesy of the Xerox Corporation.)

Developments in the Workstation Network

The basic objective of the Workstation Network has been to provide autonomous user workstations with communications facilities and access to various shared resources. There is, however, another way to view the same system. It can be seen as a single multi-processor computer whose components happen to be physically separate.

Locally distributed applications have been reported in the fields of simulation (Chandy, Holmes, and Misra, 1979), experiment support (Pohm *et al*, 1979), computer-based instruction (Shirer, 1982), and database management (Nickens, Genduso and Su, 1980).

Shoch and Hupp (1980b) have reported research at Xerox's Palo Alto Research Center aimed at realizing the potentialities of this approach in a systematic way.

PARC has developed a number of 'Worm' programs which run concurrently on several machines, liase between themselves, and cause further worm 'segments' to be loaded onto workstations (Alto personal computers in this case) that fall idle. This distributed computing facility may be used in several ways:

1. By replicating data between worm segments, a super-reliable system can be constructed. Segments on machines that fail are automatically replaced so long as the network remains live.
2. By distributing the parts of a large job to many machines, the effect of a very large computer may be realized. This provides a valuable way of using up the spare capacity that would otherwise exist overnight.
3. By using both principles, a large and super-reliable computing facility may be obtained.

Shoch and Hupp report the use of worms to provide a reliable alarm clock, an electronic mail system with active delivery, a computer animation system, and a diagnostic program for testing transceivers in pairs.

Real applications of this interesting principle require further study but it does promise the ability to overcome one significant disadvantage of the workstation network—the comparatively modest limit on the size of the largest job that can be run. The key problem at present is the difficulty of partitioning serial programs into parts capable of parallel execution. This remains an active research area (see, for instance, El-Dessouki, Huen, and Evens, 1981; and Whitehouse, 1981).

Systems in which the computers are linked more closely have been built for process control purposes, for instance by Jensen (1978). With an appropriate operating system, a set of computers linked by a LAN could serve as a very powerful distributed system. Network operating systems are being developed in several places (Coyne, 1981; Forth, 1980; Guillemont, 1982; Huen et al, 1977; Liu, Tsay, and Lian, 1982; Manning and Peebles, 1977; Sedillot and Sergeant, 1980, Swan, Fuller and Siewiorek, 1977; Wittie, 1978, and Wulf and Levin, 1975.)

Workers in this field seek either to integrate the facilities of incompatible machines or to develop powerful computing systems based on a number of similar machines.

Some of the options for more closely linked systems have been discussed by Stack and Dillencourt (1981) who propose a distributed operating system implementing a common command language. The definition of a common command language has itself proved difficult (see, for instance, Beech, 1980), suggesting that a distributed operating system will prove a major task unless the workstations and servers are themselves fully compatible.

Many researchers expect that, by linking a number of similar computers, it will prove possible to produce computers of very high performance, resilience, and cost-effectiveness. Such a machine might be called a Closely Coupled Network Computer. It is clear, however, that, for general-purpose computing, this goal is some years away.

Though a complex and fascinating research area, there are few firm conclusions from the research and no commercial products. I shall therefore not discuss it further.

The Economics of the Workstation Network

The workstation network may be seen as a means of delivering computing capacity to a population of users, and hence as an alternative to the shared use of a mini or mainframe computer through terminals. Figure 23.7 shows the relevant hardware costs of supporting users on a shared minicomputer, or on a network of 64k microcomputers. The costs shown are those ruling during the early part of

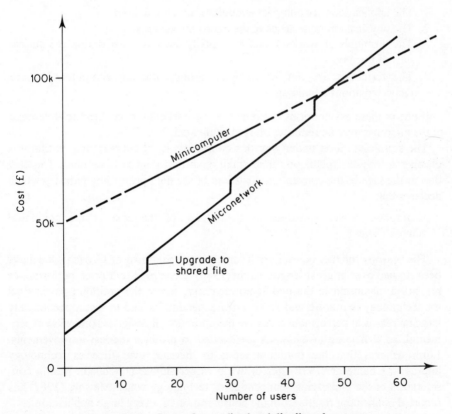

Figure 23.7   Costs of centralized and distributed systems.

1982, though similar results might have been obtained at any time during the previous two to three years.

It is clear from this figure that the microcomputer network is cheaper where there are fewer than 48 users. The position of the workstation network is, in fact, more favourable than that since:

1. The minicomputer will, for most applications, be unable to provide as many as 48 terminals with acceptable response. Therefore, although the mini may be cheaper for a large number of uses, it is likely to provide inferior service.
2. Extensions to the minicomputer system will often lead to a degraded response to existing users. The addition of another micro to the micronet, by contrast, will have no effect on existing users unless they make heavy use of shared resources that are already close to overload. It may then be necessary to add a further shared resource.

This conclusion depends on a number of assumptions about the particular installation, notably that:

1. The applications are compact enough to run on a 64k micro.
2. The physical characteristics of the micro are acceptable.
3. The terminals or workstations are heavily used, at least during the busiest part of the day.
4. The terminals are not all clustered around the minicomputer, but are dispersed about a building.

If one of these assumptions is not met in any particular case then the advantage of the micronet may be reduced, or even eliminated.

The key assumption underlying this conclusion is, of course, the fact that it is cheaper to buy computer power in small quantities than in large ones. This fact flies in the face of the conventional wisdom of the data processing industry which declares that:

'Computer power increases as the square of the cost of the computer' (Grosch's law).

The reasons for the, possibly only apparent, breakdown of Grosch's law have been argued over at great length. Lorin (1980) has argued that price/performance reaches a maximum in the middle power range. Below the optimum power level the technology is mature and small extra expenditures lead to disproportionately large increases in performance. Above the optimum all design is somewhat experimental, so that large investments are needed to produce modest improvements. Lorin believes that the optimum tends to increase over time as technology improves. Champine (1978) has drawn a rather similar conclusion from a consideration of the underlying semiconductor technology whilst Meisner (1982) has reported confirming results from the consideration of a very large application.

It is, however, a mistake to look only at hardware. Software provides two more reasons for the failure of Grosch's law:

1. Multi-user computers spend a significant amount of their processing power on switching between the various tasks and deciding what to do next.
2. Software for small systems has been written to be more efficient than that for larger systems, since the available power and the range of application have been limited.

Also, two more reasons are associated with marketing and with production volumes:

1. Small systems are produced in much larger volumes than larger ones due to the low cost of individual components and the ease of assembly and testing.
2. Small systems are sold as products with limited (or no) support and streamlined sales procedures. The vendors and distributors provide substantially less support to users than has been usual on larger computers.

For all these reasons the economic advantage of small systems is likely to persist for some time, and will extend to favour networks of minicomputers over mainframes. The falling cost of electronic components relative to electromechancal ones will tend to reduce the significance of this advantage, but this will itself be balanced by moves towards more powerful and, hence, expensive processors with larger memories. The advantage of distributed over centralized systems will thus remain a significant factor well into the 1980s.

As noted, however, electromechanical components are a significant part of system costs. The most significant electromechanical peripheral is the disc drive, and this does exhibit large economies of scale. But the workstation network exploits this by incorporating disc devices in shared file servers anyway. The argument for printers is more ambiguous (and was given at greater length on page 249), but the architecture allows printers to be either dedicated to individual users or shared as is most appropriate.

It is more difficult to form a view about the costs of buying or developing applications packages for workstation networks.

There seems to be no good reason why a networked micro should be more difficult to program than a minicomputer. Practical experience shows that micro systems can more often be developed by people without much formal DP expertise but, conversely, that these systems are typically simpler than the corresponding systems that would have been developed for the larger machines. As with minis in the 1970s, the limitations of the machine serve as a valuable discipline in software development.

For the first few years, micros shared with the minis of a decade earlier a deplorable lack of good software, and especially of system building tools such as query languages, DBMSs, and screen formatters. This deficiency began to be remedied during 1982 (Dearnley, 1982) and it seems likely that the lessons learnt on minis will soon be embodied in system building tools (sooner, very probably, than they are applied to software for mainframes).

The use of a mini, or mainframe, for program development often causes a marked worsening of the response to users running operational systems. This effect is sometimes so uncomfortable as to cause development work, or at least compilations, to be banished to evenings, or to a separate machine. Individual microcomputers are obviously free of this problem.

In fact the availability, in a micro workstation, of a dedicated processor makes possible much better methods of systems development than can be provided on a shared system. This is most obvious in the extensive use of interpreted languages, principally BASIC, on 8-bit micros. Interpretation permits a much closer interaction between user and computer than does compilation, though it requires much more processing power to run any particular program.

Where compilation must be used, it is often quite painfully slow. The need to wait for the compilation to finish may be avoided in several ways:

1. By cross-compiling for the micro on a shared and much more powerful compiler server.
2. By providing programmers with a more powerful, but fully compatible, version of the workstation.
3. By providing programmers with two workstations.

Sixteen-bit workstations, such as the Xerox 8010, allow a great deal more to be done to assist the systems developer. Possible approaches here include:

1. Minicomputer operating systems such as Unix[tm]. Unix provides a process-based development environment of the kind recommended in Chapter 3 (Begley, 1982).
2. Systems such as Xerox's Smalltalk that exploit the interactive and graphical properties of the workstation (Teitelman, 1977).
3. Integrated text and data systems that exploit the multi-programming capability of the workstation to correlate specifications, source code, and reference documentation.

Each of these approaches has distinct advantages, though there is insufficient comparable experience to say which is the best.

In the area of software packages, we may note that there are many more packages available than for minicomputers though unfortunately they vary greatly in quality. However, since micro software is typically rather cheap, it is possible to acquire a package speculatively and to discard it should it not come up to expectations. For the larger business (i.e. for a business that might actually be able to justify a minicomputer) there are probably more suitable packages for a minicomputer than for an individual micro. Certainly there are very few packages available that exploit the power of a network of microcomputers.

I conclude from this discussion that there is nothing in the nature of the workstation network that will make it less suitable than a minicomputer for the development of applications software. It will, of course, be impossible to develop such software until workstation networks have stabilized, and independent vendors will hardly wish to invest much effort in doing so until the products are established in the market.

We expect this to happen by 1983 for networks based on micros, but to be several years later for systems based on the 16- and 32-bit 'supermicros'.

Overall, the workstation network provides a cost-effective way of delivering computer power to users. The architecture is likely to remain viable in purely economic terms for the immediately foreseeable future. As the costs of processing power fall, this point will become less significant anyway, and the arguments for and against the Workstation Network Architecture will focus on convenience, flexibility, and extensibility rather than on 'bang for the buck'. The power dedicated to each individual user, and the consequent ability to work autonomously, will then be the key advantages of the workstation network.

Some of the earliest commercially available workstation networks are listed in Table 23.2. Most of these are limited to a single kind of workstation computer, the

Table 23.2 Systems based on minicomputer LANs and integrated office networks.

Supplier	System	LAN	Comments
Datapoint	Attached Resource Processor (ARC) Network	2.5M bit/s token-passing star	Used for data and word processing; many installations
Xerox	System 8000	Ethernet	Intended for word processing and office automation
Xionics	XiBus	XiNet; a 10M bit/s slotted ring	Intended for office automation; supports voice and data
Linotype-Paul	Typesetting System	5M bit/s empty slot ring	Used for typesetting, etc.
Prolink Corp	Prolink	10M bit/s	Support for data and voice
Apollo	Domain	10M bit/s token-passing ring	Used for graphics, CAD/CAM; and scientific and engineering calculations
Three Rivers Computer Corp.	PERQ	Ethernet	Used for graphics, and scientific and engineering calculations
Convergent Technologies	Integrated Workstation	307k bit/s polled	Marketed by CTL, Burroughs, and NCR, as well as by the developer, for office systems

main exception being the Datapoint ARC. The ARCNet can connect a range of Datapoint's own processors (including their digital PABX, the ISX) and, from 1982, accepted Tandy TRS-80 micros as well. Xerox has always intended to support a range of workstations on Ethernet, though the initial announcement provided direct support only for the 8010 workstation and for word processors.

THE OFFICE MACHINES NETWORK

The office machines network goes beyond the workstation network by providing interfaces for a wide range of office machines—preferably all the machines in one office.

The use of a single LAN for a wide range of machines has obvious attractions. Only one cable is needed and the various machines should be able to interwork. Amongst the kinds of machines that might be connected are facsimile transceivers, telephones, terminals, word processors, personal computers, electronic files, high-speed printers, and minicomputers.

The LAN must therefore have all the capabilities of the workstation network plus the ability to support data circuits and telephony. Data circuits pose few problems; connection-orientated LAN protocols were discussed in Chapters 16 to 19 and the other facilities needed by terminal users have been discussed by Davidson (1982), Biba (1981a,b), and others.

Because telephones require continuous circuits there are some LANs that are not very suitable for telephony. To support telephones on such LANs requires considerable extra complexity in the telephone interface (Ravasio, Marcogliese, and Novarese, 1982). It may also require a higher operating speed than would otherwise be necessary. As a result of this, the telephone interface is likely to be rather expensive.

Most organizations already have reasonably satisfactory telephone systems, however, so perhaps it would be best to leave out support for telephones. It will still be necessary to operate the LAN at minicomputer speeds, and this will inflate the cost of attaching slower devices such as terminals and micros.

To support this wide variety of machines the OMN must provide a range of communication services including:

1. Workstation network service, as specified for that architecture.
2. Data circuit, to allow terminals and other simple machines to interact with computers.
3. Variations on the file transfer and electronic mail protocols to allow for word processors without graphics capabilities.
4. Extensions to the electronic mail protocol to allow delivery of text to a facsimile transceiver.
5. Extensions to the file transfer protocol to allow facsimile transceivers to address the filestores.

6. Extensions to the data circuit to provide connection to utilities for file access, word processing, and other functions.

None of these tasks is individually very difficult, but taken together they amount to a substantial amount of diverse systems software, the construction of which is made more complex by the need to retain compatibility between the various extensions, and with the basic facilities.

It is possible to provide an OMN that provides transparent connections between dissimilar machines. This is a fairly simple task since the network needs to provide only three basic services:

1. Datagram (e.g. IEEE 802 mode I).
2. Virtual circuit for packets (e.g. IEEE 802 mode II, or X.25).
3. Data circuit.

The OMN may then provide conversion between these services where that is sensible. More specifically:

1. A data circuit can be converted to a packet circuit through a packet assembler-disassembler (PAD).
2. A packet circuit may be converted to a sequence of datagrams. Equally, a datagram may be carried in a packet circuit environment by maintaining the circuit for a very short time—perhaps only long enough for one datagram.
3. Broadcast datagrams can be converted to a number of packet calls or packet circuits but, since devices with virtual circuit interfaces are rarely expecting to receive broadcasts, this is not usually worth while.

As in the parallel case of the Terminal Service Architecture, interworking at higher levels may be provided by conversion to a network standard form or by protocol convertors. Where all the machines to be supported have been developed by a single supplier, the resolution of the higher level incompatibilities is a daunting task. (Xerox has encountered this problem in linking the 810 Intelligent Typewriter, 820 Personal Computer, 850 and 860 Word Processors, and 8010 Professional Workstation.) To address the problem with regard to documents, IBM has developed a proprietary Document Interchange Architecture (DeSousa, 1981).

Where the individual machines are supplied by a variety of vendors the problem is, in practice, insoluble.

Despite its complexity, and consequent expense, the office machines network has many attractions. Seen from the viewpoint of the integrated system it extends, downwards, the range of possible workstations. It also allows existing digital machines to be connected.

The principal disadvantages are cost and complexity, but these will both become less significant with the passage of time because:

1. New office machines will become available that can use the network's own protocols directly.

2. The costs of the interface units will fall.

The office machines network thus provides one good long-term solution to the local communications problem. It represents the full practical realization of the 'data ring main' of our title.

The first moves towards the OMN were made in 1981 when Xerox announced Ethernet access for typewriters, fax machines, word processors, and micros and Datapoint announced a fax interface for ARC and access for future Tandy micros.

THE DISTRIBUTED COMPUTER COMPLEX

Mainframe LANs have to coexist with highly centralized operating systems but a modern mainframe is, in itself, a set of cooperating computers. (Figure 23.8 shows the internal structure of a large ICL 2980 computer.)

Future large computers are likely to comprise even more cooperating elements and each of those elements will have more autonomy than was usual in the 1970s. These developments are inherent in the development of various specialized storage, printing, computing, and networking processors.

The last chapter showed how a mainframe LAN can be used to provide high-speed communication between computers supplied by different vendors, to facilitate load sharing, and to share specialized peripherals among several host computers.

The LAN can also be used as the basis of a new architecture for a large computer complex, and a possible systems architecture is shown in Figure 23.9. This shows a number of computing engines, each designed for a particular kind of work. Conventional Von Neuman computers are the most generally useful, and will in any case be needed in order to run the software that has already been written for conventional computers. Array computers provide very high performance when dealing with problems in fluid mechanics and image processing. The logical inference engine is a computer specialized for logical manipulations, and thus suitable for problems in artificial intelligence and decision support. Each specialized computer has its own main memory and some may also have very fast auxiliary stores for paging.

All the computers have access to shared storage systems over the LAN. These systems will typically include:

1. A high-performance online filing system, based on magnetic discs or bubble memories.
2. A sophisticated database processor, providing selective retrieval of data and the manipulation of data structures.
3. An archive system, allowing files to be stored cheaply for long periods, yet made available for processing fairly quickly.

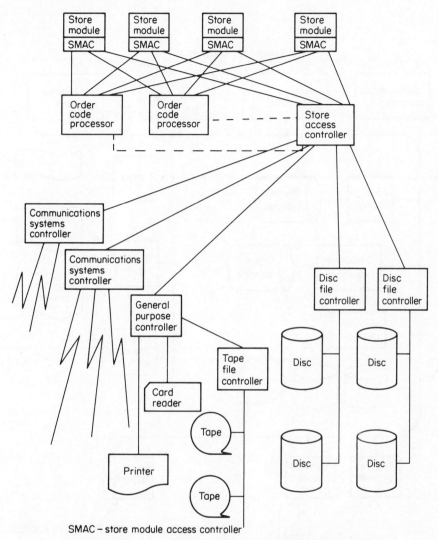

SMAC – store module access controller

Figure 23.8   Internal architecture of a large ICL 2980 System.

The computers will also share a number of bulk output facilities, possibly including conventional impact printers, laser printers, and COM units.

The computer complex will certainly need to provide online access and this may involve a wide variety of devices located both locally and on remote sites. Gateway processors will connect the mainframe LAN to appropriate networks as shown in the figure. Where dumb terminals are to be supported, the terminal

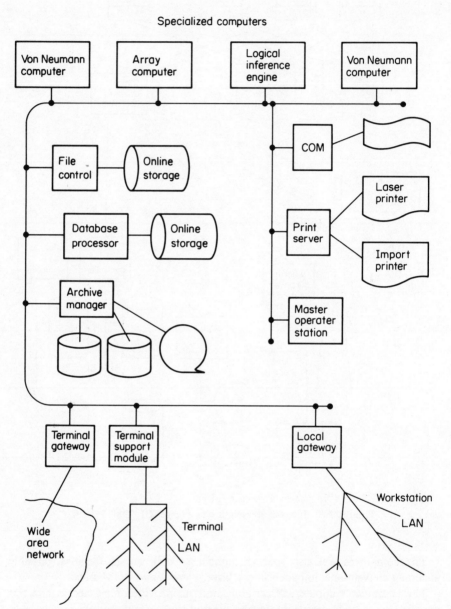

Figure 23.9   Future architecture of large computers.

support module will implement much of the dialogue with the user, leaving the specialized computers free for the functions they are best at.

A central master operator station will monitor the state of the system, assist the operator in scheduling work and in adjusting to failures, and ensure the orderly progress of jobs through the system.

The architecture will need to define the following protocols:

1. Job Control Protocol, to accept jobs from terminals and route them to the appropriate computers.
2. File Access Protocol.
3. File Transfer Protocol.
4. Virtual Terminal Protocol, used when the job must interact with interactive terminals.
5. Data Manipulation Protocol.
6. System Control Protocol, used to inform the master operator of the status of components and jobs and to pass instructions to the components.

This architecture has a number of advantages over more conventional designs for the construction of large mainframes:

1. It makes the addition of new specialised units particularly easy. They may be attached to the LAN at any convenient point and the master station notified of their existence, addresses, and characteristics.
2. It makes the development of new units straightforward since each has only one interface to honour.
3. It allows the system to be enhanced in whichever respect is appropriate; there is no need to add to main storage if the need is for faster discs.
4. It allows specialised units to make full use of the other units that are already attached.

The main disadvantage of the architecture is its incompatibility with existing systems, since most mainframe operating systems are monolithic in both concept and construction. To get the benefits from the distributed architecture it is essential to minimize the work that each specialized computer must do in order to invoke the file access routines in the file controller. Experience shows that, unless the necessary flexibility has been built in from the first (a process that can be expensive), it is very difficult to disperse the functions in the ways required by the architecture.

I nonetheless expect several major manufacturers to announce architectures of this kind during the next decade. To achieve the very high transfer speeds that are necessary the LANs will probably use an optical fibre ring. Token passing seems, according to current laboratory work, to be the favoured capacity-sharing system.

CONCLUSION

In systems architecture, as in communications architectures, the use of LANs opens up new opportunities. These opportunities are all marked by flexibility and extensibility, though they will probably also be justified in more direct terms.

All the architectures discussed in this chapter rely on the use of functionally specialized computers. The specialization may, as in the WNA, be largely restricted to configuration and software. Or it may, as in the office machine network and the distributed computer complex, also involve highly specialized hardware.

In either case the key feature of the architectures is its definition as a set of protocols. These protocols allow the component parts of the system to develop separately. They thus provide a new application of the principle that makes compatible ranges basic to every computer manufacturer's product line and that has created the various markets for 'plug-compatible' peripheral memories and processors.

In the future we may expect to see 'WNA-compatible' workstations, 'DCC-compatible' filestores and other specialized machines designed to interwork with the systems of a dominant manufacturer.

PART V

The Selection of a Local Area Network

Local area networks are different from earlier kinds of networks in their technical detail, but similar in that they should be bought to satisfy needs, rather than as a research exercise. The selection of business equipment is essentially a management task, and this part of the book treats it as such.

On the other hand, the novelty of the new networks creates new opportunities and risks, of which the decision maker must be aware. This section therefore discusses (in some detail) those technicalities that are relevant to selection.

We start, though, with the determination of requirements.

24. ESTABLISHING THE REQUIREMENTS

Any consideration of equipment selection must start with a study of the requirements. Without a clear understanding of the reasons for which a network is thought necessary, the wrong system will probably be installed, leading to frustration and wasted expense.

A SYSTEM OR A UTILITY?

The first question is whether the requirement is for an application system or for a communications utility. The term 'application system' needs to be considered broadly. It may include word processing, data processing, office automation, and process control systems. What all these have in common is that the supplier is expected to provide processing facilities to users, or data processing staff, or both. A LAN may be included in some of the configurations proposed, though not in all, and it will rarely account for more than 10 per cent. of the total cost.

The nature and features of the LAN will play only a small part in the selection of such systems. They will be much more important when buying a network to act as a data ring main, a part of the organization's infrastructure.

An organization may also decide that it needs to rationalize its communications networks in the interests of economy, ease of reconfiguration, etc. In this case the first step will be to determine the network requirements.

It is important to tackle this question carefully. A decision to buy a £50,000 data switch may, in practice, create a medium-term commitment to spend several million pounds on switches, modems, and site works. Only when the requirements have been established and agreed by those who will have to authorize the final expenditure can one proceed to the actual selection of a system.

The Relevance of LANs to System Selection

LANs supplied as part of applications systems are known as bundled LANs (Flint, 1981). Some of them use standard cables (often RS422) or 'standard' protocols at the physical and data link levels. Protocols at and above the network layer are rarely standard.

There are, at the time of writing, no *de jure* standards for LANs, though this

297

has not prevented a number of vendors from claiming conformity with them. A number of *de facto* standards do, however, seem to be emerging. The main ones are:

1. Ethernet (at levels 0, 1, and 2). This was endorsed by ECMA and IEEE in 1982.
2. Cambridge Ring, though there are incompatibilities at level 0.
3. Z-Net, for micros.
4. HYPERchannel, for mainframes and large minis requiring very high-speed communications.

Conformity with standards has clear advantages for the user. He may have multiple sources for the network components, he has a specification to work to should he wish to build his own components, and he may be able to use the LAN for systems supplied by other vendors without great difficulty.

Conformity with standards up to level 2 alone, however, does not provide interworking between conforming devices. A Xerox 8010, a DEC PDP11 under Unix/Unet, a DEC PDP11 with Decnet, and an Ungermann-Bass Network Interface Unit may be attached to one Ethernet cable. However, it is extremely unlikely that they will be able to interwork. The most one can say is that they are unlikely to interfere with one another very seriously.

For a bundled network, therefore, conformity with emerging LAN standards should be regarded as an asset, and not as an essential requirement.

The development of LANs has, as discussed in Part IV, an architectural significance, in that it has allowed new styles of distributed processing to be developed. The local distribution of processing power is desirable in order to provide system users with fast response and facilities tailored to their personal needs. In order to exploit these opportunities a system supplier will require:

1. A local network technology.
2. An understanding of the ways in which that technology may be exploited for systems construction.

In order to enable existing systems to migrate smoothly into a future distributed environment, the systems should:

1. Be modular, rather than monolithic.
2. Use message passing, rather than shared memory, for inter-process communication.
3. Be based on a coherent set of communications protocols.

The purchaser of a system generally wants to be assured that it will continue to be appropriate in the future. The guidelines given above should ensure one aspect of the necessary flexibility. They may therefore be used when evaluating systems for DP, WP, plant automation, and other applications.

The Procurement of a Mainframe LAN

We may start by dealing with the special case of a computer room network; i.e. a network providing very high speed connections between mainframes, large minis, special peripherals, and so on. If we exclude bundled networks such as Prime's Ringnet we find, at the time of writing, two products only—NSC's HYPERchannel and CDC's Loosely Coupled Network. As discussed in Chapter 23, these networks are installed largely in order to solve a specific problem, usually one associated with an expansion in computing capacity, making selection a fairly straightforward exercise.

Very few organizations are faced with the problem of choosing a computer room LAN, and they usually have very skilled systems support staff to do the necessary evaluations. I will therefore devote no further space to discussing the issues involved, which in any case more closely resemble the problems encountered in buying a new printer than those faced in the selection of a data network.

WHERE TO START

The estimation of future requirements should start from an assessment of current systems. To avoid ambiguity an exact date should be defined as the 'present' and all figures related to that date. In an organization with strong central planning this may be the opening date for the new network. In other cases a date in the immediate past should be chosen.

Table 24.1 lists the key questions that must be answered. Exact answers are rarely necessary, or even possible. Instead, crude estimates may often be used—any figures that turn out to be critical can be refined later.

Some of the questions in Table 24.1 are wholly factual but others are largely political. Managers will, for instance, often demand much higher reliability than is really justified. It is usually desirable to accept their demands because:

1. Modern communications systems can easily be made very reliable.
2. The requirement for reliability will increase as businesses become increasingly dependent on their computer and communications systems.
3. Provided that the reliability is higher than that of the machines attached, failures will typically attract little attention.

In other cases managers may indicate a low reliability requirement through not considering the costs associated with unavailability. These costs may include machine rental, staff costs (at overtime rates), lost business, and the giving of offence to customers or key staff.

The next step must be to forecast future requirements, and it is desirable to consider both the medium term, say two years, and the long term, say five years. In

Table 24.1   Key issues in network requirements.

These issues are discussed in more detail in the body of this chapter and the next.

1. How many sites are to be supported? How similar are they in their communications requirements?
2. What availability is required for inter-site communications?
3. What traffic types must be carried between sites:
    Video?
    Voice?
    Data?
    Text?
    Facsimile?
4. Between each pair of sites:
    (a) How much batch data is transferred each day?
    (b) For how many hours each day must interactive communication be maintained?
    (c) How much data passes in interactive mode?

ON EACH SITE
5. What are the requirements for video communications? Is there any requirement to integrate this with other services?
6. Are there any special data requirements (for instance, low latency, deterministic transmission times)?
7. What reliability and availability are required in local communications?
8. Is there any requirement to support computers and workstations with high transmission rates?
9. How many host computers must be supported and with what interfaces?
10. How many terminals and other simple digital machines must be supported? What interfaces and protocols do they use? Where are they and how much will they be used?
11. What special features does the site network require? (Possible features include public network gateways, gateways to existing local computers and networks, file and print servers, electronic mail.)

the past, medium-term requirements have been easily determined by consulting the development plans of the management services department, and then assuming that all projects will run somewhat late. This is still a fair basis for time-sharing and TP systems but is no longer adequate for graphics terminals, personal computers, and word processors.

The requirements in these areas must be decided by talking to a selection of end-users and line managers, as well as to data processing staff. Three tricks may be used to hold estimates within reasonable bounds:

1. Determine, preferably from existing records, recent rates of growth in terminals and traffic. Projected changes in growth rate should be looked at very critically.
2. Consider the cost implications of projected growth. A large group of extra

terminals probably implies an upgrade to the mainframe or a new computer. Will this expenditure be authorized?

3. Get a range, rather than one number, for each date. A single number stands almost no chance of being exactly right but a range can be, and it stresses the uncertainties.

It is also important to focus on patterns rather than on numbers. A new protocol or, worse, a new kind of traffic (such as electronic mail) will have a greater significance than a few terminals or workstations more or less.

Once the network has been installed it will be necessary to establish a conventional rolling plan, so as to allow decisions on network extensions to be made rationally and in good time. These data will be the starting point for that plan, as well as being used during procurement.

The remainder of this chapter discusses the requirements for inter-site traffic as they relate to local networks at the individual sites. Site communication requirements, addressed in questions 5 to 11 of the table, are discussed in the next chapter.

As discussed in the first part of this book, a number of trends are apparent in most of the advanced countries and in all parts of their economies. These may be used in extrapolating current data into the future.

1. *Communicating sites*. Data communications will be extended to a high proportion of business sites during the 1980s. The local equipment on small sites may be micros, word processors, or terminals and will generally have intelligence of its own. Larger sites will typically have computers which may be part of a large-scale distributed processing system.

2. *Inter-site availability*. Moves towards distributed processing will reduce the availability requirements for inter-site data communications in many cases, since intermittent batch transfer will become more widely used. Where centralized processing remains the norm, availability requirements will become more stringent.

3 and 4. *Traffic types*. Electronic mail will grow rapidly during the 1980s— much more rapidly than interactive data traffic. Initially restricted to data and text, it will regularly include images and speech by the late 1980s. Time sharing will also increase but telephony will probably start to decline.

The answer to each question leads to greater clarity as to the nature of the required network.

1. *The number of sites*. The requirements are simplest if just one site is concerned. If several sites must be supported then the network must include:

Transmission between sites.
Routing between sites for user traffic.

If the sites are of one kind, then the same local network technology may be used at each. In this case it should be easy to build inter-site bridges. If the sites are of different kinds then they may benefit from different networks; for instance:

A cluster of TP terminals in a small sales office.

A baseband ring at head office.

A broadband cable at a factory.

If several different networks are installed then it will be more difficult to build the inter-site bridges, adding to the cost of the network.

2. *Inter-site availability.* The inter-site links are usually the least reliable and most unpredictable element of any network. (Table 24.2 gives some examples.) If a very high availability is needed, then multiple routes between sites, and/or the ability to route traffic round a failed line or switching point, may be necessary. If even short periods of failure are unacceptable then the backup facilities must be invoked automatically and without manual intervention. Where there are more than a handful of inter-site lines, some central network management, at least for the inter-site element, is very desirable.

It may be possible to use an existing corporate network to provide these services but if, as is usual, this is not possible, then it will be necessary to buy the whole network from a company with experience in trunk, as well as local, networking, or to procure the local and inter-site elements from separate sources.

In many cases a modest availability target will be acceptable, and in these cases rather simpler inter-site links may be selected.

Whatever the requirement actually is, the local networks ultimately selected must support appropriate inter-network bridges.

3. *The nature of the inter-site traffic.* The transmission of full motion video between sites may be required in teleconferencing or educational systems. This will usually require the use of satellite facilities or of special high-bandwidth lines leased from the PTT or a common carrier. If the distances are short, it may be possible for an organization to install its own cables or other transmission plant.

Table 24.2   Reliabilities of network elements.

Element	Mean time between failures	Mean time to repair
Leased line	6 months	1 day*
Modem	2 years	4 h†
Multiplexor	1 year	6 h†
Data link with two modems and two multiplexors	2.4 months	13.6 h

* Less if there is a spare line or if the PSTN can be used for backup.

† May be less if spares are held locally.

This will require the permission of those who own the intervening land and, in many countries, the agreement of the PTT whose monopoly is thereby breached.

A mixture of leased and switched circuits, again obtained from the PTT or common carrier, will be used to carry voice traffic between sites. These will usually be analogue lines, but, from the early 1980s, digital lines will also be available in some countries. Digital lines should usually be cheaper than analogue lines with modems operating at the same speed.

Some organizations already digitize international telephone calls at much less than the standard rate (8,000 8-bit samples per second), and multiplex a number of such calls onto a single circuit. From the mid-1980s this will become attractive for trunk calls within one country, and its use will expand greatly. Digital lines favour this development.

During the 1980s most organizations will find that they have two distinct requirements for inter-site communications:

1. Tie-lines, which may be analogue, linking PABXs. In some cases there will be economies in the use of digital lines.

2. Digital transmission facilities for data, text, facsimile, and voicegrams.

Where volumes are high it may be cheaper to rent a 'group' (equivalent in Europe to 12 circuits) or even a 'supergroup' (60 circuits) than individual circuits, and to dedicate a few to data service. The remainder will be used as telephone tie-lines or lie spare as shown in Figure 24.1.

If an integrated CBX and digital lines are installed then all the lines may be terminated through that CBX, allowing the use of individual circuits to be changed rapidly. Unless, however, the devices to be connected need to transmit data at a large fraction of 64k bit/s, it will be wasteful to connect them directly. Some local data communications equipment, possibly only a multiplexor, will be interposed between the devices and the inter-site lines. (This equipment may be incorporated into the CBX in some cases.)

Since the data and voice lines are distinct, it is possible to treat voice and data separately. There is very little experience of using LANs for telephony and circuit-switched CBXs will form the telephone infrastructure in most cases. Where a few terminals on each site make infrequent off-site calls, telephone circuits may be used. In general, though, separate data and speech networks will be appropriate.

4. *The data volumes.* For the transfer of modest amounts of batch data between sites a dialled connection may be quite adequate. Such a connection, with 2,400 bit/s modems, can transfer about 10,000 bytes each minute, i.e. as much text as a fast typist can type in an hour. Expensive leased lines are therefore not at all essential for this kind of traffic and one large multinational, Hewlett-Packard, runs most of its international network with no leased lines at all.

If the volumes to be transferred are large, or if interactive communication is required to support distributed processing or online terminals, then leased lines will be necessary.

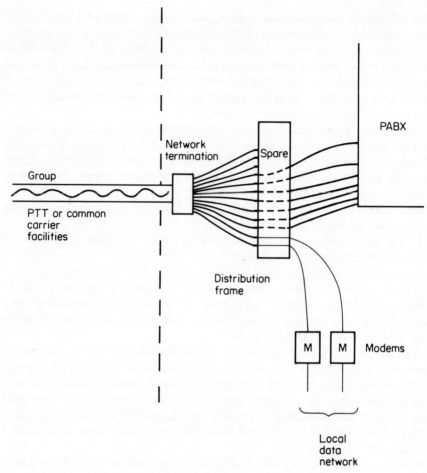

Figure 24.1   Use of a group for voice and data.

THE RELEVANCE TO THE LOCAL NETWORK

The interactions between local and wide area networking go both ways. This chapter has discussed the inter-site links that a local network must support through bridges and gateways. The selection of a suitable local network will also permit economies to be made in the inter-site network.

Table 24.3 shows a breakdown of costs for two network designs that both meet the stated requirements. Net 1 is a conventional circuit switched system, based on data switches at the sites and multiplexors for inter-site communications. Net 2 is based on 10M bit/s LANs linked through leased line bridges.

**Table 24.3   Costs of network interconnection.
(Adapted from Flint, 1981.)**

Configuration
The network has to support 200 devices on five
extensive sites. The devices are:

> 96 ASCII terminals
> 21 Synchronous terminals
> 11 RJE stations
> 19 Personal computers
> 31 Word processors
> 21 Computers
> 1 Message switch

UK prices (1980)

	$'000	
	Net 1	Net 2
Inter-site network		
Modems	202	202
Network management	84	84
Multiplexors	151	n/a
Bridges	n/a	67
Subtotal	437	353
Local networks	286	463
Total	723	816

The 19 per cent. saving achieved for net 2 is due to the ease with which the bridge can take packets from the LAN and place them, suitably encapsulated, on the leased line. The low-speed circuit boards required by net 1 in the switch and the multiplexor are omitted, with a consequent cost saving.

At the time this network was costed this saving was more than balanced by the higher cost of the LANs at the sites. However, LAN prices are falling rapidly so that the balance has moved in favour of using a sophisticated LAN to save inter-site costs.

25. THE LOCAL NETWORK

The last chapter showed that the requirements for inter-site traffic were likely, in most cases, to imply separate data and speech facilities. For the data network, some savings on the costs of inter-site traffic follow from the use of packet rather than circuit switching in the local network.

Inter-site requirements are rarely critical to the selection of a local network. It is usually the on-site requirements that determine, or should determine, the choice of system.

This chapter discusses first the likely changes in site requirements and then their implications for network selection.

EVOLVING SITE REQUIREMENTS

As in the previous chapter, it is convenient to consider requirements in terms of the questions in Table 24.1.

5. *Video requirements.* Video communications may be needed in one of three main applications:

Security.
Television distribution.
Teleconferencing.

Security video usually involves cameras at doors and on roofs, the pictures from which are viewed from a central security office. In some systems the cameras can be controlled from the security office. In the Mitre system, described in Chapter 15, door controls and a speech link are associated with the cameras. With these exceptions, data and voice services are not generally needed at the places served by the security system.

Television distribution may be required in hospitals and colleges. There is unlikely to be any requirement to integrate video with voice and data in such cases but non-integrated voice and data services may be needed at the same places.

Teleconferencing is rarely needed on a single site but its use between sites is likely to grow during the 1980s. Most current organizations with teleconferencing facilities provide them to only one or two conference rooms on each site (see, for example, the discussion in Frost and Sullivan Inc., 1980). These conference rooms will certainly require data, voice, text, and facsimile services, but they may not need full-motion video. Many organizations have found that freeze-frame and slow-scan television are quite acceptable for technical, and even some marketing, meetings. Since these services require about 50k bit/s, rather than the 2–20M bit/s digital or wideband analogue facilities needed for full motion, they are much cheaper and are likely to be generally preferred.

6. *Special requirements.* These are necessarily very specific and it is difficult to offer any useful generalizations.

7. *Reliability and availability.* During the 1980s many organizations will greatly increase their dependence on information systems for both external communications and the support of their own staff. This dependence will impose increasingly strict requirements on data networks. Like a telephone exchange, the network will be expected to be available 24 hours per day and seven days per week. It must also be able to recover quickly from component failures.

These requirements will probably not apply at first, so that the requirement is likely to be for a phased increase in availability, rather than for a very high performance from the first day of operation. For instance, an organization might specify an initial availability of 99 per cent. (30 minutes unavailability during the working week) rising over 5 years to 99.95 per cent. (one and a half minutes unavailability per week).

8. *The transmission requirements.* LANs were originally developed to support fast, bursty traffic of the kind produced by intelligent workstations. Chapter 3 argued that this kind of traffic will become increasingly prevalent during the 1980s as systems evolve to exploit the new local communications systems. Some organizations may, however, already have taken decisions that make this development unlikely, at least in the short term.

Other organizations may be in the process of committing themselves to a particular variety of workstation network. Several of these—OTL IMP, Datapoint ARC, and Convergent Technologies Intelligent Workstation for instance—are based on proprietary networks that cannot provide a general network utility. These systems will therefore have to be wired separately with, at most, a gateway to the utility network. Such organizations will, as suggested in Chapter 4, find themselves with requirements for a utility network as well as for the proprietary product.

9. *The nature and number of host computers.* Most installations restrict themselves to computers of only a few types. This is likely to remain true during the 1980s but with new types being introduced for office and factory automation.

The number of computers is likely to increase rapidly but the increase will mainly involve micros and workstations rather than conventional 'hosts'.

10. *The nature, number, and distribution of terminals.* The most important aspects of this topic are the interfaces needed to support the terminals, microcomputers, and other simple digital devices. Any network should be able to accept all the interfaces for which a continuing need exists. (Interfaces restricted to obsolete devices in process of being phased out need not be supported.)

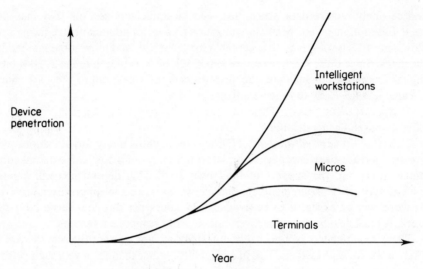

Figure 25.1   Growth in terminals.

The 1980s are likely to see a steady increase in the speeds at which terminals operate. Terminals will also become more widely distributed, but a larger growth will be in personal micros. These will, later, be succeeded by intelligent workstations, as shown in Figure 25.1.

The timing of this development will vary considerably between organizations.

11. *Gateway and service requirements.* Even if all communication is local at present, this is likely to change during the 1980s. Gateways to public data networks and the PSTN will be needed to support electronic mail and the exchange of formal business documents such as orders and credit notes.

Similarly, access to TP computers, time-sharing computers, and CAD systems may greatly enhance the value of a network originally intended to be used for office automation or terminal-to-host communications. Research by Butler, Cox and Partners Limited in 1982 showed that, in many cases, a large part of the benefits of office automation was associated with access to other organizations or to existing systems (Flint, 1982b).

The common services required on local networks will largely reflect the terminals and workstations to be attached. Services to terminals were discussed in Chapter 22 and services to workstations in Chapter 23.

THE IMPLICATIONS OF THE REQUIREMENTS

5. *Video requirements.* If video, data, and voice services will be needed at a number of places throughout the site then a broadband network may well be indicated for these locations and, in the interests of simplicity, the same network

may be adopted as the standard for the whole site if it meets the other requirements. If these requirements are uncertain, or likely to be found at only one or two places, then it will be easier to support those places with CATV cable and to make the choice of a data network independently.

In cabling a site for a network most of the expense is associated with the work of pulling cables rather than with the purchase of the cable. To pull two cables costs about 25 per cent. more than pulling one, not 100 per cent. more, so that two specialized networks may be cheaper than one integrated one.

6. *Special requirements.* In some environments a few special requirements may indicate, or exclude, whole classes of networks:

> A need to pass through areas with a high risk of fire or explosion may require the use of optic fibres.
> Very high security requirements may require encryption in the network station at an acceptable price. On some sites it may be necessary to minimize stray, but informative, radiation by special shielding.
> Particular interfaces may appear to require particular networks, e.g. Ethernet. As the market matures, however, it is likely that the same interfaces will be supported on a variety of networks. For instance, Ethernet interfaces will be provided on broadband networks.

In many cases the technical details make little difference to the functions that the network can provide. All the capacity-sharing systems described in Chapters 9 to 15 have, for instance, been successfully used as the bases of minicomputer LANs.

In other cases the technology may be of considerable significance. Table 25.1 shows how well the various capacity-sharing algorithms are able to meet the special requirements that are sometimes found.

A distinction must be made between requirements that apply to a complete site and those that apply only to a minority of devices, systems, or locations. In the latter case it may be possible to provide two, or even more, networks, on one site. Though this runs against the concept of the 'data ring main' it may well allow organizations to make major savings and such opportunities should not be ignored. Separate networks will be particularly appropriate if the special requirements are likely to remain restricted in scope or, perhaps, are likely to disappear in the long term.

7. *Reliability and availability.* Data communications equipment is typically very reliable, much more reliable than computer systems. Mean times between failure (MTBF) generally range from three months for very complex switches to 30 years for simple interfaces. Though live experience is rather limited, LAN controllers are likely to be at the top end of this range.

The availability of a local network depends also on the reliabilities of the cables and the time taken to repair, replace, or bypass failed components. Table 25.2 gives some illustrative figures.

Table 25.1 Special requirements and LAN technology.

Special requirement	Capacity sharing algorithm					
	Polling	Token passing	Contention	Dynamic reservation	Slotted ring	Register insertion ring
Deterministic response	✓	✓		✓	✓	✓
Fast response at low load			✓	✓	✓*	✓*
Good response at high load	✓	✓		✓	*	
Variable device priorities	✓	With difficulty	With difficulty	✓		
Much byte echoplex traffic				✓	✓*	✓*
Much telephone traffic		?†		✓	✓	✓

* If the maximum packet length is low.
† The practical value of the 'synchronous' mode on the IBM token ring is currently unproven.

Table 25.2 Network availabilities.

Network type	Resilience features	Electronic components MTBF (years)	Electronic components MTTR	Cables MTBF (years)	Cables MTTR	Availability (%) Common elements	Availability (%) One device
Circuit switched star	—	1	4 h	4	12 h	99.95	99.92
	With backup central logic	1	2 min*			99.9995	99.97
Broadcast LAN bus	—	2	4 h	2	12 h	99.93	99.91
	With rapid repair of cables			2	2 h	99.977	99.95
	With automatic reversion to spare cable			2	1 s	99.9999	99.977

* This is mainly the time taken to reconstruct the status of failed calls, details of which were lost with the failed switching logic.

In conventional circuit switches the central switch is complex and thus the least reliable element. For very high availability the central logic must be duplicated and a means of automatic switching to the spare logic provided.

In a LAN the cabling is the common part. For very high availability a LAN will require duplicate cables and the ability to switch between them rapidly. In military systems, which must continue to function after the destruction of large parts of the network, still higher levels of redundancy may be necessary. (The means of managing this redundancy were discussed in Chapter 8.)

In both cases, a high availability requires that planned maintenance and repair should be accomplished with the minimum interruption (preferably none) to normal service.

As the table indicates, very high availability can be obtained with both centralized and distributed network architectures.

8. *The transmission requirements.* Workstations produce traffic with a very bursty pattern, and require the ability to obtain a rapid response across the network. These requirements can only be met by a LAN or by direct links. Since the cost of direct links increases very rapidly with the number of workstations, a LAN is the best choice under most circumstances.

Almost any of the capacity-sharing algorithms can give rapid response under low load, though contention gives the fastest response. As the load increases the delay inevitably worsens, with contention worsening rather faster than the others.

Under high load some networks show rapidly worsening delay and the region of high load must therefore be avoided. This will usually involve restricting the number of devices that can be attached to the network, but these restrictions need not be at all onerous. Shoch and Hupp (1980a) measured the load on one 200-station 3M bit/s Ethernet at the Palo Alto Research Center. They found that the mean load was 0.8 per cent. whilst the heaviest load in a 1-second period was 32 per cent. Scaling these figures to the largest allowed configuration (1,024 stations) on a 10M bit/s Ethernet implies an average load of 1.2 per cent. and a 1-second peak of 48 per cent. Ethernet would certainly deliver adequate service under this load.

The performance of a micronet may suffer if several powerful machines attempt to use it concurrently for, say, file transfers.

The performance of a minicomputer LAN may suffer if several powerful machines attempt to use it concurrently for, say, file transfers.

The performance of a minicomputer LAN may suffer if attempts are made to use it to carry large numbers of telephone calls.

Where the LAN must provide rapid service to bursty traffic in the presence of high total load, the best performance is likely to be obtained from either:

A LAN with a small maximum packet size or
A LAN in which part of the capacity is reserved for the bursty traffic. This will
   be a reservation system or a broadband cable.

Where the LAN carries sufficient bursty traffic to constitute a large total load (above, say, 20 per cent.) it will usually be best to install two or more LANs, linked by filters as discussed in Chapter 18.

At their announcement, most LANs were able to accept high-speed traffic from only a limited range of devices. Those vendors who wish to offer 'open networks' have subsequently increased the range of devices supported. Nonetheless, the choice of workstation usually places severe limitations on the choice of LAN, making any detailed comparative evaluation of designs rather academic.

In the absence of a clear requirement to support intelligent workstations it may still seem desirable to choose a network which does have the capability for bursty traffic. Such a decision will incur extra costs and should, therefore, be taken only with caution.

There can also be no guarantee that such a network will be compatible with the workstations ultimately chosen. The least risky course is to choose a network with 'standard' interfaces such as IEEE 802, Ethernet, X.25, or Z-Net.

9. *The nature and numbers of host computers.* Most mainframes and minis have been designed to support terminals over a mixture of direct low-speed lines and concentrators on lines of higher speed. The protocols on the lines to the concentrators are often not published and may not be stable. Since 1980, however, suppliers have come increasingly to support the CCITT X.25 protocol.

Support for the low-speed single terminal interface is an essential feature in a local network, but the availability of a high-speed, multiplex interface to the local network is a considerable advantage. As discussed in Chapters 2 and 21 it saves money on both network and computer equipment, allows for faster transmission, and can also allow a closer interaction between computer and network.

The existence of an X.25 interface may thus be helpful. When implemented in conjunction with CCITT Recommendation X.29, it allows a number of asynchronous terminals to be supported across the network. As shown in Figure 25.2 the terminals work to a Packet Assembler–Disassembler (PAD) which converts between X.25 and the X.28 terminal protocol, under the general control of X.29. Though intended for time-sharing access on a public data network, this can also be used locally with the PAD being incorporated in the terminal interface unit.

Other implementations of X.25 are less appropriate. In IBM's case, for instance (Scantlebury, 1982), SNA's network layer and the remote concentrator protocol are both laid on top of X.25. This means that either:

The switching capability of the network cannot be used and IBM, or IBM-compatible, concentrators are essential, or

The network must include complex protocol conversion logic to decode these protocols.

These alternative arrangements are shown in Figure 25.3. The protocol conversion option, shown as Figure 25.3c, is most flexible, as it allows IBM and other equipment to interwork. It is also the most expensive, because of the need to implement and translate the SNA protocols.

The multiplex network interface may, alternatively, be supplied by the network

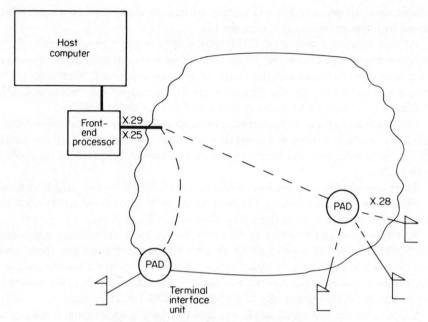

Figure 25.2   Terminal support with X.25.

vendor. Interfaces for widely used computer buses such as Qbus, Unibus, and Multibus are available on several LANs. In most cases the communications software on the computer is unable to access terminals across this interface without special supporting software which the vendor must also supply. This is a disadvantage of this approach, since there may be difficulties in integrating this software with the operating system. The non-standard software environment may also create maintenance problems.

LAN interfaces are also offered by some computer suppliers. Use of these interfaces minimizes the maintenance problems and is thus to be preferred.

In general, LANs and other packet switching networks are more likely to provide such interfaces than circuit switched networks, whether or not based on CBXs.

10. *The nature, number, and distribution of terminals.* The nature of the terminals' communications is important in network selection. Most modern terminals operate in block mode, sending and receiving one screen at a time. In transaction processing this may occur rather more than once a minute and imposes an average network load of only about 50 bit/s. A peak rate of 2,400 bit/s will usually be sufficient. Terminals of this kind can be supported on any of the various kinds of local network.

Such a terminal may be used by a typist for word processing or to page through

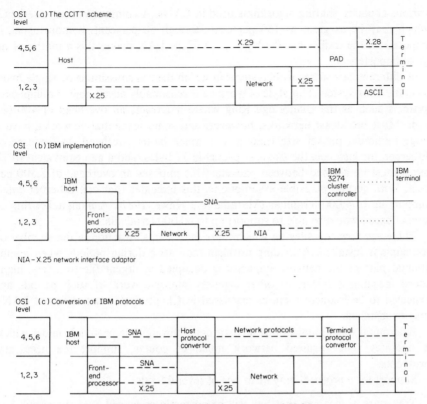

Figure 25.3   Terminal support and X.25.

a longer document. These uses imply a higher average load but, again, this will present few problems to any local network.

Graphics and facsimile terminals are likely to play a larger part in future office systems and a graphics terminal may require a much higher peak rate. Facsimile transceivers have usually been designed to operate over telephone lines at speeds below 10k bit/s, and current designs will therefore pose no problems. In the future, high-quality screens may be used to view facsimiles (which may have arrived over the public network or been captured locally) and this will certainly require higher speeds. This, in turn, implies a LAN rather than a circuit switched network.

Remote job entry stations may also have to be connected to the network. These stations are often designed to operate at speeds up to 20k bit/s, but they may be able to run much faster given suitable network connections. A continuing requirement for remote job entry across a large site may be satisfied by either separate circuits or a LAN with sufficient speed to accommodate it without overloading; 1M bit/s should certainly be enough for this.

All the kinds of terminals mentioned so far are fully compatible with all the various capacity-sharing algorithms used in LANs. A communications overhead, which may be as great as 150 per cent., though 50 per cent. is more usual, is imposed on the traffic, but the high speed of the LAN makes this a matter of no great importance.

A different case arises with systems in which the transmission is by single bytes as in the Unix system.This style of working is reasonably acceptable in minipacket systems such as the Cambridge Ring where it attracts an overhead of 400 per cent. Most broadcast networks, however, and some sequential networks, have a large minimum packet size leading to a much larger overhead. In the case of Ethernet, for instance, the smallest packet is 72 bytes, and a gap equivalent to 12 bytes must be allowed between packets. This imposes an overhead of 8,300 per cent. With certain plausible assumptions, this indicates that one Ethernet could support up to 4,000 terminals (Marathe and Hawe, 1982). A minipacket ring of similar speed would be able to support up to 60,000 terminals.

There are very few sites on which more than a small fraction of this number of terminals is installed. A loading problem may arise during periods when a substantial part of the network capacity is occupied in urgent file transfers, high-speed facsimile transfer, or other capacity-intensive work. If such periods are expected to be frequent then, as discussed in Chapter 18, a set of linked LANs may be installed.

A terminal's communications are expressed through the protocols under which it operates. The required network must, of course, support the necessary protocols.

Support for a protocol may be at one of several levels:

Transparent, meaning that bits will be correctly conveyed once the circuit has been established. Circuits will have to be established under central control or via interface boxes interposed between the terminal and the network. This is often acceptable to TP terminals which remain connected to the same host for extended periods.

Data link level (without addressing) plus character set, implying that the terminal keyboard can be used to interact with the network both to select a host computer and to access network utilities.

Full data link level, implying that any addressing functions in the protocol are supported by being mapped onto the network's own addressing functions. This is not usually available—the addressing functions are only usable with the vendor's own network.

Every local network should have a transparent virtual circuit facility over which attached devices may communicate in protocols 'that network management has never heard of, much less agreed to!' (Saltzer, Reed, and Clark, 1981).

Where the protocol is supported explicity, the second level is usually the most appropriate for simple devices. On some networks the use of transport circuits is very inefficient and can easily produce overloads. Such networks should be avoided unless it is quite clear that only a limited range of device interfaces will be needed.

If the terminals are widely scattered, the costs of installing and maintaining the physical cables will be a large part of the total cost. In these cases economy favours any network that can make use of existing wires. In most organizations, however, the penetration of terminals is likely to rise rapidly during the 1980s, so that, though cabling costs are important, they are not the only consideration.

The expected usage of the terminals is also important. If, as is likely to be the case for a private videotex system, usage is expected to be low, then the costs of the cables are again a major factor. In these cases it may well be sound to use an existing PABX to connect the terminals.

The arguments of this section are represented in Figure 25.4.

11. *Gateway and service requirements*. These will generally be consistent with the nature of the terminals and workstations to be supported, and thus impose no extra requirements on the network.

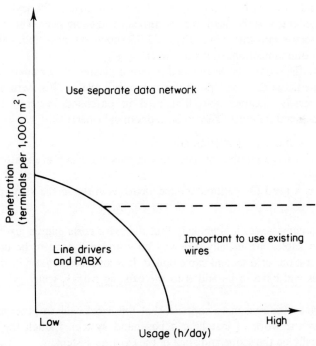

Figure 25.4   Terminal penetration and usage.

The Influence of Existing Communications Equipment

Most administrative, business, and industrial sites already have wiring for telephony. With acoustic couplers or the data support units provided with some modern CBXs, terminals may be supported over the telephone system. To avoid the use of CBX switching capacity, data may be transmitted on a carrier frequency outside the voice range and switched, as in Grapevine, by a separate data circuit switch. These methods may be used for data transmission at speeds up to 20k bit/s but are unsuitable for high-speed operation. Their use is therefore restricted to terminal support.

In many cases the multi-pair cables installed for telephony will provide spare pairs that can be used for data transmission at higher speeds. Higher speeds may also be available through digital CBXs of the kinds discussed in Chapter 5.

Chapter 5 explained why the CBX is unlikely to prove a good basis for the support of intelligent workstations. For dumb terminals, however, and where the cost of new cabling would otherwise be substantial, the use of existing telephone wires may be advantageous.

Some sites already have coaxial cable systems for television distribution, security, or CCTV. In these cases this cabling may be used as the basis of a broadband system. Broadband systems are, however, significantly more expensive than baseband systems of similar speed, due to the cost of the radio frequency filters and modems and the need to provide head-end equipment. This relationship is likely to persist into the 1980s. Figure 25.5 shows the cost trends forecast by Olivetti Telecommunications (Olteco, 1982).

The cost differential will be reduced where a cluster of terminals are able to share a single network access point through a multiplexor. Furthermore, CATV cable is generally cheaper than that used in baseband systems. Broadband technology is therefore most likely to be economical where:

1. The costs of cable installation are high.
2. There is a large number of terminals in clusters which are scattered over a large site.
3. There is a need for multiple independent networks in the same part of the site.

In other circumstances it is unlikely that the extra costs can be justified. Existing television cables are usually one-way only and will have to be upgraded to two-way operation, or a second cable pulled. It is also likely that new drop cables and branches will have to be added to the existing trunks, which will then need rebalancing.

There seems little reason to suppose that this work will, in general, be much cheaper than the work of installing a baseband system, though the costs will depend critically on the scope and state of the existing system.

This is an area in which US and European practice are likely to diverge. Televisions are often found in US offices but are something of a rarity in Europe. The

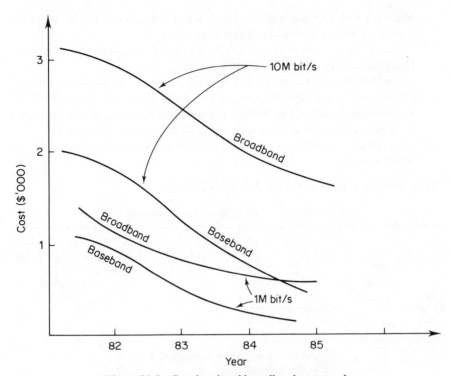

Figure 25.5   Baseband and broadband cost trends.

United States also has a larger number of experimental CATV systems which, for instance, distribute lectures from community colleges, or the proceedings of the State legislatures. Finally, the continental scope of much US business, compared to the national scope of much European business, creates a greater demand for teleconferencing. For all these reasons, and others, US organizations are more television-conscious. Broadband systems are therefore likely to be more appropriate in the United States than in Europe.

THE KINDS OF LOCAL NETWORKS

From a functional point of view we may distinguish six kinds of local networks as follows:

1. Broadband Cables, as discussed in Chapter 15. Examples include LocalNet, CableNet, and Wangnet.
2. Microcomputer LANs with terminal support. In these a LAN designed for minicomputers, such as Ethernet or the Cambridge Ring, is combined with terminal multiplexors. Examples include Net/One and the Data Ring.

3. Micronet with terminal support. These are very like the last kind except for their lower speeds and prices. HiNet is one example.
4. Terminal support network, i.e. LANs developed specifically for terminals. Examples include Clearway and Multilink.
5. Circuit switched data networks. These are based on circuit switches linked by low-speed lines. Specially designed switches include the Gandalf PACX and Infotron Timeline 460, whilst such switching functions are also provided by sophisticated multiplexors such as the Case DCX and Codex 6050.
6. Integrated CBX networks such as the Rolm CBX with data feature or the Intecom IBX.

Some key characteristics are listed in Table 25.3.

Table 25.3   The kinds of local network.

Kind	Characteristics	Typical price per port in the United Kingdom, 1982 (£)
Broadband cable	Video support Support for logically independent data networks in same area Can use existing video cables Support for bursty traffic in some cases	700
Minicomputer LAN with terminal support	Support for bursty traffic at high speed Complex terminal and protocol support functions in some cases	500
Micronet with terminal support	Support for bursty traffic at up to 1.5M bit/s	400
Terminal support network	Limited support for bursty traffic Modest peak transmission rate Cheap	200
Data circuit switching network	Spare telephone wires can be used. Existing wires can be re-used at extra cost Products and technology well proven Cheap	150 (line drivers £200 extra)
Integrated CBX network	Existing phone wires may be used	Not available

Table 25.4 Indications for the various kinds of local network.

Kind	Indication
Broadband cable	Multipoint video requirement
	Multiple overlapping logical networks
	Terminals widely scattered, with existing video cables
	Modest requirements for high-speed bursty traffic
Minicomputer LAN with terminal support	Substantial requirements for high-speed, bursty traffic
	Need for high-speed file transfer
	Need for complex terminal support functions such as encryption and protocol conversion
Micronet with terminal support	Bursty traffic requirements but with peak rate not greater than 500k bit/s
Terminal support network	Terminals and small micros—the dominant office machines
	Limited needs for complex terminal support functions
Data circuit switching networks	Plenty of spare pairs for distribution
	Many terminals within short distance of switching unit (to avoid need for line drivers or short-haul modems)
CBX data feature	Terminals widely dispersed
	Terminals in infrequent use

In many cases the choice of the network will be determined by special requirements, notably those associated with particular pieces of equipment. Thus users of the Apollo Domain CAD system must install the Apollo Domain LAN, even if it is unable to support any other equipment at all. Similarly, Wang office systems require Wangnet (though that is able to support some non-Wang terminals).

In other cases it will be possible to choose the local network that best meets all the requirements for local communications. Table 25.4 gives the indications for networks of the various kinds.

26. THE NETWORK PROCUREMENT PROCESS

Chapter 24 has discussed the creation of a statement of requirements for a communications network, and Chapter 25 the ways in which the requirements determine the general nature of the network to be installed. This still leaves open the key question as to which local network to choose for a particular site.

The selection of a communications network is best regarded as a technical procurement exercise, similar in kind to the procurement of an oil refinery, telephone exchange, or computer. This chapter therefore gives a rather abbreviated account of the process, indicating how the general principles may be applied to this specific case.

The methodology has been developed for use on fairly large projects, i.e. those where the lifetime costs are hundreds of thousands, or even millions, of dollars. For a small system the methodology may be shortened by involving fewer suppliers and using a shorter questionnaire. It may also be possible to substitute telephone calls for some of the meetings.

The selection process is divided into three phases:

1. Internal activities.
2. Liaison activities.
3. Evaluations.

Figure 26.1 shows a typical timescale for such an exercise. Where the requirements are simple, or where senior management is able to make decisions quickly, activities may be run in parallel and the activities aimed at obtaining management agreement may be completed more quickly.

INTERNAL ACTIVITIES

As soon as it is clear that a new communications network is required a small project team should be set up. There should not normally be more than three members and they should possess, between them, skills and experience in computing, telephony, systems procurement and (if there are any off-site communications) liaison with the common carriers or PTTs. If the exercise is especially complex or unfamiliar, or if an independent view is desirable in order to defuse

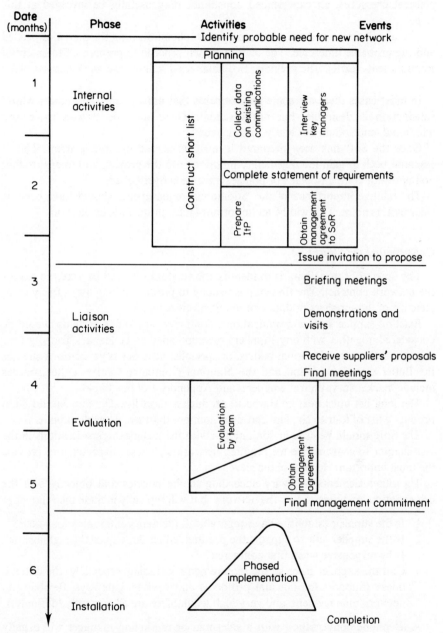

Figure 26.1   Timescale for a large network selection exercise.

political pressures, an experienced consultant may usefully be involved at this stage.

The team's first act should be to prepare a plan indicating the activities needed and the probable timescale. The team will then proceed to prepare a Statement of Requirements (SoR). The previous two chapters discussed the work necessary for this.

In most cases there are some requirements that must be met and others whose satisfaction is desirable, but not essential. These may be termed basic and additional, and should be clearly distinguished.

Once the SoR has been prepared it must be agreed by management. This is essential both to gain management commitment to the project, and to ensure that no important company plans or policies have been overlooked.

The relative importance of the 'additional' requirements should have become clear by this point. This will be an important factor in the final evaluation.

Constructing the Short List

The object of this activity is to identify the vendors who will be asked to bid for the network contract. The first step is usually to produce a long list, a fairly complete list of the suppliers of data communications equipment.

Existing suppliers of communications, computer, and office systems should be considered, together with any suppliers recommended by colleagues, friendly consultants, relevant professional bodies, or specialist advisory organizations such as the Butler Cox Foundation and the National Computer Centre. Other sources include market surveys, trade papers, and Appendix 1 of this book.

The long list must next be sieved to produce a short list. The aim should be to product a list of four to six, and certainly no more than ten, possible suppliers.

The SoR should be used in conjunction with the technical considerations in the last chapter to characterize the required network(s). These characteristics provide the most important element of the sieve.

The other elements will vary according to the policies and objectives of the organization intending to buy the network, but will typically include the following:

1. Is the supplier established and reputable in the data communications field?
2. Is the supplier able to support the product, either directly or through agents?
3. Is he responsive when first contacted?
4. Can the supplier meet all the requirements including, especially, the difficult ones? (Support for unusual protocols and devices, gateways, flexibility in network management, and very high availability are all currently 'difficult'.)

A telephone conversation with a salesman or marketing manager will usually be sufficient to answer these questions in enough detail. The temptation to include every supplier, 'just in case', should be resisted, since it wastes time on both sides and can lead to bad feeling and recriminations.

The Invitation to Propose

The Invitation to Propose (ItP) will be a written document consisting, generally, of three parts. The first part is procedural, the second gives the requirements, and the third is a questionnaire intended to impose a common structure on the various proposals.

The ItP will typically specify one or more briefing meetings for suppliers at which ambiguities in the ItP can be resolved. The ItP must state the dates of any such meetings, the date by which the proposals must be received, and, preferably, the dates of any further meetings to clarify the proposals. Four to six weeks should usually be sufficient for the preparation of proposals, but longer will be

(a) Inter-site traffic
The flow of data is mainly between the factories and head office (at which the present mainframe is located) and there is little traffic between the factories. The total volume is expected to grow slowly over the 1980s.

Inter-site traffic

	Traffic volume in direction of larger flow (bytes/busy hour)		
Site	1983	1985	1988
Ipswich Factory			
batch	50k	70k	80-110k
interactive	20k	40k	30-80k
Norwich Factory			
.			
.			

(b) Equipment installed
Current terminals are used to access the corporate mainframe. Minicomputers will be installed at all the factories during the 1980s for both administration and control of automatic assembly lines.

Equipment installed

Site	1983	1985	1988
Ipswich Factory			
3278s	2	8	10-20
RJE stations	1	2	1
minicomputers	0	1	3
intelligent workstations	0	4?	4?-10
personal micros	2	8	6-15
Norwich Factory			
.			
.			

Figure 26.2   Sample requirements tables from ItP.

required if detailed site surveys are needed (as they will be if long runs of new cable may have to be installed).

The second part gives the requirements and will be derived from the questionnaire given in Table 24.1. Quantitative values should be given whenever possible to avoid ambiguity. Figure 26.2 shows a format that might be used for the quantative data. The ItP should state clearly that suppliers that cannot meet the basic requirements will be excluded from further consideration.

An example of the required questionnaire is given in Appendix 2. Though it may appear rather formidable, the answers are largely standard information. It is also worth remembering that, as George Champine of Univac (Champine, 1978) has pointed out, the user is in the strongest negotiating position during a selection exercise. This is therefore an opportunity to get free work from the suppliers and to influence their plans for the future development of their products.

LIAISON ACTIVITIES

The statement of requirements will inevitably be incomplete, since the labour involved in documenting every point of detail is vast and most details are of no great significance. A period of liaison with the suppliers is therefore necessary if they are to prepare satisfactory proposals. The salesmen will also wish to understand the basis on which the selection will be made in order to ensure that they are giving their products the best chance of being chosen.

Though this can be done through informal contacts, it is often easier to call a briefing meeting for all the suppliers. This has the further advantage that all suppliers receive the same information, ensuring that they compete on equal terms.

It is, regrettably, usual to find that suppliers' proposals fall short of what was requested in the ItP. Proposed systems may not meet all the requirements or they may not be available for installation by the dates specified. Technical material may not be presented in the ways indicated in the questionnaire. More subtle problems may also arise:

1. The proposed network may include components which meet all the separate requirements but are unable to interwork.
2. Mistakes may have been made in the calculation of availabilities or the configurations of switches, multiplexors, etc.

These errors are usually honestly made, but they must be identified by careful study of the suppliers' product literature. It is usually necessary to ask for amplifications to, or changes in, the proposals and this is best done in person. This second round of meetings should be followed by receipt of the revised proposals, completing this phase.

EVALUATIONS

The proposals will now be available in forms that make it reasonably easy to compare one with another.

The key question, of course, is whether each proposal meets the stated basic requirements. If a proposal appears not to meet these requirements it is worth checking this point explicitly with the supplier, since the problem may be one of misunderstanding rather than a limitation of the product. The supplier may also, when he realizes the importance of the point, be prepared to offer a custom solution.

If there are some proposals that do meet the basic requirements, those that do not may be excluded at this stage.

In some cases, however, there may be no proposal that meets all the requirements. In this case there are three possible courses of action:

1. Decide to use *ad hoc* solutions for another year or two and to retry the selection exercise after that time.
2. Find a supplier prepared to develop the necessary enhancements to one or other of his standard products.
3. Decide that the requirements that cannot be met are, in fact, not essential but only additional.

Each of these courses has obvious drawbacks. The best choice will be determined by the importance and urgency of the requirements that are causing the problem, the nature of any fall-back options, and the acceptability of customized solutions.

Interpreting the Questionnaire Responses

The proposals received should be structured according to the questionnaire in the ItP. Many of the questions are intended to elucidate basic information in a consistent form but others are of greater significance.

Section A should give a good overview of the network proposed. The question on reference sites is especially important since it provides access to real user experience. Contact should certainly be made with several current users and at least one site visit is desirable. Such contacts may be valuable in several ways; they may, for instance, draw attention to particular features of the products that the users did not choose.

Section B deals with an aspect of networking that is often given inadequate attention. Being unfamiliar to staff with a data processing or conventional data communications background, the problems of cabling and physical installation are often given inadequate attention. These items may, however, account for as much as half the initial cost, and more if new ducts have to be provided in old buildings, underground, or in industrial areas. (It may be worth while trying to avoid these heavy costs by using a point-to-point link based on infrared, light-wave, or microwave technology as a bridge across such areas.)

Section C deals with the critical question of device interfaces and therefore explains what devices can be attached to the network.

Section D deals with the most distinctive feature of any LAN, the capacity-sharing algorithm. The answers given in this section provide essential background and, for capacity planning purposes, warn of the practical limits of the network.

Section E deals with the links between sites and the methods used to cope with errors. This is of considerable importance, as the trunk circuits are likely to be the least reliable part of any network. In general, a system with automatic recovery is likely to provide a much higher availability than one with only manual recovery.

Section F deals with facilities to provide interworking between incompatible machines. The call extension and receipt facilities will be important if the network is primarily intended for terminal support, but will also be useful if workstations on a LAN must emulate terminals in order to interwork with other systems. Automatic facilities are easier to use than manual ones.

Section G explores the facilities for datacalls, typically between terminals and host computers. Of the facilities listed, mnemonic addresses, clear error messages, user-specified connections, hunt groups, camp-on, and information on the current state of the system are the most generally useful. The others are more dependent on local requirements and some are, really, rather a matter of taste than of necessity.

Section H deals with the management and maintenance of the network. The answers given here will help the evaluation team to decide how the network management responsibilities should be distributed, and how many staff will have to be involved.

Section I gives the supplier an opportunity to explain his thinking on future

Table 26.1 Chapters relating to questionnaire topics.

Questionnaire		
Section	Topic	Chapter
A	General	4, 25
B	Wiring and transmission	8
C	Device interfaces	4, 6
D	Capacity-sharing algorithm	7, 25
E	Bridges	17, 18
F	Gateways	17, 19
G	Call management	—
H	Network control	—
I	Strategy	3, 4, 22, 25

network products. This may then be compared with the potential customer's own plans. For instance, an intention to introduce a compatible broadband product would be relevant to an organization with plans to increase its use of CCTV.

In each case, the earlier chapters of this book may be used to illuminate the subject area. Table 26.1 shows the relationship between questionnaire sections and the chapters of this book.

Evaluations

After studying the proposals and contacting existing users, the evaluation team should attempt to form a clear view of the merits of each proposal on a series of distinct points. These points are:

1. Success in providing for the additional requirements.
2. Initial cost.
3. Lifetime cost (over, say, 5 years).
4. Expected availability.
5. Convenience in use.
6. Reputation of the supplier and his field support.
7. Stability of the supplier.

and, of course, other points of particular interest.

The costs of installing new cables and ducts, of air conditioning, and of initial training should be included in the estimate of initial costs.

The costs of operating, maintaining, and extending the network, and of service contracts, should be included in the lifetime costs. In estimating the costs of future extensions, allowance should be made for the falling costs of LAN products and of electronics generally.

The questionnaire will have asked suppliers to calculate the availability of their proposed systems for certain, specified, communications. Salesmen are often unused to seeing these questions from the user's point of view. They will frequently ignore such considerations as:

1. The possibility of cable breaks.
2. The skills of the staff normally on-site.
3. The availability of spares on-site.
4. Time spent waiting for service engineers.
5. The need to shut the network during extensions and enhancements.

These calculations must therefore be checked carefully.

Convenience is difficult to measure but it may be assessed by 'hands-on' use of a demonstration system, study of manuals and conversations with existing users. The prospective end-users should be involved wherever appropriate, notably when considering network management.

Reputation is best investigated through contact with existing users of the same equipment and services.

The Final Decision

At this stage we have a comparison between the proposals in terms of a number, perhaps a large number, of separate items. This may be expressed in the form of a table such as that shown in Figure 26.3.

In general, no one proposal will stand out clearly from the rest. In the example shown, number 3 has the best features, number 1 is available soonest, whilst number 2 has the lowest initial cost. The decision will therefore depend upon the priorities of the prospective user.

It is now traditional to recommend the allocation of weights to the items, the

	Proposals		
	1	2	3
BASIC REQUIREMENTS Are they all met?	Yes	Yes	Yes
By when can the system be installed?	March	April	September
ADDITIONAL REQUIREMENTS Centralization of inter-site network management?	Yes, poor facilities	No, lines managed separately	Yes, good facilities
Localization of management of local network?	Yes	Yes	Not till next year
Multiplex VAX interface?	Yes	No	Yes
Multiplex 4341 interface?	Yes	No	Yes
COSTS Initial costs (£'000)	600	450	800
Lifetime costs (7 years, £'000,000)	1.4	1.2	1.2
AVAILABILITY Local terminal to host	99.99%	99.92%	99.98%
Local workstation to server	99.97%	99.87%	99.99%
Terminal to remote host	99.92%	99.80%	99.95%

Figure 26.3   Example—comparison of proposals.

reduction of each evaluation to a numerical score, followed by the calculation of a figure of merit formed by adding the products of weights and scores for each proposal. Now this is certainly a useful technique, insofar as it forces the team to consider the relative importance of the items. But it is easy to mistake this useful tool for a total solution. In the author's experience, discriminations are usually so clear as not to require the method, or so fine that trifling changes in scores or weightings will produce a different 'winner'.

Though desirable, it is generally impractical to determine the weights and scoring system at the start of the exercise. Too little will be known about the products and the capabilities of the technology to allow secure judgements to be made so early. (Exceptionally, the early setting of the evaluation criteria may be possible if the evaluation team includes a person with recent experience of a similar exercise. If no employee has such experience a consultant may be used. The presence of a consultant with the necessary skills will also expedite the technical evaluation of the proposals.)

A key consideration in the choice of a LAN is the balance between present cost and future benefit. As the use of systems expands it will become increasingly inconvenient to change from one network to another. The initial selection therefore restricts future choices and makes it essential that the system chosen should have sufficient flexibility.

It is, on the other hand, easy to spend large sums on flexibility that will never be used, or which will prove expensive, or even impossible, to exploit when the time comes. The correct balance can only be found through a careful consideration of the required flexibility and an equally careful analysis of the products offered. Many communications products exhibit much less power and flexibility than may appear at first, due to their use of 8-bit microprocessors. For instance, a 10M bit/s channel is of limited value if the interface unit is unable to accept data at speeds greater than 100k bit/s.

Often, then, the final decision will be a matter of professional judgement rather than the result of some objective and 'scientific' process. Once the evaluation team is satisfied with its decision, it must inform management and persuade it to agree. Much of the detailed study of the proposals will pay off at this stage as the team will be obliged to respond to unexpectedly astute questions and, sometimes, to combat high-level lobbying by over-eager salesmen.

SUMMARY

This chapter completes the explanation as to how and why to select a local area network. A successful outcome depends on both professional skill and managerial competence, and cannot be the application of a standard formula. I hope that these chapters will help to guide some buyers through the uncertainties of a complex and rapidly changing field.

PART VI

Conclusion

27. THE FUTURE OF LOCAL AREA NETWORKS

In its first part this book discussed some of the problems that LANs have been developed to solve, and showed how developments in electronics make LANs especially important for the systems of the 1980s. It explained the promise of the data ring main.

How far do LANs live up to that promise?

The first point to note is the sheer variety of LANs. This book has categorized LANs in several ways. It has described seven capacity-sharing algorithms (each of which exists in multiple versions), seven topologies, and nine kinds of physical medium. It has also shown that, while some alternatives are better than others for certain purposes, none is unambiguously 'best'.

Since LANs vary in their intended functions as well as in their underlying technologies, the book has also divided LAN products into five categories based on the kinds of device that each LAN is able to support effectively. Within each category almost any set of technical options may be chosen as the basis of a successful product.

It is clear that there is little likelihood of a single standard emerging from this confusion—a mixture of official standards, *de facto* standards, and proprietary designs will continue in use for the foreseeable future. Indeed, continuing product announcements show that the variety will increase before the inevitable market shakeout banishes the losers to the history books.

Despite these difficulties and the immaturity of the commercial products, (as discussed in Chapter 21), existing systems are able to provide clear benefits. These benefits include the ability for a single terminal or workstation to gain access to a wide variety of shared facilities, and savings in cabling and recabling costs. In general, though, the greatest benefits have come from the use of the high-speed LAN channel to facilitate the sharing of expensive peripherals, rather than from increased connectivity for terminals.

This finding is consistent with the general argument about changes in business communications patterns that was developed in the first part of the book. This showed that a movement away from terminal-to-host data circuits towards inter-computer communication was to be expected. This shift, and the LAN technologies, lead to the formulation of new communications architectures which can exploit the advantages of LANs, and which were discussed in Chapter 22.

It is probably for this reason that most of the initial sales of LANs have been as an integral part of some data or text processing system. It is the bundled LANs that have dominated the market. This is likely to continue (Flint, 1981) because it puts the job of justifying the LAN onto the system supplier and because it is easier and cheaper for him to implement a limited system than a more comprehensive one.

Success in the market will therefore depend more on the adoption by dominant suppliers and the availability of compatible equipment than on technical merit *per se.* It follows that ARCNet, Ethernet, HYPERchannel, Wangnet, Z-Net, and Cluster One will be with us for some while to come. The token ring will become an important competitor just as soon as IBM announces a commitment to it.

The lack of standards will have only a limited influence on the users of bundled systems but, as time passes, users will wish increasingly to open their local networks by attaching equipment from several suppliers. For this they will need standards and, as in the past, both official and *de facto* standards will be important.

Though the lack of standards will not be a critical restraint on the use of LANs, the cost of connection will be. In 1982 the cost of attachment to a micronet or minicomputer LAN was somewhere between 100 dollars and 8,000 dollars, depending on the country of purchase, the nature and speed of the interface, and the supplier. LSI and VLSI technology have the potential of reducing these prices sharply. Figure 27.1 shows the way in which the price of a full-speed connection to micronets and minicomputer LANs is expected to fall over the next decade (Flint; 1981; Frost and Sullivan Inc., 1981; Metcalfe, 1982; Olteco, 1982).

Some suppliers will use this basic trend to reduce the prices of their products. Others will seek to resist the erosion of their prices by adding such extra features as network management, bridges, gateways, servers, terminal interface units, and protocol convertors. The market will therefore become increasingly competitive during the early 1980s, leading to a major shakeout later on.

FUTURE DIRECTIONS

Existing LANs are, largely, restricted to the communication of text, data, and fixed images. Many developers are actively working on support for digital speech and this became available on a few systems during 1982. The competitive pressures will therefore force many suppliers into the speech business. But speech, and telephony especially, is a much more subtle matter than people with a data networking background are likely to suppose. We are therefore likely to see some very poor speech systems offered during the 1980s.

Several different technical options exist for the support of telephony on a LAN. Thus, separate circuits may be used for each telephone call, allowing the LAN to reproduce the functions of the CBX, but providing for additional features.

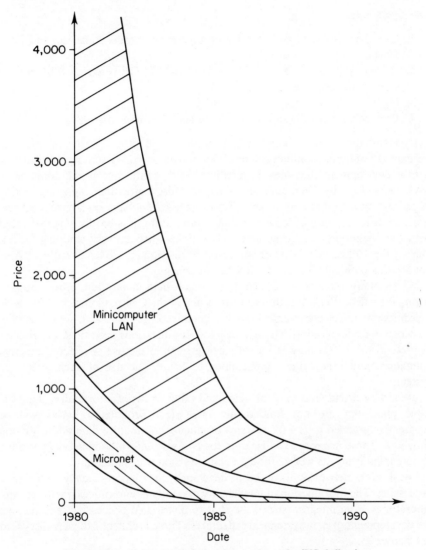

Figure 27.1   Price trends in local area networks (US dollars).

However, if voice, data and text are to be fully integrated, then they must be carried in the same channel. Speech, however, requires that the network transit time should be both short and consistent (Cohen, 1982).

Many existing LANs have difficulty in meeting these requirements (Ravasio, Marcogliese, and Novarese, 1982). To overcome these problems network developers may:

1. Use short packets, as in the Cambridge Ring (Leslie, Banerjee, and Love, 1981).
2. Reserve part of the bandwidth, as in CARTHAGE (Favre, 1982), but lose some of the promised flexibility.
3. Use much higher speeds (Limb, 1982).
4. Provide a separate operating mode for speech (Bux *et al*, 1982).

It is still too early to know which of these will prove most cost-effective. Perhaps the optimum solution will be different from anything so far published.

One development that may be predicted with confidence is the adoption of LAN technology by CBX suppliers. Chapter 5 drew attention to the distribution of processing now manifest in new CBXs. Since LANs have been developed precisely in order to support local distributed processing, it is hardly surprising that both the telephone companies and their suppliers are actively studying LANs. During the 1980s, these studies will result in distributed CBXs based on LANs but offering both LAN-like and CBX-like interfaces.

Whilst many vendors are designing for voice–data integration, others are preparing for video. Work at Litton Industries and at the Centre Commun d'Etude de Télédiffusion et Télécommunications has produced networks with some capacity for video–data integration. Though very few organizations need these capabilities at present, the 1990s may see a sufficient growth in the use of teleconferencing, animation, and other video applications to justify the use of such integrated systems.

In existing broadband systems video and other forms of information share the cable plant but are not functionally integrated. Broadband LANs will be progressively added to CATV systems producing community data and television networks. These networks will be used for two-way information services and for remote monitoring, as well as for data and television transmission.

Local area networks have been developed to support locally distributed processing. The introduction of intelligent workstations into offices, factories, and laboratories is an integral part of the shift to distributed processing, and permits the development of new systems architectures. These architectures were discussed in Chapter 23.

One of these, the Workstation Network Architecture (WNA), allows the advantages of personal computing to be combined with those of shared data and other resources. It provides an almost ideal basis for the development of office automation and other sophisticated information systems.

Many of the principles of the WNA can also be applied as between the component parts of a large computing facility producing a distributed computer complex. New large computer developments will move increasingly in this direction during the 1980s.

In both these architectures the linkage between the components is relatively loose, and each component is often able to pursue its own work without reference to other components. Research will increasingly allow a single operating system to control a group of computers, favouring the development of a closely coupled network computer (CCNC). CCNC will have high performance and reliability through the exploitation of redundancy and parallelism.

As Figure 27.2 shows, all these developments stem from the local area network and the new opportunities it offers to systems designers. It is noticeable that Figure 27.2 is, to a significant degree, the inverse of Figure 1.3, which showed

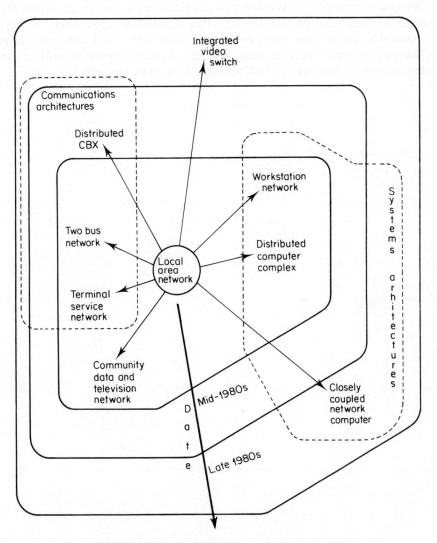

Figure 27.2 Future directions of LAN development.

how various technologies have converged to produce LANs. In this way LANs will pay back the debt they owe to their origins.

CONCLUSION

Whether these many future options are an advantage to those looking for an immediate answer to a current problem may be doubted. Indeed, the wide range of possibilities is a source of confusion rather than of enlightenment.

Despite their novelty, LANs are now established as an important part of the market for distributed data processing, office automation, and terminal support systems. The key to their value, however, lies not in the basic communications technology but rather with the things that can be done using the networks as an infrastructure. In that area the 1980s promise to be an exciting period.

APPENDIX 1

COMMERCIAL PRODUCTS MENTIONED IN THE TEXT

Product	Developer	UK Distributor
ARCNet*	Datapoint Corporation; also available from Standard Microsystems Corp.	
AWS^{tm} Workstation	Convergent Technologies	
Cable Net^{tm**}	Amdax Corp.	
Cambridge Ring	Acorn Ltd.	
Casenet	Computer and Systems Engineering Ltd.	
Clearway	Real Time Developments Ltd.	
Cluster One^{TM}	Nestar Systems Inc.	Zynar Ltd.
Comet	Computer Corporation of America	BLSL
Comtrol	Computrol Corporation	
CP/Net^{TM}	Digital Research Inc.	Vector International NV
CTOS^{TM}	Convergent Technologies Ltd.	
Data Ring	Toltec Data Ltd.	
Domain	Apollo Inc.	
Econet	Acorn Ltd.	
Ethernet^{TM}†	Xerox Corporation; also available from 3Com Interlan Sension Scientific Ltd. Bridge Communications TCL	Sintrom Ltd. Data Translation

APPENDIX 1 (*continued*)

Product	Developer	UK Distributor
Grapevine	Computer and Systems Engineering Ltd.	
Hi-Net	Digital Microsystems Inc.	
HYPERbus™	Network Systems Corporation	NSC Ltd.
HYPERchannel™	Network Systems Corporation	NSC Ltd.
IMP	Office Technology Ltd.	
IWS Workstation	Convergent Technologies	
LocalNet™	Sytek Corporation	Network Technology Ltd.
Loosely Coupled Network	CDC Inc.	
Modway	Modicon Division, Gould Industries Inc.	
Multilink	Nine Tiles Information Handling Ltd.	Hawker Siddeley Engineering Ltd.
Net/One™	Ungermann-Bass Inc.	Thame Systems Ltd.
Netskill	ICL Ltd.	
Network System™ 8000	Xerox Corporation	Rank-Xerox Ltd.
Omninet™	Corvus Inc.	Keen Computers Ltd.
OnTyme	Tymnet Inc.	
Planet	Racal-Milgo Ltd.	
Pluribus	BBN Computer Corporation	
Polynet	Logica Ltd.	
Primenet™	Prime Computer Corporation	
Prolink	Prolink Corporation	
Pronet	Proteon Associates Inc.	
QNet	Q1 Inc.	
Qube	Warner Amex Inc.	
R-Loop	IBM Corporation	
Research Machines Chain	Research Machines Ltd.	
Ringnet	Prime Computer Corporation	
Series 1 Ring (CM/1)	IBM Corporation	

APPENDIX 1 (*continued*)

Product	Developer	UK Distributor
Shinpads Bus	Sperry-Univac	
SILK^{TM}	Hasler AG	Hasler (GB) Ltd.
Transring 2000	Scientific and Electronic Enterprises Ltd.	
Ubits	Litton Industries Inc.	
Unet	3Com Corporation	Sintrom Ltd.
Videodata	Interactive Systems/3M	Ferranti Ltd.
Wangnet^{TM}	Wang Labs. Inc.	
XiBus	Xionics Ltd.	Master Systems
XiNet	Xionics Ltd.	Master Systems
Z-Net^{TM}	Zilog Inc.	

* ARCNet—compatible.

† Ethernet—compatible products are available from a number of suppliers including DEC, Intel, AMD, Fujitsu, Olivetti, Nixdorf, Thomson-CSF, Siemens, ICL, Three Rivers, Fortune, Altos, Perkin-Elmer, Intecom, Mitel, and Ungermann-Bass.

**Since withdrawn.

Trademarks

Amdax and Cablenet are trademarks of Amdax Corp.

ARC is a trademark of the Datapoint Corporation.

Convergent Technologies, Convergent, IWS, AWS, and CTOS are trademarks of Convergent Technologies.

Cluster One is a trademark of Nestar Systems Inc.

CP/M, MP/M, and CP/Net are trademarks of Digital Research Corporation.

Ethernet is a trademark of the Xerox Corporation.

HYPERbus and HYPERchannel are trademarks of Network Systems Corporation.

HXDP is a trademark of Honeywell Inc.

LocalNet, Tbox, and Tmux are trademarks of Sytek Inc.

LOCALNetter is a trademark of the Architecture Technology Corp.

Multibus is a trademark of the Intel Corporation.

Net/One is a trademark of Ungermann-Bass Inc.

Omninet is a trademark of Corvus Systems.

Primenet is a trademark of Prime Computer Inc.

Shinpads is a trademark of the Canadian Department of Defence.

SILK is a trademark of Hasler (Great Britain) Ltd.

Unibus is a trademark of Digital Equipment Corp.
Wangnet is a trademark of Wang Laboratories Inc.
Xerox, Network Systems, and NS are trademarks of the Xerox Corporation.
Z-Net is a trademark of Zilog Inc.

APPENDIX 2

MODEL SUPPLIER QUESTIONNAIRE FOR A COMMUNICATIONS NETWORK

This questionnaire is intended to be used as part of an Invitation to Propose (ItP). The ItP will also include a Statement of Requirements, as discussed in Chapter 26.

The questionnaire was developed for a multi-site engineering company in the United Kingdom and the network was intended to support various kinds of local and long-distance traffic. A local network was to be installed at each of the main sites, which would be interconnected by leased lines and which would also be connected to the PSTN and the UK Packet Switching Service. Some parts of it may be inapplicable to organizations with simpler requirements.

This questionnaire assumes that the network is to be installed in 1983 and that the SoR gave the requirements for 1983, 1985, and 1988. Different dates will be appropriate in other cases.

SUPPLIER QUESTIONNAIRE

Your proposal should answer all the questions below. If this is done by reference to other literature, such as standard technical manuals, please indicate against each question the exact place where the reference may be found.

We do not expect to find any ideal solution to our requirements. Therefore you need not feel that the inability to meet a few of the stated requirements will be, necessarily, fatal to your proposal. Where there is a shortfall please indicate this clearly, together with any proposal or plan you have for rectifying the position.

Failure to follow this guideline may result in your proposal being excluded from consideration.

A. GENERAL

1. Please give a brief description of the network you propose. (You should mention the general layout of the wiring, the capacity-sharing algorithm used, and the general nature of the devices that can be connected.)

2.   What configuration is proposed to meet the initial requirements and what will it cost? (Please indicate for each item:

> The function
> The number required
> The unit and extended prices
> The mean time between failures (MTBF)
> The mean time to repair (MTTR)

You should include all spares necessary to meet the stated availability requirements.)

3.   Are you able to meet the indicated timescale? If not, what is the earliest date that all equipment proposed could be ready for service?

4.   What upgrades would be required to meet the additional requirements? What is the price and delivery position for each item? (If you have no product that meets a requirement please indicate whether:

(a)   one can be obtained elsewhere or
(b)   you would be prepared to develop a custom solution and, if so, the likely price.)

5.   For the functions in the initial requirements what upgrades would be needed to meet:

> The 1985 numbers and volumes?
> The 1988 numbers and volumes?

For each please estimate prices in 1983 pounds.

6.   For how long has each kind of proposed equipment been available:

6.1   At all?
6.2   In the United Kingdom?

7.   How many users are there currently

7.1   All together?
7.2   In the United Kingdom?

8.   Is the proposed equipment PTT approved for connection to:

8.1   Leased lines?
8.2   PSTN?
8.3   The public dated network?

If not, what is the current position and when is such approval expected?

9.   What training and support is offered and at what price?

10. What are the maximum numbers of terminals and ports to which the proposed network may be expanded compatibly?

11. What are environmental requirements for the components? Are false floors, or other special constructions, necessary?

Availability

12. What is the availability of the system for:

Connecting an asynchronous terminal to a computer on the same site?
Connecting an intelligent workstation to a computer at the same site?

(The connections mentioned should be those of particular interest to the user community. If the reliability of some particular connections is critical this should have been stated in the preliminaries and these connections should be indicated here.)
State, in each case, the number of hours for which connection will be impossible during a year, the number of interruptions to the service that will be caused by the communications system, and the period for which something significantly less than full service will be available. If system enhancement and maintenance will cause service to cease during working hours any such periods should be allowed for.
You should assume that:

Leased lines fail twice per year and have an MTTR of 36 hours.
After an interruption to service users takes 5 minutes to reestablish their calls and contexts on remote computers.
Normal working hours are 08:30 to 05:30 Monday to Friday. Periods of failure outside these hours do not count towards unavailability.
X.25 connections to a public data network have the reliability of leased or switched lines as appropriate.
The public data network has an MTBF of 700 hours and MTTR of half an hour.
Cables laid in ducts on our sites will not be severed by accidental damage. All other local cables and wires will be accidentally broken once each year.)

These parameters were developed for a distributed processing installation in the United Kingdom in 1982. They may be different at other times and places.

Reference Sites

13.   Please name at least six users of the proposed equipment including at least
       two current users of each component.

B.   WIRING AND TRANSMISSION

1.   What cables must be installed to meet the initial requirements and where?
       Who will install the cables and how much will such installation cost?

2.   What additional cables will be needed to meet the 1985 and 1987 require-
       ments and who will install them? How much will any such extensions cost?

3.   Are there any special rules governing positioning, earthing, or the safety of
       the cables?

4.   What amplifiers, connectors, repeaters, filters, splitters power supplies, fre-
       quency convertors, etc., are needed to complete the basic site networks?
       How many of each are required and what will they cost?

5.   What signalling method is used on the cable?

C.   DEVICE INTERFACES

1.   Describe briefly the interface units used to connect terminals, computers,
       etc., to the local network.

2.   Are asynchronous and synchronous terminals supported transparently and
       what is the maximum speed available in each case? For transparent support,
       how is call addressing provided?

3.   For which of the following is protocol-sensitive support provided?

           X.25
           2780 BSC
           3270 SDLC
           ICL C03
           X.28, X.29, X.3
           IEEE 488

(Please indicate any other protocols you support.)
    In each case are the error control, addressing, and multiplexing features
of the protocol fully supported? What is the maximum speed available
through each interface?

4. If X.25 is available does the implementation:
    Avoid the need to poll terminals?
    Replace any ISO level 1, 2 or 3 protocols normally required?

5. To what extent is interworking between devices with different protocols supported?

D. CAPACITY-SHARING SYSTEM (LANs only.)

1. What system is used to share the capacity of the network between users?

2. What is the maximum capacity of the network and what happens to:

    (a) Throughput,
    (b) Traffic delay,

    if the offered load exceeds that capacity?

3. Under what circumstances, if any, can a single user occupy enough capacity to markedly worsen the service to others? What steps should be taken to avoid this?

E. BRIDGES

1. What equipment is proposed to interconnect the local networks at remote sites?

2. What network or other facility will carry signals between the sites? What is the maximum speed at which data can be transferred?

3. If leased lines are used, what is the general nature of the protocols and coding systems used on them? What modems are proposed?

4. If more than one leased line, switched line, or virtual circuit is used between two sites, is the traffic shared between them and on what basis?

5. If line noise becomes severe what corrective action, if any, will be taken?

6. In the event of the failure of a line or modem what recovery action will the system take automatically and how long will it take? How much data will be lost and how will these losses be indicated to devices with traffic on the failed link, if at all? What further action will be required of site staff and how long will this take?

7. If the direct circuit between two sites is lost but an indirect route exists will traffic be transferred to the route automatically? How long will this take and will any data be lost? If not, can the transfer be achieved manually?

F. GATEWAYS

1. How would you propose to connect your equipment to the existing data communications equipment? Can a single addressing scheme apply to both? Does this interconnection imply any loss of facilities?

2. *Datagrams.* Can local datagrams be forwarded into the public data networks and, if so, which?

3. Can datagrams be received from the public data network or other networks and presented as local datagrams?

4. *Protocol conversion.* What features exist to support interworking between incompatible:

   4.1   Terminals and computers?
   4.3   Cluster controllers and computers?
   4.4   Word processors?
   4.5   Facsimile and graphics machines?

5. In each case please state:

   5.1   The protocols or devices supported.
   5.2   The date the feature became available.
   5.3   Any restrictions on device operation.
   5.4   Whether the feature will be invoked automatically by the network or whether the user must specify the need.

6. *Call extension.* It is desirable for users to be able to access services that are not directly connected to this communications system. This may be provided by either:

   (a)   Connecting the user to another communications system from which he may request connections.
   (b)   Connecting the user to a port which has special hardware for this.
   (c)   Automatically and transparently extending calls across an appropriate communications system.

   Over which of the following communications services may calls be extended and under which of the above options?

   6.1   Public data network?

6.2   PSTN?

6.3   PABX?

6.4   A line to a similar system to this one, possibly at another site?

6.5   A line to a dissimilar system, possibly at another site, e.g. a line switch, a packet switch, an Ethernet, a Cambridge ring?

7.   *Call receipt.* It is sometimes desirable for remote users to be able to access services on the current system. Can such calls be accepted from:

7.1   Public data network?

7.2   PSTN?

7.3   PABX?

In each case what security checks may be imposed on the incoming call?

G.   CALL MANAGEMENT

This section relates to the support of dumb terminals, or of devices that emulate them, by a data circuit facility. It may be omitted if terminal support is not a requirement.

(Where the means used to initiate a call depend on the protocol used by the device or on its use of synchronous or asynchronous signalling, please answer these questions for each kind of device that behaves differently.)

1.   Is your network based on packet switching, circuit switching, or on some other principle?

2.   (a)   Circuit switching. Can a single network connection be used for several concurrent calls?

   (b)   Packet switching. Is a virtual circuit facility provided on top of or in addition to packet switching?

3.   For each site, and for the whole network, what is the maximum:

3.1   Data transmission rate?

3.2   Number of simultaneous logical connections?

3.3   Number of attached devices?

4.   What is the format and meaning of a network address? Can mnemonic addresses be understood by the network?

5.   When a user begins to use his terminal:

   Does the system automatically determine his transmission rate and, if so, within what limits?

Does the system remember such terminal characteristics as are necessary
to provide connection?
If not, what information must be supplied by the terminal user?
How is this done?

6. Are messages to users given in plain text or only in the form of codes?
(Please include a number of sample messages.) Can the texts of such
messages be varied by system management and, if so, is the variation
applied to specified users, to specified terminals, or to all users and terminals
indiscriminately? What other limitations apply to such variation; e.g.
message length, number of alternative messages for a single condition?

7. May terminal-to-port connections be made:

According to the configuration declared during system generation?
On instructions from network management?
As specified by terminal user at the time? How?

8. May all devices both initiate and receive calls, and are any special arrangements needed to ensure this?

9. *Hunting.* Assume that a single (logical) service, such as time-sharing, is
provided through a variety of ports, each limited in speed and protocol but
supporting, between them, a number of speeds and protocols. Given the
name of the service can the system automatically find:

A port that can accept the actual speed of the terminal?
A port that can accept the actual protocol of the terminal?

Or must the several groups of ports be addressed by different names?

10. *Camp-on.* If the required port is busy when called can the user opt to have
his request put in a queue for access? Can he subsequently leave the queue?
What information is given him as to his place in the queue and the likely
time at which he will be connected?
Can some users be given preference under such circumstances and, if so,
does this mean that:

They will be connected before other users who joined the queue first?
Other users will be disconnected?

11. *Conference calls.* Can calls be established between more than two devices or
ports? What is the maximum number? Is any contention or polling
discipline inherent or optional for such calls?

12. *Call redirection.* Can calls for one port be transferred to another:

> By network management?
> By the called service? How?

13. *System information.* Is the user offered any facilities whereby he may discover the state of the communications system and attached machines; e.g. congestion, lines down? Are there any features whereby network management may inform users, either online or offline, of current and future changes to the system?

14. *Access control.* Can some devices be given access to selected ports only? How many 'access classes' may be specified? Can any control be exercised over the protocol and transmission rate that may be used by a device? Can individual users (not devices) be made subject to such access restrictions? How is the user's identity established?

15. If the service of feature is not supported, in which cases would you be prepared to add it, to support it, and at what price?

H. NETWORK CONTROL

Centralisation

1. Can your network management system be run:

> From a central network control centre for the whole network?
> From each major site independently? If so, who is responsible for fixing faults on trunk lines?

2. What components are covered by your network management products and what information is maintained about each?

3. How is this information presented to central network management? (Please include sample displays, printouts, etc.)

4. When there is a failure of one of your devices does the alarm given to central network management specify the failed device? rack? board? chip? none of these? If it does not, is the information available elsewhere in the system? If not, can it be obtained through tests run from the centre? If not, how is it obtained? Is this true for all the devices that comprise the network?

5. Under what circumstances does this system break down? How often, and for how long, will this occur?

Line Characteristics

6. Can network management measure the transmission characteristics of lines whilst the lines carry live traffic? What parameters are measured? Is this done automatically and continuously and, if so, are the values automatically compared with alarm thresholds? Can changing values be shown as they vary over 10 minutes? 12 hours? 3 months? Is a graphical presentation available?

Maintenance

7. Can routine maintenance, fault location, and repair be carried out by board replacement by customer staff?

8. What maintenance service do you offer and at what price?

Error recovery

9. How are the following failures indicated to network control? What automatic recovery actions are provided and with what impact on users? What manual action would be recommended in each case?

   9.1 Severe line noise?
   9.2 Transient line failure?
   9.3 Permanent line failure?
   9.4 Transient modem failure?
   9.5 Permanent modem failure?
   9.6 Transient failure of encryption unit?
   9.7 Permanent failure of encryption unit?
   9.8 Transient failure of multiplexor or other, similar, component?
   9.9 Permanent failure of multiplexor or similar component?
   9.10 Failure of a switch?

Inter-Site Communications

10. Which of the following functions is possible within your proposal or as an optional feature (please distinguish)? Please indicate whether the function can be controlled from the centre and without assistance from the remote site.
   10.1 Switching to another bearer channel for backup.
   10.2 Reversion to PSTN for backup.
   10.3 Forcible connection and disconnection of selected terminals.
   10.4 Loop-back tests on central and remote modems.

Statistics and Accounting

11. What statistics and management information are provided? Are they machine-readable?

12. What accounting data are produced? How often and in what form? Are they machine-readable?

I.   STRATEGY

1. What, in your view, are the critical considerations for a company planning a communications network?

2. In what general directions do you expect to develop your product line in the future?

BIBLIOGRAPHY

SELECT LIST

The following books may be of special interest to the reader who wishes to consider LANs in greater depth.

Local Computer Networks, edited by P. Ravasio, G. Hopkins, and N. Naffah. The Proceedings of the IFIP TC.6 International Symposium on Local Computer Networks held in Florence during April 1982. Published by North-Holland. *The papers given at this conference include some of the most advanced research currently underway in the field.*

The LOCALNetter Designer's Handbook, edited by K.J. Thurber and published by Architecture Technology Corporation, Minneapolis. *This book includes details of many currently available commercial products.*

Tutorial—Local Computer Networks, edited by K.J. Thurber and H.A. Freeman. Second edition, published by the IEEE in 1981. *This is a collection of reprints of important articles in the LAN field.*

Local Area Networks and Distributed Office Systems, Proceedings of the conferences held in London in April 1981 and 1982. Published by Online Conferences. *Useful collections of papers, including some research and sales pitches, but focused on the practical value of LANs to business.*

The European Market for Local Area Networks, published by Frost and Sullivan, 1981.

REFERENCES

3Com (1982). *The 3Com Local Computer Network Vendor List.*

Albright, T.G. (1982). 'Radio data networks, the viable alternative to cable local distribution', *First Annual Phoenix Conference on Computers and Communications*, May 1982, pp. 286–287, IEEE.

Andersen, S.C. (1979). 'A serial data bus control method', *Computer Networks*, **3**, pp. 361–372.

Anderson, G.A. (1973). 'Interconnecting a distributed processor for avionics', *Proc. Symp. on Computer Architecture*, December 1973, pp. 11–20.

Ansaldi, W., Olobardi, M., and Traverso, A.M. (1982). 'Definition and development of a protocol for an industrial plant control network', in *Local Computer Networks* (Proc. IFIP Int. Symp., Florence, April 1982. Eds. P. Ravasio, G. Hopkins, and N. Naffah), pp. 351–371, North-Holland.

Ansart, J.P., Bloch, S., Seghaier, T., Martin, M., and Laurent, C.M. (1982). 'Danube local network interconnections via Transpac public network', in *Local Computer Networks* (Proc. IFIP Int. Symp., Florence, April 1982, Eds. P. Ravasio, G. Hopkins, and N. Naffah), pp. 279–287, North-Holland.

Arnold, R.G., Ramseyer, R.R., Wing, L.B., and Householder, E.A. (1981). 'The architecture of the MMBC system'. *J. Digital Systems*, **5(1/2)**, 39–65.

Arthurs, E., and Stuck, B.W. (1982). 'A theoretical performance analysis of polling and carrier sense collision detection communication systems', in *Local Computer Networks* (Proc. IFIP Int. Symp., Florence, April 1982, Eds. P. Ravasio, G. Hopkins, and N. Naffah.), pp. 415–437, North-Holland.

Arthurs, E., Stuck, B.W., Bux, W., Rosenthal, R., Marathe, M., Hawe W., Phinney, T., and Tarrassov, V. (1982). 'IEEE Project 802 LAN traffic handling characteristics committee report—working draft', January 1982.

Bair, J.H. (1979). 'Communication in the office of the future—where the real pay off may be'. *Business Communication Review*, **Jan.–Feb. 1979**, 3–11.

Balkovich, E.E., and Soceanu, A. (1982). 'A local computer network for performance measurement of locally distributed software', Paper given to the *IFIP International Symposium on Local Computer Networks*, Florence, April 1982.

Ball, J.E., Feldman, J., Low, J.R., Rashid, R., and Rovner, P. (1976). 'RIG, Rochester's intelligent gateway: system overview', *IEEE Trans. on Software Engineering*, **Dec. 1976**, 321–328.

Bass, C., Kennedy, J.S., and Davidson, J.M. (1980). 'Local network gives new flexibility to distributed processing', *Electronics*, **Sept. 25, 1980**, 114–122.

BCS Query Languages Group (1981). *Query Languages—A Unified Approach*, Heyden.

Beech, D. (Ed.) (1980). *Command Language Directions* (Proc. IFIP Working Conf., Berchtesgaden, September 1979), North-Holland.

Begley, A. (1982). 'The software development environment for a large real-time project', *First Annual Phoenix Conference on Computers and Communications*, May 1982, pp. 99–103, IEEE.

357

Bennett, C.J., and Hinchley, A.J. (1978). 'Measurements of the Transmission Control Protocol', *Computer Network Protocols Symposium*, Liège, Belgium, February 1978.

Biba, K.J. (1981a). 'Packet communication networks for broadband coaxial cable', *Local Networks and Distributed Office Systems*, 1981, pp. 661–625, Online Conferences.

Biba, K.J. (1981b). 'LocalNet: a digital communications network for broadband coaxial cable', *Digest of Papers, COMPCON 81 Spring*, pp. 59-63.

Biba, K.J., and Yeh, J.W. (1979). 'Fordnet: a front-end approach to local computer networks', *Proc. Local Area Communications Network Symposium, Boston, May 1979* (Eds. N.B. Meisner, and R. Rosenthal), pp. 199–215, MITRE and NBS.

Binder, R., Abramson, N., Kuo, F., Okinaka, A., and Wax, D. (1975). 'ALOHA packet broadcasting—a retrospect', *AFIPS Conference Proceedings*, **44, 1975 NCC**, 203–215.

Binney, P. (1981). 'How HYPERbus and HYPERchannel fit into a Two-Bus Local Network Architecture', *Local Networks and Distributed Office Systems*, pp. 73–83, Online Conferences.

Binns, S.E., Dallas, I.N., and Spratt, E.B. (1982). 'Further developments on the Cambridge Ring network at the University of Kent', in *Local Computer Networks* (Proc. IFIP Int. Symp., Florence, April 1982, Eds. P. Ravasio, G. Hopkins, and N. Naffah), pp. 183–204, North-Holland.

Bird, R.P. (1981). 'A dynamically microprogrammable machine as a variable function resource in a local area network', *International Symposium on Systems Architecture*, London, 1981. Also in *Microprocessing and Microprogramming*, **8(1)**.

Bittel, R. (1977). 'On frame check sequencee (FCS) generation and checking', ANSI Working Paper X3-S34-77-43.

Boggs, D.R., Shoch, J.F., Taft, E.A., and Metcalfe, R.M. (1980). 'PUP: an internetwork architecture', *IEEE Transactions on Communications*, **Com-28(4)**, 612–624.

Bucciarelli, P., and Enrico, G. (1982). 'Moving a service from a long-haul to a local network', in *Local Computer Networks* (Proc. IFIP Int. Symp., Florence, April 1982, Eds. P. Ravasio, G. Hopkins, and N. Naffah), pp. 249–264, North-Holland.

Butscher, B. (1981). 'HMINET 2—a local X.25 network connected to the German public data network', *Local Networks and Distributed Office Systems*, pp. 419–433, Online Conferences.

Bux, W. (1981). 'Local-area subnetworks: a performance comparison', in *Local Networks for Computer Communications* (Proc. IFIP WG6.4 Int. Workshop on Local Networks, Zürich, August 1980, Eds. A. West and P. Janson), pp. 157–180, North-Holland.

Bux, W., Amer, P., O'Leary, G.C.O., Gordon, R., Jabs, D., Marathe, M., Hawe, W., Phinney, T., and Tarassov, V. (1981). 'IEEE Project 802, Local Area Networks, Traffic Handling Characteristics Committee', Minutes of Meeting on 9–10 July 1981, Cambridge, Massachusetts.

Bux, W., Closs, F., Janson, P.A., Kummerle, K., Muller, H.R., and Rothauser, E.H. (1982). 'A local-area communication network based on a reliable token-ring system', in *Local Computer Networks* (Proc. IFIP Int. Symp., Florence, April 1982, Eds. P. Ravasio, G. Hopkins, and N. Naffah), pp. 69–82, North-Holland.

Cain, G.D., Morling, R.C., and Stevens, P.M. (1974). 'Comparisons of fixed and variable packet size for data communications', Technical Memorandum MN-2, Polytechnic of Central London, November 1974.

Canaday, R.N., *et al.* (1974). 'A back end computer for data base management', *Comm. ACM*, **17 (10)**.

Capel, A.C., Gilks, G.E., Basso, R.A., and Yan, G. (1981). 'A distributed local area network using non-contention protocols', *Computer Networking Symposium*, IEEE.

Capetanakis, J.I. (1979a). 'Generalised TDMA: the multi-accessing tree protocol', *IEEE Trans. Commun. COM-27*, October 1979, pp. 1476–1484.

Capetanakis, J.I. (1979b). 'Tree algorithms for packet broadcast channels', *IEEE Trans. Inf. Theory IT-25*, September 1979, pp. 505–515.

Carpenter, R.J., and Sokol, Jr. J. (1979). 'Serving users with a local area network', *Proc. Local Area Communications Network Symposium, Boston, May 1979* (Eds. N.B. Meisner and R. Rosenthal), pp. 75–85. MITRE and NBS.

Casteuil, D.S., Giovachino, D.L., and Lengyel, D.L. (1981). 'The first all-in-one local network', *Data Communications*, **Aug. 1981**, 93-102.

Champine, G.A. (1978). *Computer Technology Impact on Management*, North-Holland.

Chandy, K.M., Holmes, V., and Misra J. (1979). 'Distributed simulation of networks', *Computer Networks*, **3**, 105–113.

Chipman, J.D. (1982). 'The design of a large scale fiber optic transmission system for Vandenberg Air Base', *First Annual Phoenix Conference on Computers and Communications*, May 1982, pp. 333–339, IEEE.

Choran, I. (1969). *The Manager of a Small Company*, Montreal, McGill University, MBA Thesis (unpublished).

Christman, R.D. (1973). 'Development of the LASL computer network', *Digest of Papers, COMPCON '73*, pp. 239–242.

Clancy, Jr., G.J. (1981). 'A status report on the IEEE Project 802 local network standard', *Local Networks and Distributed Office Systems*, pp. 591–609, Online Conferences.

Clark, D.D., Pogran, K.T., and Reed, D.P. (1978). 'An introduction to local area networks'. *Proceedings of the IEEE*, **Nov. 1978**, 1497–1517.

Cohen, D. (1982). 'Using local area networks for carrying online voice', in *Local Computer Networks* (Proc. IFIP Int. Symp., Florence, April 1982, Eds. P. Ravasio, G. Hopkins, and N. Naffah) pp. 13–21, North-Holland.

Coleman, V. (1982). 'Siliconizing the local area network', A paper given to the *IFIP International Symposium on Local Computer Networks*, Florence, April 1982.

Communications News (1982). 'CATV moving to new heights in its growth', **Jan. 1982**, 40–41.

Cotton, I.W. (1980). 'Technologies for local area computer networks', *Proc. Office Automation Conf., Mar. 1980*, pp. 283–291.

Coviello, G., and Vena, P. (1975). 'Integration of circuit/packet switching in a SENET Concept', *NTC Conf. Proc., Dec. 1975*, pp. 42-12–42-17.

Coyne, R. (1981). 'Dynamic reconfiguration by a local network's operating system', *Data Communications*, **Dec. 1981**, 88–92.

Crane, R.C., and Taft, E.A. (1980). 'Practical considerations in Ethernet local network design', *Hawai Conference on System Sciences, Jan. 1980*.

Czaplicki, C.S. (1981). 'Advanced airborne executive', *Sixth Conference on Local Computer Networks*, Minneapolis, MN, October 1981, pp. 10–12.

Dalal, Y.K. (1977). 'Broadcast protocols in packet switched computer networks', Stanford University Digital Systems Laboratory, Technical Report 128, April 1977.

Dallas, I.N. (1980). *Transport Service Byte Stream Protocol*. Available from the Computing Laboratory, University of Kent, England. April 1980.

Dallas, I.N. (1981). 'A Cambridge Ring local area network realisation of a transport service', in *Local Networks for Computer Communications* (Proc. IFIP WG6.4 Int. Workshop on Local Networks, Zürich, August 1980, Eds. A. West and P. Janson), pp. 245–269, North-Holland.

Dallas, I.N. (1982). 'Implementation of a gateway between a Cambridge Ring local area network and a packet switching wide area network', *International Conference on Computer Communication*, London, September 1982.

Damsker, D. (1982). 'Totally distributed, redundantly structured hardware and software local computer control network', *Local Computer Networks* (Proc. IFIP Int. Symp., Florence, April 1982, Eds. P. Ravasio, G. Hopkins, and N. Naffah), pp. 83–99, North-Holland.

Danthine, A.A.S. (1982). 'Network interconnection', in *Local Computer Networks* (Proc. IFIP Int. Symp., Florence, April 1982, Eds. P. Ravasio, G. Hopkins, and N. Naffah), pp. 289–308, North-Holland.

Davidson, J.M. (1982). 'Connection-oriented protocols of Net/One', *Local Computer Networks* (Proc. IFIP Int. Symp., Florence, April 1982, Eds. P. Ravasio, G. Hopkins, and N. Naffah), pp. 319–333, North-Holland.

Davies, C.A. (1982). 'New systems and services for tomorrow's office', *Local Networks and Distributed Office Systems*, pp. 1–13, Online Conferences.

Day, J.D. (1981). 'Terminal, file transfer and remote job protocols for heterogenous computer networks', *Advances in Data Communications*, **1981**, 78–121.

Dearnley, P.A. (1982). 'Software development for microcomputer data processing systems', *Comp. J.*, **25**(2), 253–256.

DeSousa, M.R. (1981). 'Electronic information exchange in an office environment', *IBM Sys. J.*, **20**(1), 4–22.

Dewis, I.G. (1982). Teletex—setting the standard for electronic mail?', *Network Architectures, State of the Art Report*, **10**(1), 81–94.

DIX (1980). *The Ethernet; Data Link Layer and Physical Layer Specifications. Version 1.0*, DEC, Intel, and Xerox.

Donnelley, J.E., and Yeh, J.W. (1979). 'Interaction between protocol levels in a prioritised CSMA broadcast network', *Computer Networks*, **3**, 9–23.

Dunphy, J. (1982). 'Local fibre optics', *Systems International*, **Mar. 1978**, 21–26.

ECMA (1982). *ECMA 80, ECMA81*, and *ECMA82*. Available from the European Computer Manufacturers' Association, Rue du Rhone, 114, 1204 Geneva.

Elden, W.L. (1981). 'Gateways for interconnecting local area and long haul networks', *Local Networks and Distributed Office Systems*, pp. 391–406, Online Conferences.

El-Dessouki, O., Huen, W., and Evens, M. (1981). 'Towards a partitioning compiler for a distributed computing system', *J. Digital Systems*, **5** (1/2), 157–179.

Everett, R.R. (1975). 'The information bus', *Signal*, **Oct. 1975**, 12–14.

Farber, D.J., and Vittal, J.J. (1973). 'Extendability considerations in the design of the distributed computer system (DCS)', *Proc. Nat. Telecom. Conf.*, Atlanta, Georgia, November 1973, pp. 15E-1 to 15E-6.

Farmer, W.D., and Newhall, E.E. (1969). 'An experimental distributed switching system to handle bursty computer traffic', *Proc. ACM Symposium on Problems in the Optimisation of Data Communications*, October 1969, pp. 1–33.

Farrel, J. (1976). 'The data computer: a network data utility', *Proc. Berkeley Workshop 1976*.

Favre, J.L. (1982). 'CARTHAGE: a multi-service local network on a fiber optics loop', in *Local Computer Networks* (Proc. IFIP Int. Symp., Florence, April 1982, Eds. P. Ravasio, G. Hopkins, and N. Naffah), pp. 23–37, North-Holland.

Fishburn, M.A. (1982). 'High level protocols for office systems', *Local Networks and Distributed Offices Systems*, pp. 131–142, Online Conferences.

Fletcher, J.G. (1975). 'Principles of design in the OCTOPUS computer network', *Proc. ACM '75*, October 1975, pp. 325–328.

Fletcher, J.G., Fernbach, S., Dubois, P.J., and Boer, G.L. (1975). 'Computer storage structure and utilization at a large scientific laboratory', *Proc. of the IEEE*, August 1975, pp. 1104–1113.

Flint, D.C. (1981). 'The European market for local area networks', *Local Networks and Distributed Office Systems*, pp. 573–590, Online Conferences.

Flint, D.C. (1982a). 'The local area network as the backbone of new business systems', *Local Networks and Distributed Office Systems*, pp. 15–32, Online Conferences.

Flint, D.C. (1982b). *The Market for Office Technology*, Vol. 1: *The Technology*. Butler, Cox and Partners Ltd., London.

Forth, L. (1980). 'The null protocol network: influence and developments using microprocessors', *Data Networks: Uses and Development*, pp. 251–263, Online Conferences.

Fox, B. (1979). 'Infrared light for a new wireless revolution', *New Scientist*, 20/27 December 1979, pp. 931–933.

Fox, B. (1982). 'Why radio is running out of airwaves', *New Scientist*, 8 April 1982, pp. 81–83.

Fraser, A.G. (1979). 'DATAKIT—a modular network for synchronous and asynchronous traffic', *ICC '79 Conference Record, June 1979*, pp. 20.1.1–20.1.3.

Frost and Sullivan Inc. (1980). *The US Market for Two-Way Business Communications*.

Frost and Sullivan Inc. (1981). *The European Market for Local Area Networks*.

Gable, M.G., and Sherman, R.H. (1981). 'Carrier sense multiple-acess with feedback', *Local Networks and Distributed Office Systems*, pp. 199–214, Online Conferences.

Gardner, L.B. (1982). 'A hierarchical interlocking network for computer-controlled manufacturing', *First Annual Phoenix Conference on Computers and Communications*, May 1982, pp. 76–78, IEEE.

Gardner, Jr. P.C., and Hartman, T.C. (1980). 'VNET: how it developed and how we use it', *Data Networks: Development and Uses*, pp. 75–93, Online Conferences.

Garrow, R.A., Alker, P.L., and Rosenfeld, P. (1980). 'Technologies converge in multifunction', *Mini-Micro Systems*, October 1980.

Gates, G.W., and Tjaden, G.S. (1982). 'The INDAX two-cable CATV for Videotex services', *Videotex '82*, pp. 465–475, Online Conferences.

Gentleman, W.M., and Corman, J.E. (1981). 'Design considerations for a local area network connecting diverse primitive machines', in *Local Networks for Computer Communications* (Proc. IFIP WG6.4 Int. Workshop on Local Networks, Zürich, August 1980, Eds. A. West and P. Janson), pp. 207–221, North-Holland.

Gien, M., and Zimmermann, H. (1979). 'Design principles for network interconnection', INRIA SCH 619, May 1979.

Gordon, R.L., Farr, W.W., and Levine, P. (1979). 'Ringnet: a packet switched local network with decentralized control', *Fourth Conference on Local Computer Networks*, Minneapolis, October 1979, pp. 13–19.

Greenfeld, N.R. (1981). 'Jericho—a professional's personal computer system', *Eighth Annual Symposium on Computer Architecture*, Minneapolis, May 1981, pp. 217–226, IEEE.

Guillemont, M. (1982). 'The CHORUS distributed operating system: design and implementation', in *Local Computer Networks* (Proc. IFIP Int. Symp., Florence, April 1982, Eds. P. Ravasio, G. Hopkins, and N. Naffah), pp. 207–223, North-Holland.

Hafner, E.R., and Nenadal, Z. (1976). 'Enhancing the availability of a loop system by meshing', *1976 Int. Zürich Seminar on Digital Communications*, Zürich, March 1976.

Hafner, E.R., Nenadal, Z., and Tschanz, M. (1973). 'A digital loop communications system', *International Conference on Communications (ICC) '73*, Seattle, June 1973, pp. 50-24–50-29. Revised version published in *IEEE Trans. on Comms.*, June 1974, pp. 877–881.

Hafner, E.R., Nenadal, Z., and Tschanz, M. (1975). 'Integrated local communications—principles and realisation', *Hasler Review*, **8**(2), 34–43.

Hanna, F.K., and Wakeman, C.J. (1981). 'Teletext server for computer networks', *Software & Microsystems*, **1**(1), 8–12.

Hanson, K., Chou, W., and Nilson, A. (1981). 'Integration of voice, data and image traffic on a wideband local network', *Proc. Computer Networking Symposium*, Gaithersburg, MS, December 1981, pp. 3–11.

Harding, L. (1982). 'Contents addressable filestore as a network resource', *Sixth International Conference on Computer Communications*, London, September 1982.

Higginson, P.L., and Kirstein, P.T. (1981). 'Network inter-connection with provision for electronic mail services', *Local Networks and Distributed Office Systems*, pp. 107–121, Online Conferences.

Hopkins, G.T. (1977). 'A bus communications system', Mitre Technical Report MTR-3615.

Hopkins, G.T. (1979). 'Multimode communications on the MITRENET', *Proc. Local Area Communication Network Symposium*, Boston, May 1979 (Eds. N.B. Meisner and R. Rosenthal), pp. 169–177, MITRE and NBS.

Hopkins, G.T. (1980). 'Recent developments on MITRENET', *Local Networks and Distributed Office Systems*, Online Conferences.

Hopkins, G.T. (1981). 'Recent developments on the MITRENET', *Local Networks and Distributed Office Systems*, pp. 97–105, Online Conferences.

Hopper, A. (1978). 'Data Ring at the Computer Laboratory, University of Cambridge', *Local Area Networking*, NBS Special Publication 500-31, April 1978, pp. 11–17.

Hopper, K. (Ed) (1981). 'User-orientated job control language', Report of the BCS Working Group on JCL, Heyden.

Horton, R.E., and Miller, W.L. (1980). 'A multipoint link control protocol based on HDLC with source-destination addressing', *Fifth Conference on Local Computer Networks*, Minneapolis, October 1980, pp. 86–92, IEEE.

Hudson, D. (1981). 'PBX will be the integrating element of multi-node information systems', *Communications News*, **Aug. 1981**, 22–23.

Huen, W., Greene, P., Hochsprung, R., and El-Dessouki, O. (1977). 'A network computer for distributed processing', *Digest of Papers, COMPCON, 77* **Fall**, 326–330.

IEC (1980). 'Process data highway (PROWAY) for distributed process control systems Part I—general introduction and functional requirements', IEC Technical Committee N.65.

IEEE (1981). *Local Network Standards Committee Functional Requirements Document*, Version 5.4, October 1981.

IEEE (1982). *IEEE Project 802 Local Network Standards—Draft C*, May 17, 1982. Available from Maris Graube, Tektronix, Box 500, MS 58-240, Beaverton, OR 97077, USA.

ISO (1979). 433 Revised (ISO/TC97/sc6/N 2100): 'Consolidation of HDLC elements of procedures'. Also ISO 62: 'HDLC balanced class of procedures'.

ISO (1980). DP7498: *Data Processing—Open Systems Interconnection—Basic Reference Model*, Dec. 3, 1980.

ITAP (1982). *Report on Cable Systems* (by the Cabinet Office Information Technology Advisory Panel), HMSO.

Jackson, B., Nicholson, J., Roberts, B., and Snelling, M. (1981). 'SILK: an integrated voice and data system', *Local Networks and Distributed Office Systems*, pp. 47–63, Online Conferences.

Jacobsen, T. (1980). The ISO reference model of open systems interconnection', *Data Networks Development and Uses*, Online Conferences.

Jensen, E.D. (1976). 'Distributed processing in a real-time environment', *Infotech State of the Art Report on Distributed Systems*, 1976, pp. 304–318.

Jensen E.D. (1978). 'The Honeywell experimental distributed processor—an overview', *Computer*, **Jan. 1978**, 28–38.

Johnson, M.A. (1980). '*Ring Byte Stream Protocol*'. Available from the Computer Laboratory, Cambridge, England, April 1980.

Kahn, R.E., Gronemeyer, S.A., Burchfield, J., and Kunzelman, R.C. (1978). 'Advances in packet radio technology', *Proc. IEEE*, **66**(11), November 1978.

Kawasaki, B.S., and Hill, K.O. (1977). 'Low-loss access coupler for multi-mode optical fibre distribution networks', *Appl. Optics*, **16**(7), July 1977, 1794.

Kearns, R.F., and Basch, EE. (1982). 'Application of fiber optics for computer data links', *First Annual Phoenix Conference on Computers and Communications*, May 1982, pp. 343–345, IEEE.

Kilzer, D.J. (1982). 'Computers and materials handling', *First Annual Phoenix Conference on Computers and Communications*, May 1982, pp. 73–75, IEEE.

Kirstein, P.T., King, D., Burren, J., McDowell, C., Daniels, R., Needham, R. and Griffiths, J.W.R., 1982. 'The Universe Project'. *Pathways to the Information Society*. (Proc. 6th ICCC. Edited by M.B. Williams.) North-Holland, pp. 442–447.

Knight, J.R. (1972). 'A case study: airline reservation systems', *Proc. IEEE*, **60**(11), November 1972, 1423–1441.

Kong, I., and Lindsey, L. (1982). 'CableNet: a Local area network reservation scheme', *COMPCON '82*, pp. 182–186, IEEE.

Kuhns, R.C., and Shoquist, M.C. (1979). 'A serial data bus system for local processing networks', *Digest of Papers, COMPCON 79*, **Spring**, 266–271.

Kunikyo, T., and Ozeki, T. (1982). 'Administrator contention optical radial network—ACORN', Paper given to the *IFIP International Symposium on Local Computer Networks*, Florence, April 1982.

Leslie, I.M. (1982). 'A high performance gateway for the local connection of Cambridge Rings', *Local Computer Networks*, (Proc. IFIP Int. Symp., Florence, April 1982, Eds. P. Ravasio, G. Hopkins, and N. Naffah), pp. 267–277, North-Holland.

Leslie, I.M., Banerjee, R., and Love, S.J. (1981). 'Organisation of voice communication on the Cambridge Ring', *Local Networks and Distributed Office Systems*, pp. 465–474, Online Conferences.

Limb, J.O. (1982). 'High speed operation of broadcast local networks', *ICC '82*.

Linnington, P.F. (1982). 'File transfer protocols', *Network Architectures*, State of the Art Report 10(1). pp. 159–174, Pergamon-Infotech.

Liu, M.T. (1978). 'Distributed loop computer networks', *Advances in Computers*, **17**, 163–221.

Liu, M.T., Tsay, D.P., and Lian, R.C. (1982). 'Design of a network operating system for the distributed double-loop computer network', in *Local Computer Networks* (Proc. IFIP Int. Symp., Florence, April 1982, Eds. P. Ravasio, G. Hopkins, and N. Naffah), pp. 227–248, North-Holland.

Lorin, H. (1980). *Aspects of Distributed Computer Systems*, Wiley-Interscience.

Lowenthal, E. (1982). 'Database systems for local nets', *Datamation*, **Aug. 1982**, 97–106.

Luczak, E.C. (1978). 'Global bus computer communication techniques', *Proceedings, Computer Networking Symposium*, December 1978.

Mackie, J. (1982). 'Tomorrow's PABX/data switch', Paper given to the *Online Conference on Local Networks and Distributed Office Systems*, London, April 1982.

Malone, J. (1981). *Data Communications*, **Dec. 1981**, 101–104.

Mann, W.F., Ornstein, S.M., and Kraley, M.F. (1976). 'A network-oriented multiprocessor front-end handling many hosts and hundreds of terminals', *AFIPS Conference Proceeding 45, 1976 NCC*, pp. 533–540.

Manning, E.G., and Peebles, R.W. (1977). 'A homogeneous network for data-sharing communications', *Computer Networks*, **May 1977**, 211–224.

Marathe, M., and Hawe, W. (1982). 'Performance of a simulated Ethernet programming environment', *Electro/82*, Boston, Massachusetts, May 1982.

Martin, J. (1981). *Networks and Distributed Processing—Software, Techniques and Architecture*, Prentice-Hall Inc.

Masterman, P.H. (1980). 'The RSRE pilot packet-switched network', *Data Networks: Development and Uses*, pp. 277–292, Online Conferences.

Meijer, A., and Peters, P.P. (1982). 'Proprietary network architectures and OSI', *Network Architectures*, State of the Art Report 10(1), Pergamon-Infotech.

Meisner, N.B. (1980). 'The information bus in the automated office', in *Integrated Office Systems—Burotics* (Ed. N. Naffah), North-Holland.

Meisner, N. (1982). 'Methodology for assessing the robustness of a local network based computer system', in *Local Computer Networks* (Proc. IFIP Int. Symp., Florence, April 1982, Eds. P. Ravasio, G. Hopkins, and N. Naffah), pp. 389–394, North-Holland.

Meisner, N., and West, A. (1980). 'Report of the working session on local area networks', in *Integrated Office Systems—Burotics* (Ed. N. Naffah), pp. 228–246, North-Holland.

Melvin, D.K. (1981). 'Voice on Ethernet—now!', *National Telecommunications Conference*, New Orleans, November 1981.

Mesiva, M.F., Miller, G.E., and Pinnow, D.A. (1982). 'Mini-hub addressable distribution system for hi-rise application', *First Annual Phoenix Conference on Computers and Communications*, May 1982, pp. 346–351, IEEE.

Metcalfe, R.M. (1982). 'Ethernet—US developments', Paper given to *Local Networks and Distributed Office Systems*, May 1982, Online Conferences.

Metcalfe, R.M., and Boggs, D.R. (1976). 'Ethernet: distributed packet switching for local computer networks', *Comm. ACM*, **19**(7), July 1976, 395–404.

Mier, E.E. (1982). 'High-level protocols, standards and the OSI reference model', *Data Communications*, **July 1982**, 71–101.

Miller, C.K., and Thompson, D.M. (1982). 'Making a case for token-passing in local networks', *Data Communications*, **Mar. 1982**, 79–88.

Miller, F.W. (1979). 'Computer talk: it's a here and now technology', *Infosystems*, **Aug. 1979**, 68–69.

Mintzberg, H. (1968). *The Manager at Work—Determining his Activities, Roles and Programs by Structured Observation*, Ph.D. Thesis, M.I.T. Sloan School of Management. Cambridge, Mass.

Mintzberg, H. (1973). *The nature of managerial work*. Harper and Row.

Misunas, D.P., and Peterson, H.R. (1981). 'Replacing 3270s without sacrificing functions', *Data Communications*, **Nov. 1981**, 83–92.

Moran, D.M., and Starkson, R.O. (1975)). 'A hybrid communications switching system', *Proceedings, Electronics Components Conference*, 1975, pp. 30–36.

Mori, H., and Norigoe, M. (1976). 'Binary search polling—another technique of multiple access control', *Proc. Int. Switching Symp.*, Kyoto, October 1976, Vol. 1, pp. 143/2/1–143/2/8.

Müller, H.R., Keller, H., and Meyr, H. (1982). 'Transmission in a synchronous token ring', in *Local Computer Networks* (Proc. IFIP Int. Symp., Florence, April 1982, Eds. P. Ravasio, G. Hopkins, and N. Naffah), pp. 125–147, North-Holland.

Naffah, N. (Ed.) (1980). 'Integrated office systems protocols', *Integrated Office Systems—Burotics*, North-Holland.

Naffah, N. (1981). 'Distributed office systems', *Local Networks and Distributed Office Systems*, pp. 627–641, Online Conferences.

Naffah, N. (1982). 'Interconnection to the outside world', Paper given to the *Online Conference on Local Networks and Distributed Office Systems*, London, April 1982.

Needham, R.M. (1981). 'Design considerations for a processing server', *Eighth Annual Symposium on Computer Architecture*, Minneapolis, May 1981, pp. 501–504, IEEE.

Nickens, D.O., Genduso, T.B., and Su, S.Y.W. (1980). 'The architecture and hardware implementation of a prototype micronet', *Fifth Conference on Local Computer Networks*, Minneapolis, MN, October 1980, pp. 56–64.

Nilsson, A., Chou, W., and Graff, C.J. (1980). 'A packet radio communication system architecture in a mixed traffic and dynamic architecture', *Proc. Computer Networking Symposium*, Gaithersburg, December 1980, pp. 51–66.

Olteco (1982). Paper given to the *IFIP International Symposium on Local Computer Networks*, Florence, April 1982.

Pierce, J.R., Coker, C.H., and Kropfl, W.J. (1971). 'An experiment in addressed block data transmission around a loop', *IEEE International Convention Record*, March 1971, pp. 222–223.

Piney, C., Parkman, C., and Fluckiger, F. (1980). 'Endpoint interconnection of high-speed local packet networks in a virtual call environment', *Fifth Conference on Local Computer Networks*, Minneapolis, MN, October 1980, pp. 41–51.

Pliner, M.S., and Hunter, J.S. (1982). 'Operational experience with open broadband local area networks', *Local Area Networks and Distributed Office Systems*, pp. 71–86, Online Conferences.

Pohm, A.V., Davis, J.A., Christiansen, S., Bridges, G.D., and Horton, R.E. (1979). 'A local network of mini and microcomputers for experiment support', *Computer Networks*, 33, 381–387.

Polishuk, P. (1980). 'Fibre optics in data networks', *Advances in Data Communications Management*, 1, 174–190.

Postel, J. (1980). 'Internetwork protocols', *IEEE Trans. on Comms.*, **April 1980**, 604–611.

Pouzin, L. (1977). 'Network interconnection', Reseau Cyclades, SCH 608, September 1977.

Puzman, J., and Porizek, R. (1980). *Communication Control in Computer Networks*, p. 296 John Wiley.

Ravasio, P.C., Marcogliese, R., and Novarese, R. (1982). 'Voice transmission over an Ethernet backbone', in *Local Computer Networks* (Proc. IFIP Int. Symp., Florence, April 1982, Eds. P. Ravasio, G. Hopkins, and N. Naffah), pp. 39–65, North-Holland.

Rawson, E.G. (1979). 'Application of fibre optics to local networks', *Proc. of the Local Area Communications Network Symposium, Boston, May 1979* (Eds. N.B. Meisner, and R. Rosenthal), pp. 155–168, MITRE and NBS.

Rawson, E.G., and Metcalfe, R.N. (1978). 'Fibrenet: multimode optical fibres for local computer networks', *IEEE Trans. on Comms.*, **July 1978**, 983–990.

Reames, C.C., and Liu, M.T. (1975). 'A loop network for simultaneous transmission of variable length messages', *Proc. Second Ann. Symp. on Computer Architecture*, January 1975, pp. 7–12.

Richer, I. (1980). 'Voice, data and the computerised PABX: an electronic office', in *Integrated Office Systems—Burotics* (Ed. N. Naffah), North-Holland.

Roman, G.S. (1977). 'The design of broadband coaxial cable networks for multinode communications', Mitre Technical Report MTR-3527.

Roman, G.S. (1979). 'Alignment and performance verification of a two-way coaxial cable system', Mitre Technical Report MTR-3769.

Rubinstein, M.J., Kennington, C.J., and Knight, G.J. (1981). 'Terminal support on the Cambridge Ring', *Local Networks and Distributed Office Systems*, pp. 475–490, Online Conferences.

Saltzer, J.H. (1982). 'On the naming and binding of network destinations', in *Local Computer Networks* (Proc. IFIP Int. Symp., Florence, April 1982, Eds. P. Ravasio, G. Hopkins, and N. Naffah), pp. 311–317, North-Holland.

Saltzer, J. H., and Pogran, K.T. (1979). 'A star-shaped ring with high maintainability', *Proc. of the Local Area Communications Network Symposium, Boston, May 1979* (Eds. N.B. Meisner, and R. Rosenthal), pp. 179–189.

Saltzer, J.H., Reed, D.P., and Clark, D.D. (1981). 'Source routing for campus-wide iternet transport', in *Local Networks for Computer Communications* (Proc. IFIP WG6.4 Int. Workshop on Local Networks, Zürich, August 1980, Eds. A. West, and P. Janson), pp. 1–23, North-Holland.

Scantlebury, R. (1982). 'The evolution of X.25', *Network Architectures*, State of the Art Report 10(1), Pergamon-Infotech.

Scantlebury, R. A., and Wilkinson, P.T. (1971). 'The design of a switching system to allow remote access to computer services by other computers and terminal devices', *CM/IEEE Second Symposium on Problems in the Optimisation of Data Communications Systems*, October 1971, pp. 160–167.

Scheurer, B. (1980). 'Local network in the Kayak project', *DATA COMM*, Geneva, June 1980, pp. 314–319.

Schindler, S., and Flasche, U. (1981). 'Presentation service—the philosophy', *Local Networks and Distributed Office Systems*, pp. 233–244, Online Conferences.

Scholfield, N. (1981). 'NATO data communications interface standards', Memorandum to George White, *National Communications Systems*, 8 Jan. 1981.

Schultze, E. (1979). 'Simulation of the traffic on the SILK loop', *Hasler Review*, **12** (3/4), 76–81.

Schutt, T.E., and Welch, P.H. (1981). 'Applying microcomputers in a local area network', *Local Area Networks and Distributed Office Systems*, pp. 491–501, Online Conferences.

Sedillot, S., and Sergeant, G. (1980). 'A protocol for distributed execution and consistent resource allocation', Paper given at *COMPCON*, Fall 1980.

SERC (1982). *Cambridge Ring 82 Interface Specifications*, Draft 4 Available from The Computer Board for Universities and Research Councils, Elizabeth House, York Road, London SE1 7PH.

Shaffer, R.A. (1980). 'Home, office wiring to carry lots more than current(ly)', *Wall Street Journal*, July 1980.

Shaw Intermedia (1981). 'ITV must respond to satellite opportunities', July 1981.

Sherman, R.H., Gable, M.G., and Chung, A. (1982). 'Overcoming local and long-haul incompatibility', *Data Communications*, **Mar. 1982**, 195–206.

Shirer, D.L. (1982). 'Local communications networks for computer-based instruction', *First Annual Phoenix Conference on Computers and Communications*, May 1982, pp. 281–282, IEEE.

Shoch, J.F. (1979). 'Packet fragmentation in inter-network protocols', *Computer Networks*, **3**, 3–8.

Shoch, J.F. (1980). *An Annotated Bibliography on Local Computer Networks*, Xerox, 62 pp.

Shoch, J. (1981). 'Carrying voice traffic through an Ethernet local network—a general overview', in *Local Networks for Computer Communications* (Proc. IFIP WG6.4 Int. Workshop on Local Networks, Zürich, August 1981, Eds. A. West, and P. Janson), pp. 429–446, North-Holland.

Shoch, J.F., and Hupp, J.A. (1979). 'Performance of an Ethernet local network, a preliminary report', in *Proc. Local Area Communications Network Symposium, Boston, May 1979* (Eds. N.B. Meisner and R. Rosenthal), pp. 113–125, MITRE and NBS.

Shoch, J., and Hupp, J.A. (1980a). 'Measured performance of an Ethernet local network', *Comm. ACM*, **23**, (12), December 1980, 711–721.

Shoch, J.F., and Hupp, J.A. (1980b). 'Notes on the "worm" programs–some early experience with distributed computation', IFIP WG 6.4 Working Paper 80/19, pp. 6-1–6-16.

Shoch, J.F., and Stewart, L. (1979). 'Internetwork experiments with the Bay Area packet radio network', Xerox.

Sloman, M.A., and Prince, S. (1981). 'Local network architecture for process control', in *Local Networks for Computer Communications* (Proc. IFIP WG6.4 Int. Workshop on Local Networks, Zürich, August 1980, Eds. A. West and P. Janson), pp. 407–427, North-Holland.

Smith, S.M. (1979) 'Use of broadband coaxial cable networks in an assembly plant environment', *Proceedings of the Local Area Communications Network Symposium, Boston, May 1979* (Eds. N.B. Meisner and R. Rosenthal), MITRE and NBS.

Spiegleman, A. (1982). 'The Statmux as a productivity tool', *Telecommunications*, **April 1982**, 47–52.

Spratt, E.B. (1976). 'The future of university computer centres in the decade 1977/87—a personal view', *UMRCC Journal*, Spring 1976.

Spratt, E.B. (1981). 'Operational experiences with a Cambridge Ring local area network in a university environment', in *Local Networks for Computer Communications* (Proc. IFIP WG6.4 Int. Workshop on Local Networks, Zürich, August 1980, Eds. A. West and P. Janson), pp. 81–106, North-Holland.

Springer, J.F. (1978). 'The distributed data network. Its architecture and operation', *COMPCON 78 Fall*, September 1978, pp. 221–228.

Stack, T. (1981). 'LAN protocol residency alternatives for IBM mainframe open system interconnection', *Local Networks and Distributed Office Systems*, pp. 435–450, Online Conferences.

Stack, T.R., and Dillencourt, K.A. (1981). 'Functional description of a value-added local area network', *Proc. Computer Networking Symposium*, Gaithersburg, December 1981, pp. 24–30.

Stahlman, M. (1982). 'Inside Wang's Local Net Architecture', *Data Communications*, **Jan. 1982**, 85–90.

Sterling, T.L., Williams, R.D., and Kirtley, Jr. J.L. (1982). 'COMONET: an intra-building data link', in *Local Computer Networks* (Proc. IFIP Int. Symp., Florence, April 1982, Eds. P. Ravasio, G. Hopkins, and N. Naffah), pp. 149–163, North-Holland.

Strassman, P.A. (1979). 'The office of the future: information management for a new age', *Technology Review*, MIT Alumni Association, December–January 1979, pp. 54–66.

Strassman, P.A. (1982). 'Concepts and principles of office automation development', Xerox Executive Communications Exchange Program.

Sunshine, C. (1977). 'Interconnection of computer networks', *Computer Networks*, **1**, 175–195.

Swan, R.J., Fuller, S.H., and Siewiorek, D.P. (1977). 'CM*—a Modular, multi-microprocessor', *Proceedings, National Computer Conference*, 1977, pp. 637–644.

Sweetman, D. (1981). 'A distributed system built with a Cambridge Ring', *Local Networks and Distributed Office Systems*, pp. 451–464, Online Conferences.

Swinehart, D., McDaniel, G., and Boggs, D. (1979). 'WFS: a simple shared file system for a distributed environment', *Oper. Sys. Rev.*, **13**. November 79.

Sze, D.T.W. (1982). 'IEEE LAN Project 802—a current status', *Local Area Networks and Distributed Office Systems*, pp. 109–120, Online Conferences.

Teitelman, W. (1977). 'A display-orientated programmer's assistant', *Proc. Fifth Int. Joint Conf. on Artificial Intelligence*, Cambridge, Mass., August 1977.

Thacker, C.P., McCreight, E.M., Lampson, B.W., Sproull, R.F., and Boggs, D.R. (1979). 'Alto: a personal computer', in *Computer Structures: Readings and Examples* (Eds. D.P. Siewiork, C.G. Bell, and A. Newell), 2nd ed., 1979.

Thornton, J.E. (1979). 'Overview of HYPERchannel', *Digest of Papers, COMPCON 79 Spring*, San Francisco, February–March 1979, pp. 262–265.

Thornton, J.E. (1980). 'Back-end network approaches', *Computer*, **Feb 1980**, 10–17.

Thornton, J.E., Christensen, G.S., and Jones, P.D. (1975). 'A new approach to network storage management,' *Computer Design*, **14**(11), November 1975, 81–85.

Thurber, K.H. (Ed.) (1982). *The LOCALNetter Designer's Handbook*, Architecture Technology Corporation, Minneapolis.

Thurber, K. J., and Freeman, H.A. (1981). 'The many faces of local networking', *Data Communications*, **Dec. 1981**, 62–70.

Tobagi, F.A., and Hunt, V.B. (1979). 'Performance analysis of carrier sense multiple access with collision detection', *Proc. Local Area Communications Network Symposium, Boston, May 1979* (Eds. N.B. Meisner and R. Rosenthal), pp. 217–244, MITRE and NBS.

Tokoro, M., and Tamaru, K. (1977). 'Acknowledging Ethernet', *Digest of Papers, COMPCON 77 Fall*, pp. 320–325.

Torp, J. (1980). 'Scandinavian multi-access reservations for travel agencies, SMART', *Data Networks: Developments and Uses*, Online Conferences.

Tucker, J. (1982). 'The OSI network layer', *Network Architectures*, State of the Art Report 10(1)., Pergamon Infotech.

Uhlig, R., Farber, D., and Bair, J. (1979). 'The office of the future', *Communication and Computers*, North-Holland.

Urwick-Nexos (1981). 'Local networks: a product review', Urwick-Nexos Ltd., Slough, Berks, UK.

Vo-Dai, T. (1982). 'Throughput-delay analysis of non-slotted and non-persistent CSMA-CD protocol', in *Local Computer Networks* (Proc. IFIP Int. Symp., Florence, April 1982, Eds. P. Ravasio, G. Hopkins, and N. Naffah), pp. 459–476, North-Holland.

Wagner, P.E. (1978). 'RF modem for CATV listen-while-talk bus interface unit', Mitre Technical Report MTR-3572.

Warner, C.J. (1979). 'Local network transmission control protocol (LNTCP)', Technical Note 793, Naval Ocean Systems Center, San Diego, Calif., December 1979.

Warner, C. (1980). 'Connecting local networks to long haul networks: issues in protocol design', *Fifth Conference on Local Computer Networks*, Minneapolis, October 1980, pp. 71–76, IEEE.

Way, D. (1981). 'Build a local network on proven software', *Data Communications*, December 1981, pp. 70–73.

Wecker, S. (1980). 'DNA: the digital network architecture', *IEEE Trans. Comm., COM-28*, **4**, April 1980, 510–526.

Wheeler, D.J., and Hopper, A. (1979). 'Maintenance of ring communications systems', *IEEE Trans. on Communications, COM-27*, **1979**, 760.

White, H.E., and Maxemchuk, N.F. (1974). 'An experimental TDM data loop exchange', *International Conference on Communications (ICC '74)*, Minneapolis, June 1974, Paper 7A.

Whitehouse, P. (1981). 'Design of application programs for distributed systems', *Local Networks and Distributed Office Systems*, pp. 85–95, Online Conferences.

Wilbur, S. (1980). 'Low-level protocols in the Cambridge Ring', *Data Networks—Development and Uses*, Online Conferences.

Wilkes, M.V., and Wheeler, D.J. (1979). 'The Cambridge digital communication ring', *Proc. Local Area Communications Network Symposium, Boston, May 1979* (Eds. N.B. Meisner and R. Rosenthal), pp. 47–61, MITRE and NBS.

Willis, P. (1982). 'An implementation of a token ring', *International Conference on Computer Communication*, London, September 1982.

Wittie, L.D. (1978). 'MICRONET: a reconfigurable microcomputer network for distributed systems research', *Simulation*, **31**(5), November 1978, 145–153.

Wolf, J.J., and Liu, M.T. (1978). 'A distributed double-loop computer network (DDLCM)', *Proc. Seventh Texas Conf. Computing Systems*, pp. 6-19–6-34.

Wolfendale, G.L. (1980). 'Development of a distributed resource sharing local computer network on CSIRONET', *Fifth Conference on Local Computer Networks*, Minneapolis, October 1980, pp. 111–119. IEEE.

Wood, D.C., Holmgren, S.F., and Skelton, A.P. (1979). 'A cable-based protocol architecture', *Sixth Data Comm. Symp.*, Pacific Grove, November 1979. pp. 137–146.

Wulf, W., and Levin, R. (1975) 'A local network', *Datamation*, **Feb. 1975**, 47–50.

Xerox (1981a). *Internet Transport Protocols*, Xerox System Integration Standards (XSIS 028112), December 1981.

Xerox (1981b). *Courier: The Remote Procedure Call Protocol*, Xerox Corporation.

Yada, K., Suzuki, Y., Takahashi, O., and Yatsuboshi, R. (1981). 'The large scale integrated service local network using optical fiber data highway', *Proc. Computer Networking Symposium, 1981*, IEEE.

Yajima, S., Kambayashi, Y., Yoshida, S., and Iwama K. (1977). 'Labolink: an optically linked laboratory computer network', *Computer*, **Nov. 1977**, 52–59.

Yeomans, J.M. (1982). 'Micronets: self-contained, low cost and available now', *Local Networks and Distributed Office Systems*, pp. 51–59, Online Conferences.

Zimmermann, H. (1981). 'Progession of the OSI reference model and its applications', Paper given at *NTC '81*, New Orleans, November 1981.

Zimmermann, H., and Naffah, N. (1978). 'On open systems architecture', *Proc. International Conference on Computers and Communications, 1978*, Kyoto, Japan, September 1978, pp. 669–774.

INDEX

370